WOMEN EMPOWERMENT IN POLITICAL INSTITUTIONS

An Indian Perspective

About the Academy of Grassroots Studies and Research of India

The Academy of Grassroots Studies and Research of India (AGRASRI) is an autonomous, non-profit and Non-Governmental Professional Organisation, Registered under the Societies Registration Act xxi of 1860 in the year 2001, being headquartered at Tirupati (A.P.), a World renowned Hindu pilgrim centre. The Academy was formally inaugurated by Shri Mani Shankar Aiyar, a champion of democratic decentralisation movement in India, on 20th August, 2001 at Tirupati.

The Academy works to provide an environment suitable for the study and promotion of academic research, training, education and consultancy in grassroots democratic institutions for self-sufficient Village Republics in India. The Grassroots Governance Journal (Bi-annual) and Grama Sabha Magazine (Monthly) are the official publications of Academy, besides books, working papers, occasional papers and monographs.

In pursuance of the aims and objectives, the AGRASRI is organising the Bharat Ratna Rajiv Gandhi Memorial Lecture and presenting the Bharat Ratna Rajiv Gandhi Outstanding Leadership and Bharat Ratna Rajiv Gandhi Best Panchayat Awards at three levels—District, Taluk and Gram Panchayats—on 20th August every year since 2002, in recognition of Shri Rajiv Gandhi's significant achievements and services to the nation as Seventh Prime Minister of India.

About the Editor

Dr. D. Sundar Ram is a Founder and Director of Academy of Grassroots Studies and Research of India (AGRASRI), being headquartered at Tirupati (A.P.). He is heading the Rajiv Rural Development Foundation (RRDF), Tirupati. He is Editor of The Grassroots Governance Journal (Bi-annual) and Grama Sabha Magazine (Monthy). He is a prolific writer, author, researcher and analyst. He has written extensively on Indian governance, parliamentary studies, electoral reforms, decentralisation, federalism and state politics, with over 20 books and 150 research papers to his credit. He was earlier Reader in Public Administration, Sri Subbaraya and Narayana College P.G. Centre (Acharya Nagarjuna University), Narasaraopet, Guntur District (A.P.); UGC Research Associate in Political Science at Sri Venkateswara University, Tirupati; and Parliamentary Fellow at the Institute of Constitutional and Parliamentary Studies, New Delhi.

He is a Member in many professional bodies and organisations of national repute. He is actively involved in imparting Capacity Building Training for the elected representatives of PRI's and SHG's in Andhra Pradesh state, under the aegis AGRASRI, Tirupati. He is conferred the Man of the Year Award-2004; Man of the Achievement Award-2005 and Man of the Year Commemorative Medal for the Year-2006, by the American Biographical Institute, USA.

Presently, he is the Chief Organiser of the Bharat Ratna Rajiv Gandhi Memorial Lecture programme and Convener of the Bharat Ratna Rajiv Gandhi Outstanding Leadership and Best Panchayat Awards Jury, under the aegis of AGRASRI and Rajiv Rural Development Foundation, Tirupati (A.P.).

WOMEN EMPOWERMENT IN POLITICAL INSTITUTIONS

An Indian Perspective

Edited by

D. Sundar Ram

Director, AGRASRI

Tirupati (A.P.)

Academy of Grassroots Studies and Research of India, Tirupati (A.P.)

By

KANISHKA PUBLISHERS, DISTRIBUTORS

NEW DELHI-110 002

KANISHKA PUBLISHERS, DISTRIBUTORS
4697/5-21 A, Ansari Road, Daryaganj
New Delhi-110 002
Phones : 2327 0497, 2328 8285
Fax : 011-2328 8285
E-mail: kanishka_publishing@yahoo.co.in

First Published 2009

ISBN 978-81-7391-161-5

PRINTED IN INDIA

Published by Madan Sachdeva for Kanishka Publishers, Distributors, 4697/5-21A, Ansari Road, Daryaganj, New Delhi-110 002, Typeset by Sunshine Graphics, Delhi, and Printed at Rajdhani Printers, Delhi.

Preface

The political empowerment of women in India is very complex one and highly debatable, since the introduction of the Women's Reservation Bill in Lok Sabha. Although women constitute half of the India's population, their participation in political life has been negligible all along. It is often noticed that the suitable representation of women in Legislatures remains a distant dream, excluding their representation in the Local Self-Government Institutions. Since Independence, the position of Women in politics has always been marginal in India. Women's participation in the Lok Sabha has not come up to even 10 per cent, although we had 14 General Elections since 1952. Similar situation is visible even in Rajya Sabha, where money power and muscle power matters the most. From 1952 to 2004, number of women members elected to the Rajya Sabha, a Lower House of Indian Parliament was only 465. At the level of Upper House of Parliament and various State Legislatures also, the picture is gloomy.

The reservations of seats for women in the Parliamentary Institutions have raised many doubts and apprehensions in the male dominated Indian society. Even after Six decades of Independence, the status and position of women in political participation and their representation in Parliament and State Legislative bodies is a myth and distant dream. The reservation of seats and due representation for women in Parliamentary Institutions and polity is the need of the hour not only to improve the self-respect of Indian women but also to ensure the political empowerment of one half of the Indian society.

The present book is a collection of fourteen original essays presented by prominent policy makers, academicians, researchers, social workers and women activists at the National Conference on 'Empowerment of Women in Parliament and Local Self-Government Institutions in India: Role, Status, Participation and Decision-

Making', held during 19 and 20 August, 2008 at Tirupati, which was organised by the Academy of Grassroots Studies and Research of India, Tirupati and sponsored by the National Commission for Women, New Delhi. This valuable book brings together a range of perspectives concerning the causes of and solutions to the problem of women political empowerment in India. The focus is not simply on describing challenging situations or the un-met needs of women in political arena, but also to offer examples of positive solutions and successful initiatives on behalf of Indian women. This book looks at the practical policy dimension of reconciling two valid policy perspectives: the need to boost the political representation of women at all levels from Gram Sabha to Lok Sabha and the need for 50 per cent women reservations across all levels of institutions in India. The purpose of this book is to synthesise critical lessons learned about women empowerment in political institutions, emphasising the role of women in Indian society, for good governance and better service delivery.

As Director of the Conference, I am extremely grateful to *Padma Vibhushan Dr. C. Rangarajan*, Hon'ble Member of Parliament (Rajya Sabha) and Former Governor of Andhra Pradesh and Reserve Bank of India, New Delhi; *Dr. (Mrs) Haripriya Rangarajan*, eminent educationist and social activist, New Delhi; *Smt. Prema Cariappa*, Chairperson, Central Social Welfare Board, Government of India, New Delhi; *Smt. Rajinitai Satav*, Chairperson, Maharashtra State Commission for Women, Mumbai, *Smt. K. Ramadevi*, Chairperson, Andhra Pradesh State Social Welfare Board, Hyderabad; *Shri R. Dileep Reddy*, State Information Commissioner (RTI), Government of Andhra Pradesh, Hyderabad; *Padma Shri Dr. Jaya Arunachalam*, President, Working Women's Forum, Chennai; *Late Professor C. Ratnam*, the then Vice-Chancellor of Sri Venkateswara University, Tirupati; and *Shri S. Ramachandra Reddy*, Former Member of Parliament (Rajya Sabha), Hyderabad, for their august presence and academic contributions in the National Conference as well as the Seventh Bharat Ratna Rajiv Gandhi Memorial Lecture, Bharat Ratna Rajiv Gandhi Outstanding Leadership and Best Panchayat Awards programmes, held at Tirupati, during 19 and 20 August, 2008. I thank all contributors of the book, for their enriched papers.

I am very much indebted to the Board of Governors, the Executive Council, my colleagues and well-wishers of AGRASRI for their valuable support and encouragement, extended to the National

Conference as well as the Seventh Bharat Ratna Rajiv Gandhi Memorial Lecture and Awards programme. The financial support provided to the National Conference by the National Commission for Women, Government of India, New Delhi, is greatly acknowledged.

Last but not the least; I thank *Shri Madan Sachdeva* of Kanishka Publishers, Distributors, New Delhi, for having brought out this book in an elegant form at a short notice.

D. Sundar Ram

Director,

AGRASRI

Contents

APPENDICES

List of Contributors

Dr. C. Rangarajan is Hon'ble Member of Parliament (Rajya Sabha), New Delhi. He has earlier been the Governor of Andhra Pradesh and Reserve Bank of India; Chairman, Twelfth Finance Commission of India and Economic Advisory Council to the Prime Minister of India, Government of India, New Delhi.

Prema Cariappa is Chairperson, Central Social Welfare Board, Government of India, New Delhi. She has earlier been Member of Parliament (Rajya Sabha), New Delhi.

Dr. Jaya Arunachalam is President, Working Women's Forum (WWF), Chennai.

Jagat S. Mehta, *IFS (Retd.)* is Trustee, Vidya Bhawan Society, Udaipur (Rajasthan). He has earlier been a Foreign Secretary and Indian Ambassador, Government of India, New Delhi.

Dr. Sam Pitroda is Chairperson, National Knowledge Commission, Government of India, New Delhi. He has earlier been Advisor to the then Prime Minister Shri Rajiv Gandhi and a father of Indian Telecom Revolution.

Dr. Devaki Jain is Trustee, Sri Singamma Sreenivasan Foundation, Bangalore.

Ahalya S. Bhat is associated with the Sri Singamma Sreenivasan Foundation, Bangalore.

Padmini Ananth is associated with the Sri Singamma Sreenivasan Foundation, Bangalore.

H. Anand is associated with the Sri Singamma Sreenivasan Foundation, Bangalore.

Dr. U. Kalpagam is Professor, G.B. Pant Social Studies Institute, Allahabad (Uttar Pradesh).

Dr. M. Kunhaman is Professor, School of Rural Development, Tata Institute of Social Sciences (TISS), Tuljapur, District Osmanabad (Maharashtra).

Dr. Nupur Tiwari is Consultant, Ministry of Panchayati Raj and Ministry of Development of North-East Region, Government of India, New Delhi.

Dr. O.P. Bohra is Associate Professor, National Institute of Public Finance and Policy, New Delhi.

R. Rakshit is Consultant, National Institute of Public Finance and Policy, New Delhi.

Dr. B.S. Bhargava is Senior Fellow, Institute of Social Science, Bangalore.

Dr. Jogendra Kumar Das is Selection Grade Lecturer in Political Science, D.K. College, Kamrup (Assam).

Dr. P. Arjuna Rao is Adjunct Professor, School of Public Policy, ICFAI University, Hyderabad (Andhra Pradesh).

Dr. Bayineni Srinivasulu is Faculty Member in Economics, ICFAI University, Hyderabad (Andhra Pradesh).

Dr. Alok Pandey is associated with the Society for Participatory Research in Asia (PRIA), New Delhi.

Dr. D. Sundar Ram *(Editor)* is Founder Director, Academy of Grassroots Studies and Research of India (AGRASRI); Secretary-General, Rajiv Rural Development Foundation (RRDF); Editor, The Grassroots Governance Journal (TGGJ), Tirupati (Andhra Pradesh).

Introduction: Empowerment of Women in Indian Polity and Governance: Promises and Realities

Dr. D. Sundar Ram

Empowerment is a process of awareness and capacity building leading to greater participation, to great decision-making power and control, and to transformative action which enables individuals or groups to change balances of power in social, economic and political relations in society. The political empowerment of women in India is very complex one and highly debatable, since the introduction of the Women's Reservation Bill in Lok Sabha. Although women constitute half of the India's population, their participation in political life has been negligible all along. It is often noticed that the suitable representation of women in Legislatures remains a distant dream, excluding their representation in the Local Self-Government Institutions. Since Independence, the position of women in politics has always been marginal in India. Women's participation in the Lok Sabha has not come up to even 10 per cent, although we had 14 General Elections since 1952. Similar situation is visible even in Rajya Sabha, where money power and muscle power matters the most. From 1952 to 2004, the number of women members elected to the Rajya Sabha, a Lower House of Indian Parliament was only 465. At the level of Upper House of Parliament and various State Legislatures also, the picture is gloomy.

The women, who started as a small minority in the domain of politics in India at the time of Independence, have not become a large minority even after 60 Years of Independence. The number of Women Ministers in the Union Cabinet has not exceeded 60 since 1952. In fact, the election of Mrs. Indira Gandhi as the first Prime Minister of India in 1966 was historic event not only for India, but for the World as well, since there were only two nations which had a woman head of the government. Subsequently, many women representatives have been occupied the gubernatorial positions like the President of India, the Chief Ministers, the Governors, the Speakers, the Ministers at the national as well as state level. However, this does not mean that there has been a general improvement in the condition of Indian women.

In the fast changing political scenario, more and more countries are beginning to realise the crucial role played by women in Parliamentary and Local Self-Government Institutions in achieving development goals. In India, Shri Rajiv Gandhi took initiatives for reservations in Panchayats at all levels of 30 per cent of the seats for women. With a farsighted vision of Shri Rajiv Gandhi, today, no less than 10 lakh women have been elected to our Panchayati Raj Institutions, constituting some 37 per cent of all those elected. However, the under representation of women in high level political decision-making structures in as universal phenomenon and therefore, there inclusion is considered essential. The issue today should be not as much the participation of women in politics but how women are able to improve their lot through participation, because participation in politics is not a goal in itself but a means and a strategy for achieving something more fundamental. Today, at the World level only 10 per cent of Parliamentary positions and 6 per cent of Cabinet Ministerial positions are occupied by women. Only a few European countries like Sweden (40%), Norway (39.4%), Finland (35.5%) and Denmark (33%) have crossed 30 per cent representation of women in their respective Parliaments. On the whole, it is clear that women are not able to improve more than 10 per cent of their political representation in Parliamentary and State Legislative bodies in India, even after 60 Years of Independence.

The reservations of seats for women in the Parliamentary Institutions have raised many doubts and apprehensions in the male dominated Indian society. Even after Six decades of Independence, the status and position of women in political participation and their representation in Parliament and State Legislative bodies is a myth and distant dream. The reservation of seats and due representation for women in Parliamentary Institutions and polity is the need of the hour not only to improve the self-respect of Indian women but also to ensure the political empowerment of one half of the Indian society. Hence, the theme of present Volume, particularly the role, status and decision-making components of women empowerment in political institutions show higher significance and relevance in contemporary India.

Moreover, keeping in view the backdrop of the initiatives of the respective Governments at the Centre as well as States for enhancing the political empowerment of women in contemporary India, the Academy of Grassroots Studies and Research of India has organised a 2-day National Conference during 19 and 20 August, 2008 at Tirupati (Andhra Pradesh) on the theme '*Empowerment of Women in Parliamentary and Local Self-Government Institutions in India: Role, Status, Participation and Decision-making*' to map the spectrum of our new culture and formulate a new vision for gender equity in political participation.

II

In order to promote the political empowerment of women in India, the present Volume explore the following objectives: *(a)* To assess the real status of the political participation of women in Parliamentary as well as Local Self-Government Institutions since Independence; *(b)* To analyse the gender equality and reservations of seats for women in democratic institutions, in proportion to their population in India; *(c)* To highlight the role and performance of women policy makers in decision-making at national, state and local levels, in delivering a good governance; *(d)* To examine the level of participation of women in Local Self-Government Institutions, in the wake of 73rd Constitution Amendment Act; *(e)* To visualise the future vision and action plan for the women empowerment in India, in view of the proliferation of their representation in Parliament and State Legislatures.

The present book aims at looking the pros and cons of the empowerment of women in Indian polity and governance and draw out a blue print for the vision and perspectives of various political parties towards the reservation of seats for women in Indian Parliament and State Legislatures in proportionate to their population.

III

To find out the ways and means towards the role, status, participation and decision-making of the women elected representatives in Indian Parliament, State Legislative bodies and Local Self-Government Institutions over a period of 60 Years in Independent India, the experts and scholars are requested to present their views and opinions vividly on the present volume, with larger context of the tremendous demand for 33 per cent reservation of seats in legislative bodies. For the purpose, the following sub-themes were discussed and debated at length in the 2-day National Conference. Panel-I: Women Empowerment in Parliament and Local Self-Government Institutions since India's Independence—A Symbol of Power or Powerless, Panel-II: Gender Equity and Emerging Pattern of Leadership of Women in India Polity and Governance: Searching for Alternatives, Panel-III: Grassroots Movements and Local Governance in India: Performance and Participation of Women in Decision-making and Panel-IV: Reservation of Seats for Women in Indian Parliament and State Legislative Bodies: Future Vision and Action Plan.

IV

In an introductory Chapter, the Editor of the book D. Sundar Ram explores the current debate on the women political empowerment in contemporary India at the time of the 60 Years of India's Independence. After presenting a realistic view on the women political empowerment, he feels that the governments at the centre and states must consider and provide an adequate representation for women in various political institutions, in proportionate to their population, for delivering good governance and transparent delivery of services.

Extending a scope of activities of the organised financial system to the vulnerable groups like farmers and women, include rural masses and low income groups, C. Rangarajan, in Chapter-1, advocates that what is required now is not creating new institutions for extending their out-reach but finding ways and means to effect improvements within the existing formal credit delivery mechanism and evolve new models for extending out-reach. In a broad sense, we need to address issues on the supply side as well as demand side. Strengthening the credit delivery system in rural areas of Commercial Banks, Regional Rural Banks and Micro-finance Institutions, C. Rangarajan proposed the following seven useful approaches: First, a critical factor required for providing credit to marginal and sub-marginal farmers as well as other small borrowers is the empathy of the bank officers. Secondly, rural branches must go beyond providing credit and extend a helping hand in terms of advice on a wide variety of matters relating to agriculture and other allied activities. Thirdly, in districts where the population per branch is much higher than the national average, commercial banks may be encouraged to open branches. Fourthly, there is need for the simplification of the procedures in relation to granting of loans to small borrowers. Fifthly, the SHG bank linkage scheme has proved to be an effective way of providing credit to very small borrowers. This needs to be further strengthened. Sixthly, adoption of the Joint Liability Groups (JLGs) concept could be another effective method for purveying credit to small farmers, marginal farmers, tenant farmers, etc. and thereby reduce their dependence on informal sources of credit. Finally, the business facilitator and correspondent model needs to be effectively implemented. Supporting the financial inclusion plan in India, for the micro credit finance movement to gather momentum, C. Rangarajan opines that it is necessary that the various legal forms of micro-finance institutions should be encouraged. Each legal form has it own special advantages. However, it needs to be noted even the most successful micro-finance institutions in the corporate sector depend to a large extent on funding by the banks. Thus, the banks will continue to play a key role either directly or indirectly in micro-finance. Looking at the picture as a whole, C. Rangarajan concludes that two initiatives that will bring about a significant surge forward of the micro-finance sector will be the growth of the bank-SHG linkage programme and the induction of individuals as business correspondents. The two will constitute the main pillars of the future development of bank related micro-finance, even as other forms of micro-finance institutions will continue to grow. The goal of making a significant progress towards financial inclusion seems attainable. Financial inclusion is no longer an option but a compulsion.

In Chapter-2, Prema Cariappa outlines that the political empowerment of women alone would ensure participation of women in decision-making and shaping India's future. While evaluating the real picture of the women political empowerment in contemporary India, Prema Cariappa emphasises that it is necessary that women should be part of the decision-making process of the nation and further she argues that political empowerment is essential for gender justice and equitable society. Expressing concern over the delay in the passing of the Women's Reservation Bill in the Parliament, Prema Cariappa outlines that the very legitimacy of every decision taken without the consensus of women is questionable because it was taken by only 50 per cent of the population, which belongs to men. Praising the initiatives and reforms by the policy makers towards the 73rd Constitution Amendment, Prema Cariappa said that the credit for 10 lakh women getting elected to the Panchayati Raj bodies every year in the country should go to the former Prime Minister Shri Rajiv Gandhi. Discussing the radical transformation of Indian society through women participation, Prema Cariappa feels that women must be given a change not because they were necessarily better than male politicians but because they cannot do any worse. Explaining the salient features and contributions of the Central Social Welfare Board for the Women Empowerment and Development, Prema Cariappa has called upon women to stand united and fight for their rights.

Following a comprehensive review of the initiatives and efforts made by various International Organisations and Institutions like United Nations Organisation, Jaya Arunachalam, in Chapter-3, believes that the Indian Government too under the dynamic leadership of Smt. Indira Gandhi enacted two landmark social legislations in favour of poor rural women workers at the grassroots. Having been the champion of the poor and vulnerable, Smt. Indira Gandhi further took up the challenge of the feudals and the rural rich by enacting these two legislations, i.e. Minimum Wages Act and Equal Remuneration Act. But at the enforcement level it is still very weak both due to the complacency of the bureaucracy and the strong-rooted feudal forces who stand in the way as great impediments at the grassroots. Stressing the need for passing of the Women's Reservation Bill for 33 per cent seats in the Parliament and State Legislative bodies, Jaya Arunachalam pleads that as this gender bias goes on unabatedly despite India achieving 61 Years of Independence, it is time to think of corrective mechanism i.e., a policy on reservation for women so that they should take care of atrocities and establish gender justice. Tracing roots of concern for gender equity in India, Jaya Arunachalam opines that women today are at crossroads and in a minority everywhere. Despite being one half the human kind in an independent nation where many social legislations are in favour of them along with the constitutional guarantee assuring them equality of sexes that was assured quite late in many other countries, women feel today that they are no where in the National Agenda in all fields. However, we can't forget the historic Constitutional Amendments in the local bodies governance through 73rd and 74th Amendment Acts in favour of women. No doubt it is landmark event and as a result we see today few women panchayat leaders who not only are accomplishing well but also are awarded for their excellence in their governance.

In Chapter-4, Jagat S. Mehta visualises that India now is in transition from too much reliance on the state to too self-centered pre-occupation with the market values. Gandhiji depended on good secular NGOs, which will enable them to turn away from cynicism to the exercise of civic responsibilities. By and large women respond more readily to development needs of the rural areas and so awareness of civic responsibilities, courage to identify corruption to defy the bureaucracy. But we the elite have a great responsibility. Our forefathers led the struggle for independence and had no hesitation in making sacrifices. The suppression of ages has disappointed 'aam admi.' While attempting the sorry state of affairs in contemporary India, Jagat S. Mehta feels that the efficiency of the Central Government in giving legislative directions cannot be negated but it is for the Panchayat to check the arrogance of bureaucracy, exercise the Right to Information (RTI), expose false muster roles, rampant abuse of NREG and JYRY and generally the ignorance of the villagers not exploited.... India has shown that democracy demands equality of sex and we must again become pioneers. The Panchayati Raj legislation like the Hindu divorce legislation of 1955 was incomparably farsighted. Neither has been strictly enforced but there were small steps in the right direction. Highlighting the advantages of the women empowerment in plural societies like India, Jagat S. Mehta concludes that the democracy can only thrive with the equality of sexes. India as a pioneer in Women's rights should consciously reject the residue of a male dominated heritage.

Sam Pitroda postulates the crucial role of women in Indian polity and governance, in Chapter-5. Assessing the importance of the gender equity in civilised society, Sam Pitroda argues that the status of women in a society, and the level of equity and empowerment accorded to them are crucial components of understanding the development index of a country. And one of the key benchmarks for understanding the level of empowerment is the role of women in the decision-making process of a country. Analysing the initiatives taken by the successive governments towards women empowerment in India, Sam Pitroda feels that women still continue to face considerable handicaps to their involvement in politics. The conservative attitude in rural areas, patriarchal values, religious views, family responsibilities, lack of education and economic dependency often make women in rural areas unequipped to effectively participate in the political process. To begin our journey to empower women in Parliament, State Governments and Local Government Institutions, Sam Pitroda recommends that we use the growing power of the Information and Communication Technology with access on mobile phones to help create an environment for openness, transparency, networking, sharing, training, education, awareness and collaboration by establishing various portals in all major Indian languages at national, state and district levels.

In Chapter-6, Devaki Jain, Ahalya S. Bhat, Padmini Ananth, and H. Anand project the overall national experience of decentralised developmental planning and implementation with the experience of one of the NGO's located in Karnataka which has been working with Elected Women Representatives (EWR) for almost 15 years. Discussing the ground realities of the women elected leaders in Karnataka Gram Panchayats, they find that the history and review reveals not only women's capability in political, economic and social participation in Local Self-Government but also the overall value of giving more leadership space to Elected Women Representatives (EWRs) to plan and implement the flagship schemes such as National Rural Employment Guarantee Scheme (NREGS), National Rural Health Mission (NRHM), as well as several other schemes that are on the anvil. Experience shows that women more deeply committed to localised governance than men.

U. Kalpagam, in Chapter-7, opines that Gender-sensitive grassroots governance under the present system of democratic decentralisation through the PRIs can become possible and effective only if elected women members are made aware of the systemic gender exclusion and of how the process of development further marginalises them. Such an understanding has to be further bolstered by a critical mass of grassroots support by the community women who could collectively transform the nature of grassroots governance. Highlighting the nature of systemic exclusion and discrimination that women face in the development process, Kalpagam argues that gender sensitive grassroots governance under the present system of PRIs is possible only if women gain 'Voice' and 'Rights'. It also requires that synergies be built with CBOs, NGOs and social movements.

Highlighting the need for increasing the number of women's representatives in legislative bodies, Kunhaman, in Chapter-8, contends that the question of reservation for women in legislatures raises not only gender issues, whatever these may be, but also many larger and systemic and structural questions which are quintessentially socio-economic and political in nature. Discussing the broad contours of women empowerment through political institutions, Kunhaman, however, reveals that the present debates and discourses predicated mainly on concepts such as 'gender revolution', 'gender politics' etc. do not seem to give due attention to these questions. Hence, Women's participation is required not ensuring gender justice (justice is not just a number game) nor for articulating women's issues (male members can also do that), not for steering debates in legislatures especially with regard to development policies (there is no guarantee that this will happen) but to make legislatures more representative.

Praising the initiatives of the State Governments of Bihar, Rajasthan, Madhya Pradesh, Chhattisgarh, Himachal Pradesh and Uttarakhand for 50 per cent seats of reservation available for women in Panchayati Raj Institutions, Nupur Tiwary in Chapter-9, explores that this has given exposures to backward, dalit, poor and illiterate has given political and social empowerment. As a result of this development more important issues like education, water, road and health have started getting more important in the agenda of Gram Panchayats.

While discussing the concept of women and development at the global level, O.P. Bohra and R. Rakshit, in Chapter-10, opine that the rank of India is far behind in terms of economic participation, educational status and political empowerment. It ranks far below than its neighbours in South Asia (Sri Lanka and Bangladesh), however higher than Nepal and Pakistan. Surveying the concept of gender budgeting and decision-making initiated by the Government of India, they examine these issues through the primary survey carried out in the two villages of Rajasthan (a Feudal State) and presented for the view of common masses particularly for the rural India. Some inferences can be drawn from this to replicate them at the other parts of India and the higher level of governance, if found suitable.

B.S. Bhargava, in Chapter-11, describes that in many panchayats, women Chairpersons/Vice-Chairpersons are becoming assertive because of increasing awareness about their role and rights and working of the Panchayati Raj System in India. Deepening of participatory democracy and broadening of its social base, and the phenomenon of 'shifting of dominance' towards non-dominant castes and communities (numerically speaking) are really encouraging trends. Tracing roots of ground realities and emerging challenges, Bhargava, believes that the socio-economic background of several women, muscle and money powers in electoral process, role of local elites, lack of presence in political parties' structures, conflict between domestic and public roles, proxy phenomenon, attitudinal aspects and unwanted behaviour of local bureaucracy are some among other factors/constraints, coming in the way of their empowerment.

Jogendra Kumar Das examines the social background features of the women leaders at the grassroots in an empirical setting based in the District of Kamrup in the Indian State of Assam in order to explore the nature of women representation in the PRI's constituted aftermath of the new dispensation with an objective to look whether women are able to come up to the leadership position breaking out all the traditional barriers associated with women empowerment lies in our hard patriarchal social set up, in Chapter-12.

Tracing briefly the working of the Panchayati Raj Institutions after an enactment of 73rd Constitution Amendment Act, P. Arjuna Rao and Bayineni Srinivasulu, in Chapter-13, assess the impact of increased representation of women in the Gram Panchayats, particularly in the leadership positions as Sarpanchs, on democratisation at one level and weakening of patriarchy at another level. Discussing the radical transformation of rural society through women empowerment, the conclude that the 73rd Constitution Amendment Act transforms the very character of democracy through an integrated representative (Gram Panchayat) and participatory (Gram Sabha) system of grassroots governance and likewise it reverses the development activities from supply driven to demand driven.

Examining available opportunities for participation in politics and express the voice and shape public policies, Alok Pandey, in Chapter-14, feels that the lack of personal skills in terms of education, awareness and structural constraints like lack of support from male colleagues and government functionaries, from family and society and economic constraints hinders the effective participation of women in polity and governance at the grassroots level in India.

The issue of women political empowerment has become a matter of international concern while gaining prominence in national developmental efforts. The United Nations Convention on Women Empowerment, which has a higher rate of ratification by the nations of the world than any other UN convention, signals a new global awareness of the importance of this issue. This book is a collection of fourteen original essays presented by prominent policy makers, academicians, researchers, social workers and women activists at the National Conference, organised by the Academy of Grassroots Studies and Research of India, Tirupati and sponsored by the National Commission for Women, New Delhi. This valuable book brings together a range of perspectives concerning the causes of and solutions to the problem of women political empowerment in India. The focus is not simply on describing challenging situations or the un-met needs of women in political arena, but also to offer examples of positive solutions and successful initiatives on behalf of Indian women. This book looks at the practical policy dimension of reconciling two valid policy perspectives: the need to boost the political representation of women at all levels from Gram Sabha to Lok Sabha and the need for 50 per cent women reservations across all levels of institutions in India. The purpose of this book is to synthesise critical lessons learned about women empowerment in political institutions, emphasising the role of women in Indian society, for good governance and better service delivery.

1

Financial Inclusion in India: Need for Institutional Changes

DR. C. RANGARAJAN

It gives me great pleasure to be in your midst this evening and to deliver the Seventh Bharat Ratna Rajiv Gandhi Memorial Lecture. I am grateful to the Academy of Grassroots Studies and Research of India for their decision to confer on me the Bharat Ratna Rajiv Gandhi Outstanding Leadership Award for the year 2008. I accept the Award in all humility. I am also grateful to His Excellency, the Governor of Andhra Pradesh, Shri Narayan Datt Tiwari, for his kind presence this evening.

Rajiv Gandhi will go down in history for two reasons: First, he gave a new orientation to politics in our country. He recognised the importance of technology and gave to technology development a major thrust. The various technology missions that he initiated have brought about significant changes in the Indian economy. Second, he gave Constitutional recognition to the third-tier of government in our country. The village panchayats and municipalities acquired a new status because of the Constitutional amendments introduced by him. Let us hope that his dream of making local self-governments the real levers of progress becomes a reality.

I propose to speak to you today on financial inclusion and the role that the various institutions which provide micro-finance can play in bringing about greater inclusion.

Nature of Inclusion

Financial inclusion denotes delivery of credit and other financial services at an affordable cost to the vast sections of the disadvantaged and low-income groups. The various financial services include savings, credit, insurance and payments and remittance facilities. It will be wrong to classify all those who are not borrowing from the organized financial system as excluded. What is relevant is that those who want credit should not be denied the same provided they are bankable. The criterion of being bankable should not be interpreted narrowly to exclude the vast majority. The objective of financial inclusion is to extend the scope of activities of the organized financial system to include within its ambit people with low incomes. Through graduated credit, attempts must be to lift the poor from one level to another so that they come out of poverty. Financial inclusion may, therefore, be defined as a process of enabling access to timely and adequate credit and other financial services by vulnerable groups such as weaker sections and low-income groups at an affordable cost.

Extent of Exclusion

NSSO data reveal that 45.9 million farmer households in the country (51.4%), out of a total of 89.3 million households do not access credit, either from institutional or non-institutional sources. Further, despite the vast network of bank branches, only 27 per cent of total farm households are indebted to formal sources (of which one-third also borrow from informal sources). Farm household's not accessing credit from formal sources as a proportion to total farm households is especially high at 95.91, 81.26 per cent and 77.59 per cent in the North Eastern, Eastern and Central Regions respectively. Thus, apart from the fact that exclusion in general is large, it also varies widely across regions, social groups and asset holdings. The poorer the group, the greater is the exclusion.

Institutional Changes

The question that is before us is how to extend the scope of activities of the organized financial system to include low income groups. The institutions which currently provide financial services in the rural areas include branches of commercial banks, regional rural banks, cooperative societies and micro-finance institutions. What is required now is not creating new institutions for extending their outreach but finding ways and means to effect improvements within

---

*Text of the *Seventh Bharat Ratna Rajiv Gandhi Memorial Lecture* delivered by *Dr. C. Rangarajan*, on 20th August, 2008 at Hotel Bliss (Darbar Hall), Tirupati, Andhra Pradesh, under the aegis of Academy of Grassroots Studies and Research of India (AGRASRI) and Rajiv Rural Development Foundation (RRDF), Tirupati (Andhra Pradesh).

the existing formal credit delivery mechanism and evolve new models for extending outreach. In a broad sense, we need to address issues on the supply side as well as demand side. The formal banking system, the rural cooperatives and non-governmental organisations must be strengthened organizationally to extend their outreach. The financially excluded sections require products which are customised to meet their needs. Financial exclusion is also caused by demand side issues. Unless steps are taken on the demand side that is in the "real sectors" mere supply side solutions from the financial sector will not work. Credit is necessary for this, but not sufficient. Credit has to be an integral part of an overall programme aimed at improving the productivity and income of small farmers and other poor households. Putting in place an appropriate credit delivery system to meet the needs of marginal and sub-marginal farmers must go hand in hand with efforts to improve the productivity of such farm households.

Let me place before you some thoughts on strengthening the credit delivery system in rural areas of commercial banks, Regional Rural banks and micro-finance institutions.

Commercial Banks

The commercial banks have a large outreach. There are, at present, 33,500 commercial bank branches in rural and semi-urban centers in the country. The critical question is how to make these rural branches more effective in terms of delivering credit to the small and the very small borrowers. List below some approaches in this regard.

First, a critical factor required for providing credit to marginal and sub-marginal farmers as well as other small borrowers is the empathy of the bank officers. Rural lending requires a specific type of organizational ethos, culture and attitude. Rural branches of banks have to be farmer-friendly. Lending to the low-income groups needs motivated bank staff. Such motivation is a function of attitude and beliefs as well as a system of incentives. The possibility of creating a separate cadre of rural bank employees does not appear to be feasible. Several studies have shown that there is a positive co-relation between the extent of training undergone by the managers and their overall attitude. More needs to be done in this regard.

Second, rural branches must go beyond providing credit and extend a helping hand in terms of advice on a wide variety of matters relating to agriculture and other allied activities. We may have to think in terms of branches on the lines of agricultural development branches of SBI where advice on farm and non-farm issues were provided by technical staff attached to the branches. As the Committee on Financial Inclusion has suggested, at least, one branch of the lead bank at the block or taluka level can be designated as a nodal branch to address the issue of exclusion. These branches must be strengthened with technical staff for provision of developmental services in the farm and non-farm sectors. All banks could make use of the advice provided by such branches.

Third, in districts where the population per branch is much higher than the national average, commercial banks may be encouraged to open branches. 139 districts in 15 states have been identified by Reserve Bank as inadequately served by the banking system.

Fourth, there is need for the simplification of the procedures in relation to granting of loans to small borrowers. In some cases, enabling legislations have to be passed. Stamp duty exemption for loan documents relating to small borrowings is also needed. On the whole, a simplified document for the grant of small loans must be evolved. Some steps have already been taken in this regard by NABARD.

Fifth, the SHG bank linkage scheme has proved to be an effective way of providing credit to very small borrowers. This needs to be further strengthened. The SHG-bank linkage programme has worked well and has contributed significantly to financial inclusion. The cumulative number of groups financed by the banking system is close to 2.3 million. The financial inclusion attained through SHGs is sustainable and scalable on account of its various positive features. One of the distinctive features of the SHG-bank linkage programme has been the high recovery rate. However, the spread of SHGs is very uneven and is more concentrated in southern states. This regional imbalance needs to be corrected and special efforts in this regard may have to be taken by NABARD. SHGs also need to graduate from mere providers of credit for non-productive purposes to promoting micro enterprises. Several State Governments have been very active in the promotion of SHGs.

However, there is no need to provide any interest rate subsidy to SHGs. Banks do provide them credit at reasonable rates of interest. The financial support of the State Governments could be better directed towards building appropriate capacities in the self-help groups and providing technology support and marketing facilities. There are other quality issues which have arisen in the wake of the sharp quantitative expansion. These need to be addressed. Federations of SHGs at village and taluka levels have certain advantages. However, the disadvantage is that banks may lose their direct contact with SHGs, if federations act as intermediaries between the financing banks and SHGs. Perhaps, the best course of action would be to make the federations act as facilitators rather than as financial intermediaries. Federations, if they emerge voluntarily from amongst SHGs, must be encouraged.

Sixth, even though SHG-bank linkage has emerged as an effective credit delivery channel to the poor clients, there are segments within the poor who are left out such as share croppers/ oral lessees/ tenant farmers, whose loan requirements are much larger but who have no collaterals to fit into the traditional financing approaches of the banking system. To service such clients, Joint Liability Groups (JLGs), an up-gradation of SHG model, could be an effective way. The Committee on Financial Inclusion had recommended that the adoption of the JLGs concept could be another effective method for purveying credit to small farmers, marginal farmers, tenant farmers, etc. and thereby reduce their dependence on informal sources of credit.

Finally, the business facilitator and correspondent model needs to be effectively implemented. In order to increase the outreach of the banking sector, the Reserve Bank have permitted banks to use the services of specified institutions as intermediaries for providing banking services. However, this scheme has not taken off. This model has a high potential. Banks must take the initiative to remove the obstacles that come in the way of an extended use of facilitators and correspondents. Rules, at present, permit not only institutions but also certain category of individuals to function as business facilitators. This list can be further expanded to include such people as ex-service men as has been done recently. At present, individuals are not allowed to function as business correspondents. Perhaps, a relaxation can be made here. I believe this has also been done recently by RBI. Individuals who have served as bank facilitators and have shown to have a satisfactory record may also be used as business correspondents. In fact, the appointment of well-chosen individuals holds out the best promise in this regard. However, one critical issue in the effective use of this model revolves around as to who should bear the additional transaction costs resulting from the employment of facilitators and correspondents. There has to be some flexibility with respect to the charging of interest rate. These transaction costs can still be accommodated within the present stipulation that the interest rate charged should not exceed the PLR.

Regional Rural Banks

Regional rural banks were originally conceived as low cost institutions having rural bias, local feel and pro-poor focus. The original assumption regarding the low cost nature of these institutions was belied. In fact, they soon turned into loss making institutions. With the changes introduced in the post-liberalization period, there is a remarkable turn around in the financial performance of the RRBs. RRBs are yet another instrument to achieve the goal of financial inclusion. At present, RRBs have close to 15000 branches in rural areas. The share of RRBs in the loan account of all scheduled commercial banks in rural areas is an impressive 37 per cent. However, they account for only 21 per cent of the total credit outstanding in rural areas implying thereby that the clientele comprises of small borrowers. RRBs have done well also in relation to the promotion of SHGs. Of the total 22.4 lakh SHGs credit linked by the banking industry, 33 per cent linkage is done by RRBs. Strengthening of the RRBs could be one major policy intervention for promoting greater financial inclusion. The operations of RRBs could be expanded to 80 hitherto uncovered districts. I understand action is already being taken in this regard. RRBs may also usefully adopt the business facilitator and business correspondent model to achieve greater inclusion.

Role of Technology

In the task of making banking services available to everyone, technology has an important role to play. The required outreach into interiors with low operational costs is only possible with the use of appropriate technology. Technology has to be leveraged to create channels beyond branch network to reach the unbanked and to extend to them banking services similar to those dispensed from branches. In short, technology has to enable the branch to go to the customer instead of the other way round. The RBI has set up an Advisory Group for IT enabled financial inclusion to facilitate development of information technology solutions for delivery of banking services. It is understood that the Group will prescribe certain minimum parameters and standards that are essential for setting up robust technology solutions. The essential ingredients of all the models under consideration include:

(a) the issue of a smart card to the client in the village on which all the transactions are recorded;

(b) a hand-held terminal with the business correspondent at the village level; and

(c) a Central Processor Unit (CPU) linking the smart cards and BC terminals with the banks.

It is necessary to ensure that every transaction made is accompanied by a print out being provided to the farmers or other clients. The operating costs of these models are expected to be minimal and can be easily absorbed by banks. As the transaction increases in volume it will become easier to absorb the incremental operating costs. More importantly, the costs of the technology solutions will be substantially lowered if the infrastructure is shared. The Report of the Committee on Financial Inclusion has recommended the setting up of a Technology Development Fund. The Central Budget has also made a provision for this. This fund can be utilised to strengthen the technology base for financial inclusion.

Micro Financial Institutions

Micro-finance institutions play a significant role in ensuring financial inclusion. There are several legal forms of Micro-Finance Institutions (MFIs). There are about 1000 NGO-MFIs, 3000 cooperative MFIs and about 20 company MFIs. However, the company MFIs are the major players accounting for over 80 per cent of the micro-finance loan portfolio. Ten such MFIs are reported to have an outreach of 100000 micro-finance clients. However, an overwhelming majority of MFIs are operating on a smaller scale with clients ranging between 500 to 1500 per MFI. The geographical distribution of MFIs is skewed with concentration in southern India where the rural branch network of banks is also strong. It is estimated that MFIs added during the year 2006-07 3 million new borrowers and this takes the total coverage to 10.5 million borrowers.

With respect to the operations of MFIs, a number of issues have arisen in the recent period. One such issue relates to the rate of interest. It is recognised that the transaction costs for delivering credit to very small borrowers are high. Also to the extent to which various advisory services are provided, the cost further goes up. It is necessary for MFIs to separate the pure interest costs from other costs which are charged to the borrowers because of the additional services provided. Overall it is necessary to ensure that the burden on the borrower is not such as to make him default. MFIs need to ensure that the earnings capacity of the borrowers is sufficiently enhanced enabling them to bear the cost of borrowing. Taking a holistic view, it is necessary for micro-finance institutions to keep the overall cost to the borrowers maintained at a level that is consistent with the repaying capacity of the borrowers.

As the Committee on Financial Inclusion has recommended, there is a need to recognise a separate category of Micro-Finance—Non-Banking Finance Companies (MF-NBFCs). This should be done without any relaxation on the start up capital. They should also be subject to all the regulatory prescriptions applicable to NBFCs. Such MF-NBFCs could be defined as NBFCs that provide credit up to a specified amount to the borrowers. Consistent with the definition of micro-finance that is prescribed in the new bill, it may be specified that MF-NBFCs are those with 80 per cent of the assets of in the form of microcredit of up to Rs. 50,000 for agriculture, allied and non-farm activities and in the case of housing, loans up to Rs. 1,50,000, per individual borrower, whether given through a group mechanism or directly. The supervision of MF-NBFCs could be delegated to NABARD by RBI. These MF-NBFCs could be recognised as business correspondents of banks for providing savings and remittance services. They will not, however, serve as correspondents on the lending side as there could be a conflict of interest.

For the micro-finance movement to gather momentum, it is necessary that all the various legal forms of micro-finance institutions should be encouraged. Each legal form has its own special advantages. However, it needs to be noted even the most successful micro-finance institutions in the corporate sector depend to a large extent on funding by the banks. Thus, the banks will continue to play a key role either directly or indirectly in micro-finance.

National Rural Financial Inclusion Plan

The Committee on Financial Inclusion has recommended that a National Rural Financial Inclusion Plan may be launched with a clear target to provide access to comprehensive financial services, including credit, to at least 50 per cent of financially excluded households, say 55.77 million by 2012 through rural/semi-urban branches of Commercial Banks and Regional Rural Banks. The remaining households, with such shifts as may occur in the rural/urban population, have to be covered by 2015. Semi-urban and rural branches of commercial banks and RRBs may set for themselves a minimum target of covering 250 new cultivator and non-cultivator households per branch per annum, with an emphasis on financing marginal farmers and poor non-cultivator households. This is an achievable target.

Looking at the picture as a whole, two initiatives that will bring about a significant surge forward of the micro-finance sector will be the growth of the bank-SHG linkage programme and the induction of individuals as business correspondents. The two will constitute the main pillars of the future development of bank related micro-finance, even as other forms of micro-finance institutions will continue to grow. The goal of making a significant progress towards financial inclusion seems attainable. Financial inclusion is no longer an option but a compulsion.

2

Women Representation in Political Institutions in India: Role, Status, Participation and Decision-Making

PREMA CARIAPPA

I am delighted to be amidst you here today to Inaugurates the National Conference on very vital theme 'Women Political Empowerment in Indian Parliament and Local Self-Government Institutions'. I also congratulate Dr. Sundar Ram and his dedicated team for organising a national level conference at the temple town Tirupati, under the aegis of Academy of Grassroots Studies and Research of India (AGRASRI), in collaboration with the Rajiv Rural Development Foundation (RRDF), Tirupati.

Moreover, it is my great privilege and honour to address you today on the eve of Shri Rajiv Gandhi's 64th birth anniversary. I think everyone who is gathered here will agree with me that if he was still present among us today our country would have followed a very different path of development. Shri Rajiv Gandhi was a true champion for women's rights. That was the reason why he took up the 73rd amendment as a personal mission and piloted the Bill through Parliament. Today, the women of India can thank him for this landmark step that he took for their advancement on the path of political empowerment.

The political empowerment of women is essential for a gender just and equitable society. This goal is a basic requirement for bringing about peace, development and equality in society. The representation of women in the highest legislative bodies of the country is based on the constitutional freedoms granted to all citizens–equality between the genders, women's right to develop their potential and pursue any career and their right for representation in the political institutions.

Interventions for the empowerment of women must take into account the fact that political empowerment are one of the most important aspects of the whole process of empowerment. So that women can participate in decision-making and can shape the future of their communities it is necessary that they should be a part of the political process of the nation. Shri Rajiv Gandhi had given the women of India a tremendous boost when he steered the 73rd Amendment through Parliament. As a result, the women at the grassroots were given 33 per cent reservation in the panchayati raj bodies. With every panchayat election, 10 lakh women enter the democratic process of the country and they are involved in tasks of village welfare. This exposure has created a whole new cadre of women workers at the village level who are being groomed at the entry level of the democratic process.

For millennial ever since the dawn of time, women have played a role that is subordinate to men. During the Stone Age it was necessary for Man to be the provider and Woman to be the nurturer. Unfortunately, a lot of men are still living in the Stone Age in spite of all their erudition and learning. When we ask for a place in Parliament they tell us to go back to the kitchen!! Women are challenging the authority of men because they are sick and tired of the scams, crime, violence, liquor and drugs which are a part of our politics today.

The world of politics in India is so much surrounded by an aura of crime and corruption which is synonymous with politics; it is also true that if we want to bring about a change and cleanse the political system we will have to give reservation to women.

The experiment at the Panchayat level has given us certain pointers. Initially the women who are elected to these seats are a large proportion of the wives and daughters of members who could not get seats due to reservation. Such women are seen as pawns in the hands of their male relatives and they are somewhat looked

---

*Text of the Inaugural Address delivered by *Smt. Prema Cariappa*, on 19th August, 2008 in Tirupati, Andhra Pradesh, at the National Conference on *'Empowerment of Women in Parliament and Local Self-Government Institutions in India: Role, Status, Participation and Decision-Making'*, organised by the Academy of Grassroots Studies and Research of India (AGRASRI), in Collaboration with the Rajiv Rural Development Foundation (RRDF), Tirupati (Andhra Pradesh). The Conference was Sponsored by the National Commission for Women, Government of India, New Delhi.

down upon. However, these women also serve a very useful purpose of increasing the visual impact of women in power, which is the first step towards changing the attitudes of society towards the idea that women can also exercise authority and can assume a seat of power. On the other hand, it is also true that an equal if not greater proportion of women who have been elected to the local bodies are genuine workers who have forged valuable bonds of partnership at the grassroots level.

Women must be given a chance not because they are necessarily any better than male politicians but because they cannot do any worse. Male leaders indulge in crime and corruption, they concentrate their energies in fighting for greater power, greater privileges, mega-projects etc. If women are given power they will fight for a cleaner political system, anti-corruption, better health and sanitation for villages, appropriate technologies, education for girls, vocational opportunities for adolescent girls and young women, anti-dowry practices, greater property and land rights for women and for the actualization of empowerment in its truest terms.

Today there are thousands of women working at the village level for development agencies. They are far better suited and qualified to enter politics than the local 'dada' who puts on garlands and goes around with a loudspeaker at election time. Women cannot muster money and muscle power and therefore they are not seen as good candidates. Reservation will ensure that at least women are given an entry-point. History shows that once they come into power and begin to make a difference, women usually stay in power.

The Central Social Welfare Board is working towards making women aware of their political rights through its Awareness Generation Programme. Under this programme, Camps are held at the village level in which several resource persons give lectures to groups of women on subject relating to their civil and legal rights and responsibilities as citizens of the country. These camps have a range of topics from health, hygiene, sanitation, low cost nutritive food, child care and other women related issues. The camps provide an ideal entry point for disseminating information about the programmes of the Board and other development schemes of the Government for women. The Central Social Welfare Board also implements several other programmes for the social and economic empowerment of women. The Rajiv Gandhi National Crèche Scheme for Children of Working Mothers provides a safe and secure environment along with facilities for supplementary nutrition, early childhood education and basic medical care for the children of working mothers. The Voluntary Action Bureaus and Family Counseling Centre provide counseling and rehabilitative services for women who are victims of domestic violence or family discord. Our Short Stay Homes give shelter and immediate relief to women who are rendered homeless owing to violence, discord or moral danger. The Board also runs a 24 hours Women Helpline which women can dial if they feel threatened by violence, atrocities or exploitation. Another of the support services offered by the Board is grants to Working Women's Hostels which provide a protected atmosphere for working women who are living away from their families.

For the special uncovered and disadvantaged groups such as children of prostitutes, prisoners, leprosy patients and rag pickers, the Board provides special services under its Innovative Schemes. The Board is also carrying on a campaign against Female Feticide for the past several years and in the coming years it is envisaged that this campaign will be scaled up into a countrywide effort.

Women are endowed with greater sensitivity to vital issues and with the sincerity and devotion that is necessary to stay with the task till it is completed. They have not been able to grasp opportunities so far because they suffer from inherent problems and burdens. That however does not mean that they should not be given a chance to do something better. One million women have been elected to the local bodies. How long do you think it will take them to learn their new jobs and realize their true status? And even in the Parliament if our handful of women leaders, are able to create such a storm, can you imagine the strength of nearly 200 women? Perhaps men are scared because the future belongs to women!!

The proper representation of women in terms of numbers and quality is absolutely essential for their meaningful partnership in the progress of the nation. When we do not allow women to be a part of decision-making at the highest levels we are denying half of humanity the right to be represented and given a voice. The very legitimacy of every decision taken without the consensus of women is questionable because it has been taken by only 50 per cent of the population (the men). In this great nation of ours that is emerging as a global leader, can we allow this kind of discrimination? I conclude by placing the aforesaid pertinent questions before you.

3

Towards Social Transformation in India: Indicators of Women Empowerment

DR. JAYA ARUNACHALAM

I am indeed very pleased to present the Valedictory Address today at this Conference and thank the organisers particularly Smt. D. Bharathi Sundar and Dr. D. Sundar Ram, Founders of Academy of Grassroots Studies and Research of India, for giving me an opportunity to speak where an eminent personality and economist will be present here today with whom I had the opportunity to work. Dr. C. Rangarajan has been instrumental in nominating me for the International Activist Award.

It also happened to be the year of 64th Birth Anniversary of the visionary of modern India Shri Rajiv Gandhi. It gives me pleasure to be here in Tirupati due to its Academy of Grassroots Studies and Research of India (AGRASRI) and Rajiv Rural Development Foundation (RRDF) serving the rural masses in Andhra Pradesh.

> "A society can be judged by how well half the society progresses and if they are to progress, half the talent and energy cannot be ignored. Women should be allowed full freedom and action."
>
> *Rajiv Gandhi,* NAM 1985, New Delhi.

True to his words our late former Prime Minister Shri Rajivji showed great interest in grassroots initiatives in the country. He was a great supporter of the *Worldwide Women's Movement* and was keenly interested in improving the status of the women. As an astute, socio-political reformer Shri Rajiv Gandhi started visiting grassroots initiatives and one such initiative is *Working Women's Forum (India).* Rajivji visited the forum twice i.e. he visited the *fisher women members* of WWF in August 1988 at the *eastern coast of Tanjore, Tamil Nadu* and his second visit was to the *women beedi rollers* centre in the same year on November 1988 at Vellore where about 5000 *women beedi workers* met him in a village. In both places he patiently listened to the grievances of women and took action immediately on the need based petitions that women presented on the immediate requirements such as *desilting of the canal in the fisher women area* and *non-payment of stipulated wages* to women beedi rollers at Vellore.

As a supporter of worldwide women's movement, Sri Rajivji initiated several *national missionaries* to enhance the status of the women in the country that was greatly appreciated in the *UN Fourth World Conference* at *Beijing* and India is considered as one of the pioneers in establishing such national missionaries for the enhancement of status of women unlike in other countries who were lagging far behind.

Shri Rajiv Gandhi appointed *several committees*, prepared a *perspective plan for women* and personally presided over some of these committees to implement actions. Some of us were actively involved in these committees in one way or other and worked so closely. Realising that the discrimination inflicted on the girl child is a reflection of patriarchy and overall gender bias, he declared the *year 1990* in the *SAARC Conference in Pakistan* as the *Year of Girl Child* and called female children as "*Future Women*" who otherwise are a victim of neglect in India. What made Sri Rajivji appreciate *Working Women's Forum (India)* – product of worldwide women's movement its salient features are presented below. The facts describes the efforts of WWF in enhancing the social/financial status of women at various stages.

WWF now has completed 30 years of its work. Having recognized long before that this half the energy and half the talent particularly are women, Working Women's Forum (India) initiated itself in 1978 with *800 women* at the grassroots is a social movement of over *a million* women today. The Forum moved from a single branch of poor women entrepreneurs from Chennai urban slums to 14

---

*Text of the Valedictory Address delivered by *Dr. Jaya Arunachalam*, on 20th August, 2008 in Tirupati, Andhra Pradesh, at the National Conference on '*Empowerment of Women in Parliament and Local Self-Government Institutions in India: Role, Status, Participation and Decision-Making*', organised by the Academy of Grassroots Studies and Research of India (AGRASRI), in Collaboration with the Rajiv Rural Development Foundation (RRDF), Tirupati (Andhra Pradesh). The Conference was Sponsored by the National Commission for Women, Government of India, New Delhi.

branches, and moved beyond one state to *three southern states* in different cultural and linguistic context spreading its activities over *3644 villages* and *2256 slums*. In its 30th year one feel quite gratified that the endeavour of mobilizing/empowering poor women in WWF has been possible through *micro-credit extension to the poor as an inclusive process* combining the same with *micro insurance* and several other welfare *measures/benefits*.

Indicators of Empowerment

Several studies conducted so far on WWF both by outside experts besides our own periodical impact study every 5 years where quantitative and qualitative indicators proved both the degree of empowerment women achieved and the progress made by women both at home and in the workplace.

Women workers in WWF have demonstrated that in these three decades they gained self-confidence, articulation and self-perception. They have understood and accepted their roles/responsibilities but also have learnt to confront violence within the family/community. Further women proved beyond doubt that they are an alternate leader in the family and certainly can stand up to question injustice in the neighbourhood. They refused to accept not only the imposition of superstitious out-moded traditions of patriarchy such as dowry, child marriages, widowhood, desertion and other social evils as a curse, fought against oppressive actions/human right violations inflicted on girl children such as feticide and infant mortality. WWF took up special effort to empower these women through an intensive reproductive healthcare programme that heightened women's awareness, enhanced their decision-making efforts both to decide on the number of children in each family, their nutrition requirements, the choice of contraceptive practices that each of them desired. Her knowledge on legal rights made her to assert for her rights and share in family property, custody of her income and other legal matters.

Quantitative Indicators

Several WWF studies indicate quantitatively that within the family there is an increase in marriage age of girl children, fewer children in family, visible changes in physical and nutritional status of the family. Enhancement in the literacy status of both her children and herself that are quite appreciable. Women in WWF is able to visualise a need for collective strength and collective consciousness as a way to succeed instead of fighting alone.

Women in WWF like other women's group never go in search of women in slums/villages rather it is the other way round. Spontaneously, many new groups approach the cadres of the Forum in their neighbourhood, results of which is the phenomenal growth of WWF as a social movement.

Combating the Influence on Class, Caste, Gender—Towards Social Transformation

The activism of the *class nature* became imminent when WWF organised agricultural labourers, export workers, piece rate and contract labourers such as Cigar, Agarbathi, Handicrafts, Lace and Weavers of Textile industry.

The *class question* was focused when women workers confronted wage questions in contract labour/piece rate wage operations in the workplace particularly in many of WWF branches in Andhra Pradesh/Tamil Nadu. The earnings of these workers in the unorganized conglomeration of work options were not only irregular but also too meager and very low to make both ends meet. For workers in the urban centre, struggle for housing, water and civic-amenities aggravated their miseries. But on the other hand it was not anyway better with their landless counterparts in the rural areas who equally suffered unemployment, underemployment and low wages, sometimes limited to even 45 to 60 days of work a year. If they happen to be living in drought prone areas (Bidar, Dindigul) a demand for regular employment was quite imminent. Thus it is more than an annual feature that even today 'rural poor workers' are on their *migrating journey* to the already over crowded city slums in search of new work options and continue to be victims of vicious cycle of poverty. Recently even the *100 days work a year programme* introduced by the Government of India in rural areas is so tough for the worker to perform, that a single day work puts him/her off from work for two successive days as the working conditions are so harsh.

Forum also concentrated on the oppressive *caste* and *gender* aspects in the urban centres where more of gender (violence) and caste bias (as most service workers are SC/ST Class) were quite visible as most of the vendors and food hawkers in the city belong to the Schedule Caste. High prevalence of alcoholism further aggravated poverty/gender violence. Further, men's income contribution to the family was either low or nil. Therefore, the character of the initial urban groups had been more a solidarity/ neighbourhood groups of grassroots initiative, in furtherance of building up their leadership effort to fight such caste/ gender bias.

Hence, to expose the caste/ class/ gender character of vested interests and strengthen bargaining power of women workers, WWF had to create a subsidiary union on trade lines called the *"National Union of Working Women"* that was inaugurated by *Mr. Phill Neck,* the then Director ILO, South Asia Office on *7th May 1982,* a landmark decision to create *visibility* to women workers and to their valuable economic role. This strategy revealed a sharper focus to the class nature of the exploitative elements in their productive effort. The continuous *trade union lessons* enhanced their awareness on labour issues.

The Forum had come a long way in its journey in their facilitation to poor workers in these three decades facing many problems, taking up struggles/ challenges for these workers. It was not a smooth sail for the forum to tackle issues of *wage-workers, micro entrepreneurs* such as *vendors / hawkers* of *Chennai, lace artisans* of *Narsapur* or *Silk weavers* of *Kancheepuram* who worked as contract/ piece rate workers or *Bidri workers* of *Bidar* or *Agricultural workers* of *Dindigul* or *Fisher women* of *Adiramapattinam* or *Agarpathi rollers* of *Bangalore* or *match stick makers* of *Vellore, Seri culture* workers of *Chennapatna* or handling *Devadasi issue* at *Bellary.*

What Prompted WWF to Spread Itself?

In the year 1979, a peasant woman from *Dindigul district* approached the President WWF to start some non-farm employment programme on the same line as in Chennai. The initiative of the *Forum* thus moved from the urban areas to rural areas slowly and a branch of *Co-operative Bank (ICNW)* was also initiated there. WWF strengthened the traditional occupations of the rural women in Dindigul through *Micro Credit support* that became an *alternate employment* potential besides agricultural wage work. It was nothing new for them as the women head loaders who go round selling greens/ vegetables in the street of villages have been now assisted to procure produce like Banana, Tamarind and Chilies from the villages and sell them to the rural market in the nearby rural fairs. The credit provision strengthened their ventures and lessened their dependence on landlords/ employers. Such alternate employment helped the agricultural workers towards *revision of wages* by the landlord around the area where workers were paid even below the minimum wages as stipulated by social legislations.

Some of them were even able to get *dairy cattle* through WWF's micro-credit options to pursue the sale of milk and other dairy products as an alternate option. In *Adiramapattinam* in the eastern costal areas of Tanjore even as in 1980s due to upcoming of large scale prawn farming activities in the coastal districts by the well-to-do business men due to economic liberalization policies led to the destruction of livelihood economies of the fisher folk who are totally dependent on the sea for their daily survival. Such promotion of prawn farming even created severe shortage of salt affecting fisher women's dry fish trade. Here *Forum's credit intervention* through *ICNW provided* to fisher folk in *1981* strengthened women's fish trade business, from auctioneers who often supplied perished products, when supplied on credit. Additionally the problem faced by fisherwomen was that the selection of auctioneers in fishing villages was in the hands of village leaders who mostly did not have any consideration for women's fish trade. Therefore they allowed all kinds of contractors to engage in fish auctions with a result, women never had a say in the selection of good auctioneers despite being entrepreneurs and playing a major role in overall fishing economy. Later forum's awareness/orientation programme led women to fight for a say in the auction of the fish catch of their villages. Forum's intervention made women to fight for their rights decide on *fair trade practices* in auctions sending petition to higher authorities for the desilting of fishing canals and for *transportation facilities* to travel to other market centres.

In a region of agricultural prosperity i.e. in the fertile area of West Godavari in the coastal Andhra Pradesh, the Forum's work exposed the exploitative/oppressive conditions women went through as the *lace artisans* in the shanty towns of *Narsapur, Palakol* and *Bhimavaram* numbering *80000,* in the region, despite their producing for the world market. Thus in 1981 President WWF replicated the experiment of Chennai slums at Narasapur and the surrounding villages taking the women artisans into confidence and facilitated them with access to credit and a *marketing outlet.* As the wages of the lace artisans was very low, WWF later negotiated with the exporters and bargained to increase their wages from Rs. 3 to Rs.10 per reel of thread which eventually has increased today to

Rs. 80. In introducing an organisational platform and finding a marketing outlet, WWF keenly followed study findings of *Marie Mies* a German Researcher who focused on the conditions of lace artisans.

The forum at the outset brought the lace artisans into the *organizational frame work,* later had set up production-cum-design center to acquaint them with *new/modern designs,* initiated a *credit cooperative enabling* lace artisans to have access to micro-finance and become *entrepreneurs,* later facilitated in sale of their products in the *open markets* in nearby *shanties.* Some of the lace artisans have been sent as trainers to other districts of Andhra Pradesh to train young women workers. Later on, Forum brought into its fold the rope makers and weavers of Malkipuram and other micro entrepreneurs in Bhimavaram, a shanty town in Andhra Pradesh.

To bring into the limelight the oppressive conditions of *Beedi rollers* and *Match Stick makers* in Vellore district of Tamil Nadu a branch was initiated in Vellore in *1983. Child labour* and *Child mortgage* was rampant among both beedi rollers and *match stick makers.* The *International Labour Organisation* later facilitated WWF's Vellore branch to practice the alternative employment programme as a part of the *anti-tobacco campaign* world over; besides the occupation in cigar rolling had been falling down due to the closure of many factories in that area. The alternate skills facilitated better income for the poor women and lessened the hazardous effect of cigar rolling/match stick making. It was here, a grievance petition was handed to the late Prime Minister Shri Rajiv Gandhi when he visited *Forum in the year 1988* regarding low wages that was even far below the minimum wages. Then the State Government was asked to intervene to get right wage through the *intervention of Prime Minister's Office.*

In *1983 the Bangalore* branch was initiated to provide relief and credit to *Agarbathi workers* who mostly are migrant workers in the slums of *Bangalore city* where the trade of Agarbathi rolling mostly using these migrant workers from Tamil Nadu has been prevalent in highly exploitative conditions. The forum mobilised the migrant Tamil workers at the outset, that created feelings of neglect among the non-migrant local Kannada Agarbathi workers. Realising this forum quickly brought both the groups as neighbourhood solidarity groups and opened a credit Co-operative (ICNW) to facilitate both collective bargaining of the workers in the trade led to increase in wages from Rs. 2.50 to Rs. 60 per thousand Agarbathi sticks rolled in the factories. *Bidar* is a backward district of *Karnataka* and is a drought prone region receiving very poor rainfall.

The *Government of Karnataka* earlier in the 80's initiated the *Bidar Integrated Rural Development Project* (BIRD) to improve the quality of life particularly of the rural poor women/children who are engaged in agricultural wage work, cattle, goat poultry rearing, also engaged in blanket weaving, bidri handicrafts (special handicrafts of that area). Having spent about substantial amount through UNICEF's assistance on the *Bidar Integrated Rural Development Project* (BIRD), the Karnataka Government decided to hand it over to a community organization to take over the project from them in the *year 1987* i.e. after 5 years Working Women's Forum (India) was considered as their choice. Accordingly the President WWF was invited by the Karnataka State Government to take over the project as they felt WWF as a community based organization will deliver goods in reaching the people in large number. WWF commissioned a *feasibility study* to learn about what went wrong in the earlier approach of the project of the government particularly the reason for failures and have a healthy discussion with the local women. The study revealed the real situation that the earlier project did not involve the local community participants particularly the women from *Schedule Caste* and the *minorities* who are dominant in the district. The President of Mahila Mandals appointed by the Government project authorities were upper caste, well to do women, who did not visit colonies/ bastis even once during the project time. Later placing all these information before the government WWF President accepted to take over this project to work and informed the Government of Karnataka that they will utilize only WWF's methodologies to restructure the entire programme strategies to suit the local poor.

As in other places, here too the Forum initiated Co-operative bank i.e., ICNW to initiate the *Microloan programmes* to help the alternate employment options to women agricultural workers of the district encouraging them to take up goat, cattle and poultry rearing and help blanket weaving, chumki work and bidri handicraft production train the young women to see that such products would find markets in Mumbai. The forum's emphasis on non-farm employment programme and access to financial services enhanced their quality of life among the landless poor women in Bidar. Though silk weaving has been carried on in *Kanchipuram* from ancient times as part of India's heritage slowly the other products like polyester products have resulted in less demand for heavy/costly Kanchipuram silk sarees. Besides the policies of the government benefited only the male weavers in the government co-operatives and admitted only male heads of household despite women too had been major components of weaving occupations. The assistance of the government in cash as well as in kind (in the form of *gold thread*) was pledged by the male weavers of the family to moneylenders and cash being spent on liquor and personal expenses. The *establishment of an ICNW branch and the intervention of the Forum* in the year *1990* helped the women strengthen their employment potential and their role in weaving occupation made visible and helped many women weavers to redeem their bonded children to other weaving families. The strategies adopted by the forum as in other places resulted in the enhanced resource position in weaving families, reduction of *indebtedness* and fight *child labour*. Further the *visibility of women weavers* helped government to admit women weavers too to production and marketing societies on par with male weavers. Strengthening adult employment particularly led to redeem their children from bondedness. Further frequent buyer-seller meet of the Forum periodically became a *marketing outlet* for the weavers.

Forum initiated *Chennapatna* branch in 1991 to extend credit activities through ICNW to women mostly engaged in *sericulture work*, toy making, raising mulberry plants etc. The problem in sericulture work is that the silk worms could be reared only in a moderate weather. Extreme heat and rain destroys these worms. Women faced the same discriminatory process as men are paid Rs. 80 while the women get Rs. 30 for the same volume of work. Credit extension has been provided to them therefore to diversify their activities like wooden toy making or other occupations to suit the seasons. *Dharmapuri* a drought prone area was *initiated in 1993.* The abysmal poverty condition gave place to socially disadvantaged practices such as female foeticide/infanticide, infant mortality in Dharmapuri and in the neighbouring districts. This is because of the superstitious belief around the area that the female children are drain on the family. Therefore several workshops and education/orientation programmes by WWF in addition to strengthening adult employment helped the few girl children being sent to school but it cannot be said that this practice is totally done away with.

Forum is fighting very hard to fight this human right violation. The women engaged in cotton handloom weaving in this district receive very meager wages. Education, training, credit assistance and other Social Security Measures is slowly improving their economic/food security situation. The *Bellary* branch of Karnataka was an initiative of the then *Central Minister* for *Women and Children* asking President WWF to replicate WWF's experiment in Bellary in the year 1994 there, where large scale exploitation of women/ children who not only practiced all kinds of superstitious social evils induced them into prostitution. WWF President, at that time was part of the *National credit fund* i.e. Rashtriya Mahila Kosh to help women NGOs in the country. The government made Rashtriya Mahila Kosh to provide financial assistance to help women to initiate this Bellary branch in the *year 1993*. WWF's immediate priority at Bellary was to stop the untold suffering and the oppression that was inflicted on girl children. The evil practice as mentioned earlier was dedication of these children to the female deity to become Devadasis later or child prostitutes lifelong. Forum thus strengthened women's economic roles at the outset and started helping their mothers to take up some gainful employment in that area and encouraged them not to induce these young girls into prostitution but instead send them to school that are provided by government in all poor areas in large numbers.

The women in *Hyderabad* are mostly engaged in zari embroidery, chumki work, basket making and bangle making. The problem was to organize *minority women* in the slums of *Hyderabad* and *Secunderabad*, where women of this neglected communities mostly lived in dire poverty and exploitation. The women get a very meager wage for the chumki work, i.e., Rs. 200 for 2 sarees that takes one month to complete the work. Similarly in making Bangles, the wages are also very meager. If the bangles require intricate complicated designs they would complete only 4 Bangles per day that would fetch them hardly Rs. 20 to 25. The forum initiated the *credit cooperative in 1997* that enabled these minority women from the closed societies to come out and mobilise other women. Apart from its original grassroots character, WWF now had acquired an additional strength through this unionization process to protect women from *hazardous economic role* and started helping her through health care services. These integrated health service is designed in such a way to facilitate her as a worker and as a mother along with other benefits (insurance, maternity benefits, medical aids).

To describe the strategy adopted in the process of building this movement of Working Women's Forum, the strategy has not been a sophisticated one but the same indigenous sustainable one that followed by Gandhiji even before and during the struggle for India's freedom. Despite such strategies being indigenous, it worked in building up a commitment/solidarity among poor women, facilitating other poor women in smaller communities and neighbourhoods.

Having described the poor women's experiment in WWF the question that looms large in our mind is where will they find themselves in the *National Agenda* in every spear of human activity. An ordinary educated women feel that they are in a small number in many fields. No doubt democratic process and electoral systems of course has thrown up a few women leaders such as Late *Smt. Indira Gandhi,* Late *Benazir Bhuto in Pakistan, Khalida Zia* and *Sheikh Hasina* in *Bangladesh* and Late *Srimavo Bandaranayaka and Chandirika Kumaratunga* in *Sri Lanka* at the helm of affairs particularly in *South Asia* after their freedom struggle fighting colonial powers. Such emergence of few leaders in politics neither provided full *gender justice* nor made an impact on the *status of women* particularly at the grassroots. No one can forget that large number of women came out on the roads in the 19th century to fight for the freedom of the country at the call of *Father of Nation* to oppose the *British colonial powers* during *freedom struggle*. However it is no exaggeration to say that the fruits of freedom did not reach women directly particularly when the *National Government* was formed. Their services are totally forgotten.

Therefore, reason for the emergence of women's movement worldwide demonstrated similar gender bias world over. Thus the *UN declared the year 1975* as the *International Women's Year*. In India too, *Smt. Indira Gandhi* using this opportunity took up the challenge with the feudal and the rural rich to help poor women agricultural workers and enacted two legislations i.e. *Minimum Wages Act* and *Equal Remuneration Act*. But at the enforcement level it is still very weak even today due to the complacency of the bureaucracy and the strong-rooted feudal forces that stand as impediments/road block in the implementation of such laws.

The glaring example of the gender bias of *this millennium* is the fate of *Women's Reservation Bill,* though it is a much debated subject today, but not being taken up seriously for consideration to be passed in the Parliament. In comparison, we cannot forget the *historic constitutional amendment* in recent years regarding local bodies governance the enactment of 73rd and 74th Amendment to integrate women into the political process particularly at the grassroots. Undoubtedly this landmark event happened during the time of late *Former Prime Minister Shri Rajivji* resulting in more and more women *panchayat leaders accomplishing everywhere today. We often hear about the excellence in their governance* at the grassroots. This landmark decision took place because of the exceptionally strong political that was demonstrated by *Shri Rajivji,* the then Prime Minister of the country. Today we witness conspicuously absence of such strong political will among our current politicians in replicating the same process to pass the *Women's Reservation Bill assuring women 331/3 per cent seats in the Parliament.*

Women are not asking for any charity but the following statistic shows the poorest representation of women in all the institutions i.e. *8.2 per cent in the Lok Sabha* and *11.4 per cent in Rajya Sabha* as on the year 2004. Equally their representation in *Central Council of Ministry* in the year 2004 has been at *10.29 per cent.* Also the participation of women in executive positions in *IAS,* was *10.42 per cent* in the year 2002 and *IPS 4.44 per cent* in the year 2005. Women occupied *4.5 per cent* in the year 2005 of total number of judges in *Supreme Court* and *3.31 per cent* in the *High Court* as on 2003 statistics. *(Women in India; National Institute of Public Co-operation and Child Development, New Delhi 2007).*

As a person who has been closely associated with *Rajivji* I want to share few thoughts here. The reason why women insist on this reservation bill is, such a strong political action alone is the way to fight the prevalent discrimination, exploitation and struggles, that women go through in their every day life both at home and in work place. The gender bias and the discriminatory process that goes on unabatedly even after India's 61 years of independence, requires a corrective mechanism i.e. a policy reservation for women to put an end to atrocities against women and establish *gender justice.* As champion of women's causes *Rajivji* was well aware of multiple burden of women that were crucial obstacle to their development who said very emphatically that *"it is really at the grassroots, at the daily level the discrimination must be removed."*

Once again I thank the organisers of the Conference for giving me an opportunity to address the august body.

REFERENCES

U. Kalpagam, Labour and Gender—Survival in Urban India, 1994.

Nandini Azad, World Employment Programme—ILO Study—Rural Women and Development Lessons from the Field, 1983.

Andrea Menee Singh & Anita Kelles—Viitanen, Invisible Hands—Women in Home based Production, 1987.

Juan Migul Luz, Salehuddin Ahmed Evesto and D. Garilao, Managing the Informal Sector—1991.

Paul Ekings, A New World Order—Grassroots Movement for Global Chamber, 1992.

Ponna Wignaraja, Women Poverty and Resources, 1990.

Marty Chen, The Working Women's Forum: Organizing for Credit and Change, 1983.

Jennefer Sebstad, Women and Micro Enterprises an Assessment of UNFPA Experience, 1994.

Jaya Arunachalam/Brunhild Landwehr, Structuring the Movement and Spreading it on, 2003.

Working Women's Forum (India) Impact Study & Evaluation Report—1996-2000, 2002-07.

Dr. Loes Schenk-Sandbergen, Evaluation of WWF, Amsterdam University, Holland, 2001.

Maria Mies, ILO Study—House Wives Producing for the World Market, 2004.

4

Women Empowerment and Local-Self Government in India: Some Reflections

JAGAT S. MEHTA, *IFS (Retd.)*

No doubt there has been progress in the empowerment of women after the Panchayati Raj was established. The 73rd and 74th Amendments to our Constitution enacted in 1993 and 1994 added distinction and refinement to our democracy; it has really surged ahead of long-established democracies which had built-in preferences for women. The third tier (with the Central Parliament and State Assembly providing the other two tiers) with one-third of office bearers posts reserved for women exists nowhere else. From traditional suppression of women, we held forth the promise of political equality for the weaker sex. The reservations for the handicapped members of the society—the Scheduled Castes and Scheduled Tribes (another inherited curse)—have been preserved (but, alas without a time-limit or waver for the emancipated or educated creamy layer). By prescribing a rotational basis, no constituency can turn into a pocket borough. Elections have been held under the new amendments in many Union states. In some the Panchayats were elected as early as 1970s, but in Rajasthan, though it was the first to launch a Panchayat in 1959, the electoral stipulation has been enforced only since 1995 and, this means only three quinquenial elections have been held.

Some forms of Panchayats existed in much of India even during the colonial period but they were mostly caste based. The promise of political power devolved to the third tier grassroots level only after it was constitutionally sanctioned by these amendments in the nineties. They can still gather strength or be abused, but our own experience in Udaipur, as subsequent paras will make clear, has been guardedly positive. A beginning has now been made, but it will remain a moot point that, knowing Gandhiji's inclination and the extensive debate in the Constituent Assembly, why the Panchayat System should not have been embodied from the very beginning. The two tier system was dominated by motivated first generation guardians of public interest who had undergone personal sacrifices in striving for a democratic self-government. This Panchayati Raj Initiative may have been the confidential recognition of the failure in the eighties after the deterioration of values and the unforeseen discovery of the cancerous virus afflicting the succeeding two generations, who had turned politics not as a commitment but a profession disregarding or selfishly circumventing the spirit of the constitutional directives. The Congress lost its credibility in 1967. Or was it because in imitating the British parliamentary democracy, we made the fundamental mistake of overlooking that the average size of the constituency in the House of Commons is about 60000-70000 while for the Lok Sabha Constituency, even then numbered over a million and now sometimes exceed 2 million. The latter may be the reason for elections becoming the root cause of the prevalent corruption with deliberate hesitation in enforcing limits to election expenditure enabling the state to restrict use of money power.

The Logic of the Panchayati System: Pluses and Anxieties

In the flush of exhilaration of independence, we rampantly destroyed forests and made them a source of capital accumulation for electioneering. The Panchayati System at its base level has only 200-300, which gives a much better chance of electoral franchise being uninfluenced by ulterior factors like money or muscle power. By the eighties, at the village level, the deliberate intention was also to inoculate against the hazards of party system deflecting local development.

It is openly acknowledged that we were given one of the most enlightened constitutions in democratic history, but the aam admi (public in general) is cynical about its functioning; he is disgusted with the widespread corruption, the denial and distortion of individual rights, laws perversion and the flagrant abuse of power. Many flaws have certainly crept in contaminating the ugly features of national and state politics in the first forty years. The old domination of caste still persists – a fear voiced by Dr. B.R. Ambedkar in the Constituent Assembly – the Panchayati System has the ingredients of providing a corrective balance to the functioning of democracy in India by initiative in rural development in the hands of the base level and not social legislation coming from top downwards.

The fact that all parties have been voted out of office and that in several states the governments are now of SC/ST or OBCs, is proof of a functioning democracy, notably the rejection of an artificially justified Emergency is proof of its constitutional provisions. Equally those in office have illegally made fortunes is a slur not only on individual morality but a constitutional lacunae of inability to prosecute known violators. The arrogance of the bureaucracy has got worse as compared to the imposed steel frame; indeed, it is believed that not only has their independence of civil servants generally gone but the bureaucracy has shown the way to corruption to the elected leaders. The rich are able to rely on wealth; male domination has not been sufficiently reduced. We would be doing democratic India a disservice if we were not more vocal in acknowledging our own failure in working a near perfect constitution.

In 2008 we can therefore only make a tentative balance sheet to judge whether the Panchayati System has succeeded as much was expected by Rajiv Gandhi and his colleagues and whether such shortcomings are likely to be aggravated or ameliorated in the years ahead. My appraisal will be largely anecdotic and not based on measured national statistics. It is, in fact, based on the limited experience of a Capacity Building Institution started in 1997 and confined to Udaipur district. Before appraising the negative and the positive features of our experience, it may be useful to describe the Institute, called Vidya Bhawan Institute of Local-Self Government and Responsible Citizenship.

Vidya Bhawan Institute of Local-Self Government and Responsible Citizenship

The Institute is a part of Vidya Bhawan—an Educational Society established with a Middle School in 1931—which now has 10 other institutions. Unlike other Vidya Bhawan Institutions, it has no building and is utilising an existing guesthouse constructed by the Old Boys of Vidya Bhawan. The permanent faculty is small (of about 7) but it is helped in "training" by the next door sister institute—Seva Mandir—which for 40 years has been working in adult education and rural development, is also confined to Udaipur district and parts of Rajsamand district. One of *the* Vidya Bhawan Institutes, Krishi Vigyan Kendra, has space and residential capacity to accommodate in two hostels (for men and women), which are used by the Panchayati Raj Institute. (A nearby hill also belonging to Vidya Bhawan is earmarked to build an independent institution, but it was felt that first we must get the institute going before any capital expenditure is assembled with a working corpus to cover the running expenses).

What is unique about the institution that it imparts a 6-day in-house training for those who have been elected under the Panchayati System either as Ward Panches, Sarpanches or as members of the Panchayat Samiti. They are mostly tribals. The programme consists of volunteers who decide to come to attend the course with no governmental or financial lure to attract them. The in-house programme enabled day and night interaction between elected representatives from different villages.

The original capacity envisaged was 25. Initially only 6 or 8 persons came in the first courses, but by the help of Seva Mandir and the word of mouth publicized at monthly melas at the block headquarters—there are 11 blocks in the district—the institute has become well known. We have had as many as 40-50—sometimes even 70—volunteers in courses, and that speaks volumes for the spreading confidence. Each volunteer is given the bus fare and Rs. 50 only in lieu of wages or earnings lost, but this is inadequate to cover minimum wages. So far in 11 years, some 7000 have gone through this capacity enhancing "training." The total number of electoral offices of the Panchayats in Udaipur district is 6400. We have not yet covered all of them. The excess are explained by new selectees, some coming for refresher courses, and special parallel programmes run for women only. Anyway, the number of volunteers itself is proof of the respect and the interest the Institute has come to command. The Institute has throughout been open and conscious of the ideal of being accountable to the rural constituencies and the city cognoscenti. The representative advisory committees have met regularly.

Apart from the small faculty of motivated persons, mostly retired and living on their pension but deeply interested in strengthening grassroots democracy and aware of Human Rights. We have been helped by a large group of experts numbering nearly 20. It includes serving and retired – a Block Development Officer, a retired Chief Conservator of Forests, an agricultural specialist, a retired sessions judge, two doctors and two woman activists, etc. The total budget expenditure has, however, been minimal. In fact, while budget when drawn up envisages full salaries, some did not accept honorarium. So far we have stretched a three-year grant to efficiently run the institute for four years. The programme has made many training innovations like games of snakes and ladders to drive home the importance of what should be the ingredients of development and the values which must be emphasised.

The institute has brought out 25 publications. A well-illustrated manual is given to each participant. They are encouraged to literacy and to correspond with the Institute and select letters in Photostat of their own writing are published in the newsletters which are distributed to Panchayat headquarters. As a matter of fact, the Institute's publications, specially the manual has been sent all over the Hindi speaking belt, including the Government Institute in Hyderabad but in response to their demand only.

The institute was launched by a grant from the Human Rights Division of the European Union for one year but with purposeful austerity, this was spread over nearly two years. Thereafter it has received sustained support from Sir Dorabji Tata Trust. Two years ago, as part of Sir Dorabji Tata Trust scrutiny, Sudhir Rao with India-wide knowledge of the Panchayat System, was nominated to spend a whole week looking at the working of the institute. He attended all training sessions, met the faculty individually, had talks with the visiting lecturers and interviewed several of the participants in one-to-one session behind closed door. We were truly gratified that in the report to his principals in Mumbai, while offering suggestions for improvement, he expressed that these grassroots democrats groomed by Vidya Bhawan were being truly 'empowered.' Indeed, he felt that there was no other institute in India, which had similar programme and promise.

I myself have been interested in the programme and must have attended at least 300 concluding sessions. In each case I have asked the new comers – and most came for the first time – whether there was anything in the course content to make suggestions or which they found redundant or already knew about from their working experience or through the officially nominated "Sachiv." I was truly astounded that almost invariably the participants articulated that they had not known most of what was imparted in the six days training programme. Many gave instances of how the Sachiv almost deliberately kept them ignorant and sometimes even the BDO refused to return the register of works and employment. Even allowing for exaggeration, I believe this has the basis of truth.

Some corroboration to our positive claims comes from statistics. In the elections of 2000—3 years after we started—the voting percentage was 15th in the whole of Rajasthan's 32 districts. (In 1995 Udaipur was 24th). In the 2005 elections, the voting percentage in Udaipur Zilla rose to No. 1 slot. What perhaps had some significance was that the percentage of women voting had jumped by 14 per cent compared to the year 2000.

The Social Problem of Women Empowerment in Rajasthan

What are the other visible signs of progress in Women's empowerment? As is well known, even compared to much of India, the tradition of Purdah, the seclusion of women with total denial of equality, was prevalent in the rural areas and even cities of Rajasthan. In middleclass homes, no men were allowed in the Zenana section. 99 per cent of marriages were still decided by parents based on caste and dowry. Poverty is endemic. Women were treated like chattels and girl child was denied education and paired before attaining the legal age and this has not gone. An anecdotal instance might illustrate the prevailing poverty. 100 miles of railway line cuts across the district. In one of our courses for women, the poverty and hardship of women was to the extent that out of 40 participants, 10 had never seen a railway and 28 had never boarded one. Our course therefore took them to 2 stations of Udaipur only 4 miles apart to give a firsthand experience of buying a ticket, boarding, and seating in a railway compartment for this journey between the City Station and Rana Pratap Station, one woman started screaming when the train was crossing a medium-length river bridge thinking it was hurtling to a crash. She had never seen a railway bridge!

Positive Gains but Insufficient

We have, however, seen proof of emancipation which can be traced to the Panchayati Raj System. In the early years, even the elected women, either Ward Panches or Sarpanches, used to come with faces in veils, often accompanied by their husbands and not ashamed to acknowledge that they exercised their power on the advice of their male spouses. Currently, only 10 years later, all women are unveiled; they come without their husbands. Some women are no doubt educated, but most are illiterate, and they are no longer unaware of their administrative responsibilities.

Although this too cannot be corroborated by statistics, women Sarpanches have been more objective and more effective in supervision of schools, health clinics, anganwadis in their jurisdiction. It depends greatly on whether the women have independence of livelihood such as provided by Seva Mandir under the Sadhna scheme of piecework sewing allotment. Women empowerment in NGO villages has probably more vigour at the grassroots than in the lower middleclass of cities.

In land transactions irregularities and preference continue. There is still gender abuse, child labour, under-payment of wages to women, diverse proofs that women are inferior and have no right of independence in earning and equality, but where a new beginning has been made. Some households can see sights of emancipation like in Bollywood films with women and girls dilly-dallying prior to marriage. The reservation of one-third of offices for women is having its impact. One exceptional story might be summarised.

Champabai, a woman Sarpanch, got a Talab (lake) traditionally appropriated by landlord made into a common heritage by sheer force of collective strength. Champabai has studied up to the VIII class but she is likely to become the Pradhan of the Block even in a general seat and could well be the earnest to grassroots democracy making their way to the Vidhan Sabha and eventually the Lok Sabha.

General Observations on Women's Emancipation: Bureaucratic Corruption

Let me now revert from the local experience to the general question of women's empowerment. Many studies have been made, only some I have read and, therefore my judgement is perhaps superficial. But let me pose some questions, which may be relevant. The first- Whether the introduction of the Panchayati System when it is third-tier was a consequence of the unexpected degeneration of our democracy and particularly the alienation even of those belonging to the Scheduled Caste, Scheduled Tribes has not actually belied the expectation that democracy will be a corrective to inherited wealth and power. It could be argued though not proven that the grassroots electoral system would expose the elite dominated society of the past. The awful truth is that social values have further degenerated and non-connected are more amenable to ulterior factors like caste and connections. This is particularly because either deliberately or with the connivance, the bureaucracy, the Panchayat Office bearers are kept in the dark about their responsibilities and powers. The Sachiv (Secretary of the Panchayat) instead of being the accountable, attempts to run the Panchayat. He decides whether and when Gram Sabha is called twice yearly or not called. Thus the very social legislation which was to empower the Panchayat such as in National Rural Employment Guarantee Scheme or the Jawahar Yuva Yojana becomes the instrument for more corruption, which spreads upward. This may be a temporary phenomenon. What is further significant is that only nominally women are not being elected against general seats. One asks whether leakage and waste would not be reduced if by a special method dues are credited to their respective bank accounts. This would eliminate the middle bureaucracy and yet raise the purchasing power. It would not help create capital accumulation but that remains almost as dubious as before the NREG scheme was started.

What then are the prospects of translating the constitutional vision of political equality for the female sex? There is an ever-growing feminist movement. Not just a Prime Minister, the leader of a major party, but there is growing number of women in influential positions, but the resistance to women empowerment politically and in the private sector remains strong. There is clash in the positive implementation of women's empowerment at the decision-making level. But none can argue this publicly and so the progress is slow. Girls are still seen a burden to be got rid of marriages. Instances are there of foeticide and the present alarming imbalance between the total number of men and women. We are far off from the envisaged corrective that political power must come from below. It must be better imposed by the Central and State Legislatures.

There is, however, a beginning of emancipation towards gender equality. Our own experience has shown that by non-political voluntary organizations a more effective corrective can be made. A somewhat greater emphasis on education for the girl child would mean less influence of the male spouse. Already the old system of women not sitting on the durries is forgotten.

My limited experience underlines the importance of good NGOs who will empower rural society. The country now is in transition from too much reliance on the state to too self-centered pre-occupation with the market values. Gandhiji depended on good secular NGOs, which will enable them to turn away from cynicism to the exercise of civic responsibilities. By and large women respond more readily to development needs of the rural areas and so awareness of civic responsibilities, courage to identify corruption to defy the bureaucracy. But we the elite have a great responsibility. Our forefathers led the struggle for independence and had no hesitation in making sacrifices. The suppression of ages has disappointed "aam admi." The efficiency of the Central Government in giving legislative directions cannot be negated but it is for the Panchayat to check the arrogance of bureaucracy, exercise the Right to Information (RTI), expose false muster roles, rampant abuse of NREG and JYRY and generally the ignorance of the villagers not exploited.

Role of Good NGOs

My final thoughts are that we cannot do without Government for social legislation but also we cannot end up in the failure in implementation. There are Good NGOs and superficial NGOs. An impartial body outside bureaucracy and the elected members should determine the NGO to be entrusted with the selection. Spirited NGOs could provide the bridge for the empowerment of women. India has shown that democracy demands equality of sex and we must again become pioneers. The Panchayati Raj legislation like the Hindu divorce legislation of 1955 was incomparably farsighted. Neither has been strictly enforced but there were small steps in the right direction. Democracy can only thrive with the equality of sexes. India as a pioneer in Women's rights should consciously reject the residue of a male dominated heritage.

5

Women in Indian Polity and Governance: A Symbol of Participatory Democracy

DR. SAM PITRODA

The theme of 'women and politics' have emerged as a critical issue, especially over the last two decades. This issue is connected to larger questions of gender, social development and the role of power in society. The status of women in a society, and the level of equity and empowerment accorded to them are crucial components of understanding the development index of a country. And one of the key benchmarks for understanding the level of empowerment is the role of women in the decision-making process of a country. This awareness was reflected in the platform for action developed at the 1995 Fourth World Conference on Women in Beijing, one of the goals of which was to increase women's participation in political institutions.

In India, while the constitution ensures equal rights to both men and women, women representatives in politics have been negligible, even after 60 years of independence. Women were at the forefront during the independence movement, and since then the country has seen some powerful women politicians. This has, however, not translated into strong representation of women at all levels of the political process. As of 2004 a mere 9 per cent of women were involved in decision-making in Parliament and that too of a certain class profile. A truly vibrant political democracy requires all members of civil society to participate fully in making and implementing decisions. In 1992, the Government of India took a step forward towards addressing the issue of women's minimal presence in the political process through a constitutional amendment that sought to empower women in panchayats and municipal bodies by reserving 33 per cent seats for them.

Empowerment of women at the grassroots level organisations has ensured a participatory form of decentralised governance. There are now over one million elected women at the village, block and district level. Women have gained a sense of empowerment by asserting control over resources, addressing problems of the community and challenging stereotypical notions. Panchayati Raj Institutions (PRIs) have also given many women a greater understanding of the workings of politics, in particular the importance of political parties. There is now a notable surge of women in Local Self-Government Institutions, even crossing the mandated 33 per cent level. As women enter the structures of governance in large numbers, they are changing these structures so that they reflect more closely the concerns of women. The presence of women at the local level in politics has initiated a positive domino effect and the impact can be felt in progressive action on neglected issues such as girls' education, domestic violence, corruption, health etc.

While the overall picture is upbeat, there are some concerns as well. It is essential to understand that the ability to take advantage of this positive discrimination is mediated by class, ethnicity, caste and power structures. The constitutional provisions have ensured representation of women in local governance, but merely becoming members does not ensure effectiveness. It is not always the case that the most capable women are elected as leaders. Often, women who are relatives of the existing local leaders may get elected to fill up these reserved seats. Women still continue to face considerable handicaps to their involvement in politics. The conservative attitude in rural areas, patriarchal values, religious views, family responsibilities, lack of education and economic dependency often make women in rural areas unequipped to effectively participate in the political process. In some cases elected women have remained at home while their husbands have attended panchayat meetings and carried out official transactions on their behalf. Also, sometimes women have acted as proxies for men's views or for influential lobbies at the councils. Further, these elected representatives have often been from upper caste communities and hence this participatory process is not entirely free of caste and class bias.

Reservation is an important step to ensure participation of women. But this must be backed by a more concrete agenda for action involving spread of education and mass communication among women, proper training before assuming office, self-help groups for awareness, economic independence through access to micro-credit organizations, and access to health providers etc. For political empowerment institutional policies are not enough, an enabling environment is also needed. This includes a legal framework, sensitisation workshops to negotiate institutional rights, civil society cooperation and an active political constituency advocating the rights of women. Also a security structure needs to be provided to women against harassment from vested interests.

Enshrining political change within the law has forced both the pace and direction of a positive change in the status of women. There is now a real engagement between women and the political system. But this can only be a means to an end. What is also needed is an active programme for social change to encourage greater participation of women in the political process at all levels in the country. Only this systemic change can truly empower them and redefine their role in the political structures of the country. In this regard India still has a long way to go.

To begin our journey to empower women in Parliament, State Governments and Local Government Institutions I recommend that we use the growing power of the Information and Communication Technology with access on mobile phones to help create an environment for openness, transparency, networking, sharing, training, education, awareness and collaboration by establishing various portals in all major Indian languages at national, state and district levels.

6

Value of Networking Elected Women Representatives in India: The Collective Reflection

DR. DEVAKI JAIN, AHALYA S. BHAT,
PADMINI ANANTH & H. ANAND

The Fourth World Conference on Women in Beijing held in 1995 clearly delineated the need for a *"Collective Voice"* to the issue gendering governance. The 73rd Amendment to the Indian Constitution ensured that there are more than one million elected women representatives among the 3.5 million local political persons in India. Individually, these women came from diverse backgrounds, lacked political experience and the working knowledge of the state. The need of the hour was for a collective voice that could influence and drive the gendering and location of elected women representatives in Local Self-Government. It was hoped that this might shift the centuries old subordination of women.

In this chapter, we would argue:

- That Local Self-Government, *LSG* as mandated by the Indian Constitution through the 73rd and 74th Amendments—and which is now synonymous with Decentralisation in India,—is the best if not the only tool, instrument available to the poor,—as well as other excluded—from conventional—power groups, such as women, minorities and dalits in India—to *participate, direct and claim justice*. Further that Indians, need to recognise this fact, and respect it and not be ambivalent, if we honour democratic processes of development engineering.
- We suggest that these amendments and the structures they propose are *democratising development* deepening democracy and improving the quality of representation, through the most well established vehicles of democracy, namely

accountability, affirmed by universal franchise and multiparty elections at regular intervals, social justice, enshrined by the reservation of seats for women and the excluded castes.

- In the Indian context when local elected councils have been constituted, they need to be perceived and strengthened as an alternative to locally active NGOs. In countries where the democratic culture is less embedded, then NGOs are the voice of democracy, i.e. of justice, of action in times of crisis, humanitarian aid, voluntary service. But in India where locally manageable institutions exist and have the mandate of the Constitution, it would, be subversive to bypass them.
- We go on to suggest that participation, for excluded groups as well as for the poor is most valuable when it is in politics. The focus of the women's question lies in gender-relations; the inequality in power, in autonomy between men and women; and the redressal of this inequality/lack of autonomy for women is contingent on their political presence—their visibility—in conventional politics. (This was also strongly affirmed in Beijing in 1995 by the World Wide Women's Movement).[1]
- We suggest that Local Self-Government in India has however for the first time-envisaged participation; if we include participation in formal politics as a key aspect of participation, then we have massive or in-depth participation. For the first time we have more than one million Elected Women Representatives (EWRs), amongst 3.5 million local politicians. What a massive force of politicians? We would argue that the PRI system has in fact ushered in participation in the most vital sphere namely the power game and while we mock at the women, they are transforming gender relations and perceptions of themselves in their own eyes as well as in their crucial circle the family.

  Participation is usually measured in terms of *numbers* and percentages: e.g. how many women participated in a meeting, or an association or these numbers are often disaggregated according to class or caste or whatever other social group is relevant to justice and poverty. Then there is the question of in *which forum or institution*. In institutions, which are marginal like Mahila Mandals, institutions that are bypassed like the Panchayati Raj Institutions or institutions with power like financial institutions so again there is an institutional element.

Participation can also be measured by the *outcome:* has my participation influenced the decision? This is where the notion of leadership and power comes into the question.[2] Women may participate in many meetings but the outcome might not have revealed their voices.

This exposure to politics, of fighting elections even if set up as a dummy, sitting in councils even if hand and mind twisted by the men, is politicising women in formal politics and the scent of power, like the scent of honey is not easily shed. Women are flexing their muscles as well as becoming courageous and revealing their influence on local institutions. Women's strong presence in local self-government, namely Panchayati Raj Institutions (PRIs') in India has influenced many dimensions of politics – theory and practice. It has not only unpacked gender relations – namely the relations of power between men and women – but also transformed the quality and thrust of local self-government and the political landscape in India. Women critique current ideologies of political economy, the notions of power and the methods of exercising it, and demonstrate how they can mould these into institutions that are gender equitable, just and humane (Jain, 1997).[3]

- Proximity is a value to the poor and excluded. Women value proximity, whether it is to a drinking water source, a fuel source, a crèche, a health centre, a court of justice or an office of administration. Poor women have to walk miles together to access this facility, which is exhausting and consumes valuable time. Moreover, when there is an attack, a rape, a burning, a witch-hunt or other violence against a woman, seeking redress from councils, which are located far away, may not be feasible. But if these councils and the people in them are near, the chances of redress and effective action are greater.
- A case in point is a Presentation made by Mahila Samakhya, an educational programme being supported by the Central

Government now in the Eleventh Plan, and earlier by the Dutch, thrilled the audience at a National Conference on Domestic Violence—as it showed the capacity; of women not only to nurture and stay *with collectivities like the sangha or the mahila panch* or the *nari adalat* but to dispense justice through dialogue and debate amongst women only. A remarkable innovation and practice in so called backward states like Uttar Pradesh[4]—*a vivid example of the value of proximity for effective participation, for resolution of conflict and for holding state and society accountable.* In assessing the outcomes, the presenters made remarkable conceptual innovations, affirming the feminist view that it is practice that is the teacher, not theory and that practice can and should construct theory, if it has to be efficient, that assessment indicators need to be fluid and move over time, depending on the phase of a process.

- These women were showing how the most important outcome, the solution is not the end of the marital conflict. The solution is woman recognising her agency, a concept that has been developed by Prof. Amartya Sen.[5] There has been a transformation in the family and in her as well as her own power. It is here that development is converted into a right, not in the Human Development Reports (HDRs). Through these institutions like Mahila Samakhya, the Mahila Panch and Nari Adalat have enabled women to convert a development input in the form of a programme of education into a rights' affirmation programme by using skillfully the collective, by being able to belong and nurture their collectives, something which men cannot easily do.

Amartya Sen emphasises the importance of recognising the political-social participation and leadership of women if they are to be effective agents of change and not just passive recipients of welfare.[6] Women's participation in politics, the arena for the negotiation of power, is of crucial importance in removing women's poverty and subordination.[7] Furthermore, local self-government, including proximate political agencies, provides one of the best vehicles to translate the proposition of active participation into practice.[8] Development has to be democratised for its impact to be equitably distributed. Ultimately, localising government, attention to the institutional architecture of countries, and enabling participation of the poor and discriminated offers the only way of dealing with injustice and conflict.

- We would then suggest that even if nothing else happens with the PR Institutions, even if the skeptics ask for it to be made to serve the poor to quote the guidelines, "such as making the Panchayati Raj decentralisation work for the poor" decentralisation has justified itself.

A Recent example is the importance and the value of Mahila Panch and Nari Adalat—two institutions emerging out of the Mahila Samakhya programmes in Uttar Pradesh and Gujarat (already described). They have, to quote their own presenter, redefined what can be called justices. They have shown that women can dispense justice and resolve conflict by discussing among themselves only. They have shown that women not only can have redressal to let us say marital conflict, a case of domestic violence, but also the very process has led to an affirmation of *women's agency*, to transforming her complaint into asserting a *right*. They argue that women need a neutral space, a space outside of all the local alignments class, caste, political parties and trades. In these neutral spaces they are able to come to, what we can call, consensual decisions, which deeply affect their lives. There has been an identity for women in politics irrespective of caste or party. This self perception arises not only from the women's own sense of their shared experience but also from attitudes and imagery imposed on them by the men.

Hence, the Local Self-Government or the PRIs have helped to change the local government beyond simply increasing the numerical presence of women but also by enabling effective participation by them.

Women Make a Difference

Women are transforming the development agenda to address critical issues like health, education, income generation, curtailing social evils, refining leadership, changing village dynamics, etc.

To believe that women are using their new formal political space to empower themselves and to support them, four agencies in South India have initiated federating EWRs into a fluid association, since politicians are a fluid flow and not a trapped group like let us say workers in a factory. This project was coordinated by the Singamma Sreenivasan Foundation (SSF) wherein the EWRs have identified their need for an Information and Resource centre in the district, not the conventional crèche etc.

An experience from one of our partners SAKHI in Kerala affirms women's capability to develop collectivities despite the divisions of political parties, caste, gender, class. When the idea started, it was clear that elected women were part of the party hierarchy and could not form groups across parties due to the party's insistence on loyalty to party. However, over a year, they have moved away from this position and begun to examine how the decentralised fund in Kerala is used by the district bodies.

In Tamil Nadu, there are two federations of elected women politicians, namely, a federation of Chairpersons of the district panchayat and a federation of the elected members of Gram Sabhas in Tamil Nadu.[9]

But the knowledge does not stop there. Because this knowledge was developed not by an NGO, not by an outside academic consultant, but by the process in which the EWRs themselves participated, they have begun to tackle this at the governance level and raise their voice in the larger spaces.

The women's collectives and collectivities also have an additional glint, namely they are bound across class, namely poor and non poor. Women engage in issues which impact women like domestic violence or water, or reproductive health, especially in urban slums and rural areas.

SSF is also enabling EWRs to participate, to develop informed voice to *engage in policy debates and formulation*. This project looked at an innovative strategy—collection of oral histories—individually and collectives, which revealed women's impact and/or frustration in local self-government, their own views and definition of an enabling macro policy. This also included informing the elected women of the macro policies that has links, to their locale—livelihood, environment, and family structure,—so as to develop a response. The village studies also looked at the changes in respect of identifiable interventions in economic and social development spheres and promoting social justice such as improving employment/income opportunities, local food production, sanitation and the conditions of the discriminated sections of the village population. The Local Women Politicians were thus exposed through the technique of PRA (Participatory Rural Appraisal) to converse on macro policy matters such as the population policy, health policy and so forth.

The *Women designing Fiscal Policy* rests on the premise that the purpose of any transformation either of the process or the outcomes of budgets is towards removal of poverty, especially the *poverty of women*. This project (Building Budgets from Below) was undertaken in five phases across 4 districts as well as selected wards in Mysore City Corporation, Tumkur and Udupi City Municipal Councils of Karnataka. It raised awareness of various stakeholders on gender responsive budgeting and developed a user-friendly tool/methodology, which could be used not only by the women, but also for the training purpose. In addition, the women were enabled to understand on the schemes of both Central as well as State Government.

SSF has in fact been enabling elected women to prepare village development plans in 44 GPs spread over 3 districts of Karnataka after looking at the kind of fund availability under various schemes. The experience in Karnataka has shown that there is great eagerness among women to acquire this knowledge and to engage in designing how they want their village to be developed. Free hand is to be given to the panchayats/EWRs to utilise the untied funds as required by the panchayats.

We have to ensure that the district plan is not merely a tool to know *how to spend* the funds that have been decentralized and put into the districts, but a *plan that has goals*, which they have to optimise.

It is here that capacity building not merely of the officials and the technical staff, but of the elected persons and the innumerable agencies that are now spread across rural India, SHGs and other forms of mobilisation for the various missions, farmer associations etc. need to be brought into play on the design of the *district plan*.

Unless some of the sectoral schemes are allowed to be integrated as the available funds by the district to be utilised towards the district's achievement of what can be called full employment and increase in growth, it is difficult to see how district plan can be a tool for transformation. By using the flagship issue of women's well being, such a turf battle and impediment can be removed as women's empowerment cuts across all such inhibitions.

EWRs are also linking the dialogues and up linking them to *violence against women* and to Gender Audit apart from population policy. In India, the proportion of crimes committed under IPC against women towards the total crimes has increased continually during the last 5 years from 7.4 per cent in 2002 to 8.2 per cent during 2006.

The violence against women project used various research tools like group discussions, one-to-one interactions with the community members, the surveys and the street plays to understand the problem in local specific context. Besides, series of interactions with the community members (including workshops) were held in order to familiarize them with the aims and objectives of the project and the implementation strategies as well as to seek their active participation in all our activities.

The following are some of the responses by the collective voice of the women.

- *Sale of Arrack:* It was observed that consuming arrack was one of the main causes for violence against women, hence through collective action; agitation was launched to ban the sale of arrack. In the process, the Ookuta members, CBR groups and the SHGs started protesting against the illicit liquor.
- *Domestic Violence:* To bring awareness and to publicize the issue of violence against women, several posters, pamphlets and other materials were disseminated in the villages. The community which was reluctant inclined themselves to address these issues, either with village elders or judiciary.
- The other issues discussed at length are HIV/AIDS, Female Foeticide and Trafficking.

'Women's Participation in Decentralization" — a project undertaken by SSF involves continuous interaction with the elected women representatives, through its programmes for strengthening them, enabling them to perform their newly acquired roles effectively by providing gender, education in a new smooth and efficient way thus promoting the organization to assess the trends of change in a reflective manner. This action research project investigates the following aspects:

1. How far local self-government with reservation quota has enabled women elected to office has helped them to gain

'Power'. Power to self esteem, gender relations, capacity to implement developmental projects and finally to achieve a sense of liberation.

2. To examine whether intervention by feminist/women led organization makes a difference to the same above question.

1. Gram Swaraj Andolan – A Participatory Campaign

Value of collectivity – Gram Swaraj Andolan launched collectively by the federation members against the recent amendment of Panchayati Raj (Amendment) Bill, 2007 is an example of 'voice' and collectivity. According to the amendment, the Gram Sabha loses its right to choose beneficiaries for all Government funded programmes and thereby it becomes a precedent to further curtail other rights of Panchayati Raj Institutions in the state.

As there was a need to prevent the Government from passing the amendment bill, Singamma Sreenivasan Foundation through its okkuta members partnered with similar minded NGOs and launched a movement in this regard.

As a way forward, more than 2300 representatives of Gram Panchayats participated in the Convention and Rally jointly convened by some NGOs under the banner Panchayati Raj Hakkottaya Andolan 2007 on July 5th 2007 at Bangalore.

It was very heartening to see a large presence of women at the event whose participation was informal and active. These reaped results and on July 19, 2007, the Governor returned the Amendment to the Legislature for reconsideration. Thus, this initiative nevertheless has proved that through federation – a collective voice, members especially women members can articulate their voices towards injustice that curtails their rights.

2. Participation in Gram Panchayat Affairs

Over the years, SSF has observed that the elected women representatives in the initial years of intervention were reluctant to participate and articulate their views. It was learnt that these women (though they were intelligent) felt that it is a male dominant society and also they were culturally used to the notion that expressing their thoughts could be against the respect of the village elders. So this notion curbed them from articulating their perspectives and ideas.

But, over the years, with the intervention of NGOs like SSF, women have been able to come out of the seclusion and also they now feel that even in the male led society, they as representatives of the people, have a responsibility on their shoulders. Hence, women strongly feel that they should play a vital role by articulating the people's voice.

This fact was clearly observed during this project intervention and the field team who stayed with these women, to capture their views and perception of their personal as well as public life. It is strongly felt that the intervention of the NGO has brought them the knowledge and information which is adequate for any leader to express their views. This was also a learning process for SSF to know more about the village life as well as the social and cultural lives of these women.

Many obstacles to the realization of PRIs transformative potential remain. Skepticism about decentralisation persists in many quarters. There continues to be a resistance to really devolving power and funds from centres of (male) power to the periphery. Women still face considerable handicaps to their involvement in politics; for example, inadequate education, the burden of reproductive and productive roles, lack of self-confidence and the opposition of entrenched cultural and religious views.

A Woman Led Information and Development Centre – Hub for South India would help in organising activities, which would strengthen the implementation of the national programme of decentralization. It would not be limited only to the women domain but it would be for all. It could be a center to listen, learn and disseminate. Thus, it would exchange information between states, between panchayats also exchange best practices, enable capacity or skill building, prepare memoranda and policy documents with the training institutes, resource persons as well as other knowledgeable persons and with the help of Self-Help Groups/ Sthree Shakti Groups.

SSF is well positioned to undertake the responsibility of District Level Women's Information Centres.

REFERENCES

1. Conference Journeys: What Have We Not Done? Were Have We Gone Wrong? *CONGO Presentation*, June 2000.
2. *For Women to Lead... Ideas and Experience from Asia: A Study on Legal and Political Impediments to Gender Equality in Governance*, National Commission for Women, New Delhi, 1997.

3. Devaki Jain, The Poverty Thing, *Presented at a Special Event*, Organised by UNDP, New York, May 1997.
4. *Ibid.*
5. Amartya Sen, who has provided the space to understand and make the links between development, human rights and justice, has an interesting comment to make. We need a vision of mankind not as patients whose interests have to be looked after, but as agents who can do effective things – both individually and jointly. We also have to go beyond the role of human beings specifically as 'consumers' or as 'people with needs', and consider, more broadly, their general role as agents of change who can – given the opportunity – think, assess, evaluate, resolve, inspire, agitate, and through these means, reshape the world.
6. Amartya Sen, *Development as Freedom*, New York, Anchor Books, 2000.
7. Devaki Jain, Through the Looking of Poverty, *Lecture given at New Hall, Cambridge University*, October, 2000.
8. Devaki Jain, Valuing Women – Signals from the Ground, *Lecture at University of Maryland*, June 2000.
9. Women Chiefs. See. More Powers for The Panchayats, Special Correspondent, *The Hindu*, Chennai, 18th April, 2002.

ADDITIONAL REFERENCES

1. District Level Planning for Social Development, Devaki Jain, Sub Committee of Karnataka State Planning Board (1994).
2. The Importance of Federating Women Members of Panchayat Bodies, Keynote address by Devaki Jain, State Level Convention of Women Panchayat President, Chennai, 18 October 2000.
3. Capitalising on Restlessness, Inaugural Address by Devaki Jain, Commonwealth Universities Meet at SNDT Women's University, Bombay, 15 November 1995.
4. Devaki Jain and C.P. Sujaya, Does the Mahila Component Plan show the way?
5. Devaki Jain, Using the handle of regulation to revive the space for social justice, Feminisms and Globalisation: Women 2000, 7 June 2000.
6. Feminism and Feminist Expression-A Dialogue', Panel Discussion on Indigenous Feminist Concepts, Achievements and Problems, Devaki Jain assisted by Supriya Seth, Asiatic Society, Karnataka Women's Information and Research Centre, Bombay, October, 1997.
7. Kumud Sharma, From Representation To Presence – The Paradox of Power and Powerlessness of Women in PRIs, Centre for Women's Development Studies, New Delhi.
8. Devaki Jain, Participation of Women in Panchayati Raj, India Panchayati Raj Report 2001 – Four Decades of Decentralised Governance in Rural India, National Institute of Rural Development, Hyderabad, 2001.
9. Devaki Jain, Political Restructuring, Pluralism: With Special Reference to Women's Participation, India-South Africa Round Table, Cape Town, May 15-16, 1997.

7

Gender Perspectives on Grassroots Governance: The Indian Experience

DR. U. KALPAGAM

Grassroots governance is increasingly being recognised as an important requisite for the fulfillment of development agendas and goals. In the decade of the eighties (1980s) it was considered politically correct for development intellectuals to assume a critical vantage point in debates on development issues and policies and to pose the question "Development for whom?" All policies came under the scanner of that morally loaded question and only those considered politically naïve would bypass that question. The intervening years have enhanced the collective wisdom to an extent that we now realize that posing that question critically does not necessarily imply positive outcomes on the ground. Even carefully framed policies meant for the masses, for the poor and for the common man do not reach those in need. Hence many more questions of development practices need to be addressed before development could become a reality for the poor. It is in this context that 'inclusive development', 'participatory democracy' and 'grassroots governance' as ideas for development practice has assumed importance.

For development to be 'inclusive', it has to bring into the mainstream of development all groups and communities without marginalising them. Unfortunately though, the processes of capitalist development bring about both inequalities as well as marginalisation. In the name of modern development, life forms and livelihoods undergo changes and traditional occupations and means of livelihood are lost forever. Modern development by its exclusivist tendencies has resulted in inequality and marginalized sections of the population both in economic and social development. Further social structural factors such as caste, gender, and ethnicity and so on have furthered the exclusivist tendencies of modern development. For development both economic and social, to be 'inclusive', such that development does not by-pass any section of society, or that the development of one group does not lead to the underdevelopment of some others, development practices must be oriented to an 'inclusive' approach. Such an inclusive approach is possible only if development practice is participatory. Top-down bureaucratic approaches to development and market-led development can be made to become 'inclusive' in their effects, only if at the grassroots these approaches are buffeted by a participatory approach.

Top-down bureaucratic approaches became the most significant approach with planned economic development. Development schemes such as the various poverty alleviation and employment programmes like food-for-work were conceived as part of plan schemes and delivered through the bureaucracy through district, block and village level development officers. Although the importance of village-level governance through panchayats was recognised very early on, inspired by the Gandhian ideals of decentralised democracy anchored in self-governing village panchayats, their roles in participatory development were not adequately recognized, which led over time to an increasing top-down approach in development planning and practice. Mukherji (2008: 42) observes that "the period between the passing of the Indian Constitution by the Constituent Assembly in 1950, and the passage of the Constitution (Seventy-third) Amendment Act (1992) has been marked by a tortuous dialectic in the form of contestations between the forces of participatory and parliamentary democracy." It was this dialectic that led to the formalisation of the third tier of government at the grassroots level in 1992. It has been noted by many that this constitutional amendment was indeed not the outcome of grassroots demand through a process of struggle or mass movement, but rather the acknowledgement by policy makers of the lacuna in the development administration. There are three components to the PRI process of grassroots governance namely the electoral process, the decision-making process and the service delivery. Deepening democracy at the grassroots could enable the process of 'inclusive' development if and only if the three components of PRI are set up to work efficiently.

Evaluations of various development programmes have over the years highlighted the facts of corruption, siphoning of funds and appropriation of benefits by the undeserving groups, willful neglect of the very poor and marginalized sections, except in the rare instances of committed elected governments and an efficient and committed development bureaucracy coming together and acting in tandem. This accounts in part for regional variations in the performance of development programmes that it is now not wide off the mark to note that development programmes perform better in the southern states than in the Hindi belt of north India. Vested interest groups generally seek to corner development benefits such that the ones most deserving, the deprived are neglected and marginalized. Especially in rural areas, rural power structures are correlated with asset ownership, resource control and caste or the placement in the social stratification. Instituting the PRI process of grassroots governance thus faces tremendous hurdles and is expectedly fraught with contestations and struggles.

Marginalisation and exclusion does not arise only with respect to the development programmes of the state. Even the market-led development process leads to marginalisation and exclusion. Small landholders are often rendered landless when either big farmers increase their scale of operations or as is increasingly the case when corporate farming becomes established. Communities engaged in traditional occupations like rural artisans and weavers have been compelled to give up their traditional occupations when newer commodities that are factory made are substituted for the traditional products. Tribal groups who had customary rights over forests and grazing lands and their products have been pushed back or forced to join the ranks of landless labourers when market forces like the setting up of industrial plants in lands occupied by tribal groups are forcibly acquired from them under the modernization agenda. Exploitative use of natural resources by multinational and other commercial interests resulting in depletion and making such resource-dependent livelihoods unviable have exacerbated the marginalisation of many traditional communities. The social exclusion of stigmatized groups like scheduled castes, now grouped as Dalits, and different tribal groups resulted in their exclusion from the development process by and large, both on account of their low command over assets and resources and their lack of social power. In fact all these forces have now galvanized the affected social groups to prevent these tendencies of marginalisation and exclusion by their attempts to claim both "Voice" and "Rights" in the development process. We witnessed these in the controversies over the recent Narmada dam oustees and their rehabilitation, the farmers whose lands were appropriated by the Tata Singur Plant, the projects of the various SEZs now put on hold and many more that seem to be cropping up with increasing regularity.

Grassroots governance that brings about a democratic and participatory approach could counter some of these tendencies of marginalisation and exclusion and make development more inclusive. An inclusive development is one in which social justice becomes an integral part of economic growth and development.

Women as Excluded Others

Much has been written by now to show that women are marginalized and excluded from the development process. The reasons for such exclusion has been attributed to the widely upheld social ideology that women are primarily homemakers even though the large mass of poor women are economically active. Women's reproductive roles and child bearing and nurturing functions are seen to further confine women to the realm of domesticity. These ideological constructs of women have obscured the fact that women in no way constitute a homogenous group; the social fault lines that run through society makes women as much into a heterogeneous category as it does the men. Many women combine both their roles as homemakers and are economically active as well, even if the official statistics sometimes do not reveal so, contributing to the invisibility of women's work. Such invisibilising tendencies in conjunction with the patriarchal blinkers of men and of the women who have by large internalized patriarchal ideologies operate as much at the level of development policy and practice as it does in both the household and society at large.

While development policy may have become more gender sensitive and strive not to exclude women on account of the growing awareness and activism at national and international levels, development practice at the grassroots level, the point at which it affects women by exclusion or inclusion has not significantly changed. A massive and radical change at the grassroots that can prevent not only women but others as well, to become the 'excluded others' from the development process requires multi-pronged efforts of both state and non-state factors, and in which education as well as the economic empowerment of women become important factors. The growth and spread of social activism through grassroots NGOs in the last two decades, social movements as well as enabling development policies like the 73rd and 74th Constitution Amendments for local self governance and women's participation in such governance as well as policies of poverty alleviation and employment generation like the National Rural Employment Guarantee Scheme (NREGS), the Self-Help Groups and micro-credit lending and so on are all efforts that provide opportunities towards an inclusive development.

Let us now examine how and why women belong to the category of 'excluded others', by first examining the processes of exclusion and marginalisation of women viewed as a homogeneous category and then of women as a heterogeneous group. The invisibility of women's work on account of the patriarchal ideologies certainly cause their discrimination in the labour market which accounts for their lower wages, lower skill attainments, fewer entrepreneurial opportunities, and confinement to jobs in the lower rungs, often in the informal sector. Labour market discrimination is complemented with and is partly the outcome of patriarchal discrimination within families and households. Women face discrimination in terms of household tasks and the often rigid sexual division of labour that leaves them with less leisure to acquire skills, education, participation in community activities and so on. Girls face discrimination on account of the same patriarchal ideology of women being home workers and are often denied educational opportunities that is at par with their male siblings. Lack of property rights and the consequent low command over household assets along with patriarchal dominance deny most women a fair share in household decision-making. Even when women do earn cash incomes by way of employment, this does not always enhance her decision-making power or autonomy, and often times women are denied the control over even their earned incomes. All these facets of discrimination result in women being excluded from measures and means that could enhance their well-being.

This is most starkly brought out in the aggregate statistics on indices of human development such as education and health. Gender disparities do exist, even if in some regions, classes and communities, these gaps may be improving over time. The pervasive disparities and gaps as indicated in statistics clearly suggest that these tendencies of discrimination and exclusion operate at the levels of daily existence, the family/household and the work sphere. These tendencies have inhibiting effects on their public and community roles as well.

Different categories of women face discrimination and exclusion in varied ways. If girls are deprived of education, adolescent and young women face curtailment in their movement and do not often enjoy the freedom of interacting with people in an attempt to control their sexuality, that often denies them the chance of coming to learn of the various opportunities in the world. If married women face exclusion on account of their reproductive role and as homemakers, there is further exclusion within the family, based on age and status hierarchies as well. Especially among young married women in rural areas, one often hears them say that they enjoy greater freedom after marriage than before. But daughters-in-law bear a greater burden in the division of household chores and in many parts of north India at least have to abide by the norms of veiling and seclusion. While single unmarried women among the poorer classes are not so common, as the status of singleness is unviable economically, poor women also face a greater likelihood of sexual harassment in case they remain single. Female heads of household left to fend for themselves and their children also face severe discrimination much like the single women. Older widows too face neglect and are often on their own trying to subsist, doing some odd work to earn a living. No doubt there are caste and class differences both in the nature and intensity of discrimination and exclusion that women face. Dalit women face far more discrimination even in the hands of upper caste women. But it is in general true to conclude that women do form a part of the 'excluded others'.

Development programmes such as the numerous poverty alleviation and employment programmes, health and education programmes and social security programmes often bypass many of these categories of women, unless specific attempts are made to reach out to them. This is on account of the patriarchal biases operating on numerous fronts both within and outside the family. It has been widely acknowledged that many poverty alleviation programmes that needed the deserving poor to be first identified ignored female-headed households completely, and poor and destitute widows find it difficult to access social security schemes like old age pension.

Similarly patriarchal biases within the family have succeeded largely in ignoring women's health, thus giving it very low priority. Even the state's health policies have insufficiently focused only on maternal and child health programmes, thus viewing women primarily in their child bearing and nurturing roles. It can be concluded that top-down development policy approaches in which the service delivery is attempted through a bureaucratic administration that is insufficiently sensitized to the ways in which grassroots power structures including that of patriarchal power operates, has not succeeded in including women in the development process.

Market-led development processes have also marginalized women of various categories and communities. Especially since in rural areas poor women bear a greater burden of household survival through various kinds of subsistence activities like collection of forest produce, fuel and fodder in addition to waged work on others' fields or non-waged work on own farms if they are from slightly better off households, the marginalisation of women by the market-led development processes have severely impacted on the subsistence and survival strategies of poor women and their households. When rural artisans and those in traditional occupations lose their livelihood on account of the development of the modern economy, the men and women not only join the ranks of wage labourers but lose their traditional skills and knowledge. Women's knowledge of agrarian system, food processing, and water management and so on are rendered obsolete and is not even taken cognizance of. As modern methods of farming are introduced, women are often excluded from acquiring the knowledge of modern farming techniques. Resource depletion on account of marketed development such as ground water depletion has severely affected many rural women who now have to expend more time and effort in water collection. Many caste groups and ethnic communities that had earlier served rural communities through their wares and services now stand marginalized, and the women of these marginalised communities remain further marginalised on account of the new and older norms of patriarchal power affecting their lives.

An inclusive development approach can only be based on a participatory approach that is based on democratic grassroots governance. Only such an approach can attempt to counter the multiple forces of marginalisation and exclusion at work, and bring women into the mainstream of development, especially rural women.

Panchayats, Grassroots Governance and Women

The project of democratic decentralisation in India is not complete and is still evolving. Democratic decentralisation of governance envisages a three-tier system of elected representatives to help in governance at the local level, in rural and urban areas. In rural areas the three tiers are the Gram Panchayat (the body of elected representatives at the village level), Panchayat Samitis (the body of elected representatives at the Block level) and Zilla Parishad (the body of elected representatives at the District level). The landmark 73rd Constitution Amendment made way for one-third reservation of seats in panchayats for women, both in general category and in the reserved scheduled caste category. Thus women could be elected on either of these two categories. Mukherjee (2008) has highlighted through a study of the panchayat elections in Punjab and West Bengal in 2008 of the various lacunae and loopholes in the electoral system and has suggested improvements to achieve the desired result of democratic decentralisation. He like many others before him has found the widespread problem of women being used as 'proxy' candidates. This argument of women being used as 'proxy' candidates however true it may be, has been used by a large number of people to question the validity of seat reservation for women.

This stand unfortunately does not question why 'proxy' cases occur and is so widespread, nor how the situation can be changed. It also does not recognize that a single amendment or a few years experience down the line does not exhaust the possibility of moving towards a more efficient and perfect system of democratic decentralization in which women function as equal partners in development in the long run. The amendment, encapsulating a long-term vision, has conferred on women the legitimate status to become equal partners in development. Despite the criticism, the amended system of representation in the Gram Panchayats has allowed many thousands of women to become grassroots leaders for the first time (Dogra, 2001). It could also be argued that even in the case of 'proxy' candidates in which the male members of the household are the *defacto* panchayat members, it is heartening that male members prevailed upon the female members of the family in agreeing to put them up as 'proxy', thereby giving their women some public roles, however symbolic and devoid of real decision-making power, which they otherwise would not have done.

Equally, and infrequently overlooked, is the possibility of the fact that entry through the 'proxy' woman route has enabled groups that had never acquired or had power in the village before could do so now. In one of my fieldwork situations, I came across one such proxy, a young Muslim woman as village Pradhan in Lahoorpur village in Allahabad district, in her own admission, it was her husband, a shoe shop owner who conducted her affairs and she just put in her signature or thumb impression. But her self-esteem grew, when even researchers like me had to call on her before I conducted my study in her village. Most importantly, the Muslims were only a small minority, and even her family was not residing in the village habitat itself but outside near the main road nor did they own any land in the village, while the dominant landholding caste was the Kurmis in the village.

The probability of all elected women in a Gram Panchayats being proxy candidates is likely to be anyway lower than of a single elected woman being so. It is quite possible that by functioning together with others on the panchayat, they do over time learn something. The more important issue though is the fact of higher illiteracy among women, and many of the elected women are illiterates. Education and training become essential for elected women.

The question of being a 'proxy' raises the more fundamental question of patriarchal dominance and women's low status and power in decision-making in the household. Once again it is necessary to look at the optimistic side to argue that even proxies could in slow degrees give the individual woman more decision-making power in the family, for by granting her some public visibility and role, there is the unintended consequence of giving the woman a little more voice even within the family. Thus public roles and private roles are intertwined and mutually reinforcing. In the case of non-proxy woman candidates, the empowerment processes could in fact be hastened.

The other problems that equally merit some concern are situations when a woman wishes to contest for the panchayat election but is dissuaded or prevented by her spouse and family members saying that her role is primarily to take care of the family and not be concerned with community affairs as yet another instance of patriarchal domination. In some cases a woman desirous of contesting the election may be prevented from doing so, not by her family members, but by others in the village, supposedly on caste, class and other grounds. Often such attempts at dissuading women are more violent than non-violent acts of persuasion, reflecting how brute the power realities are at the village level. Even elected women representatives are debarred from holding office by family and other social forces of domination. This is more so in the case of Dalit women candidates, where it is often accompanied by caste violence. However, it is perhaps still true to say that while all these problems are prevalent, the new system of representation has thrown up a large number of women grassroots leaders, whose functioning however questionable now on grounds of efficiency, could be improved over time.

Equally, as the same set of elected representatives are not likely to prevail indefinitely, and newer and newer grassroots leaders are likely to emerge, there may be an anxiety that this inefficient and undesirable feature of 'proxy candidacy' is likely to prevail in the long run. This clearly suggests that greater awareness needs to be created among all rural women about patriarchal and social domination.

The problem of the illiteracy of elected women and lack of knowledge about rules, regulations and functioning of PRIs can be solved, at least to some extent, through functional literacy programmes and carefully designed training programmes which are already underway in many states. But the issue of sensitizing women at large on issues of patriarchal and social domination is more difficult as the multiple and intertwined layers of domination and resistance have to be cognised, understood and transformed. Social movements including that of the women's movement has now well understood that such transformative agendas require concerted collective action which in turns feeds into transformative visions and agendas at the level of the individual as well. Individual imaginations of transforming society have to be turned into a collective imagination, if it is not to be ensnared by power and engulfed with fear.

The question to be raised here is whether the existing system of PRIs allows for the possibility of recognizing these issues of patriarchal and social domination and of ways of transforming them. Mukherjee (2008) has noted that even the electoral system for PRIs varies from state to state. Whereas in some states contestants for the Gram Sabha election are not conducted along party lines, and individuals are merely allotted symbols for the voters to identify as in Punjab, in yet others it is along party lines as in West Bengal. The implications of party and non-party contestation for women in Gram Panchayats Elections have to be clearly understood.

Although in the evolution of a democratic polity with an electoral system for over sixty years, women have identified with parties, voted for parties and constitute a sizeable segment of the membership in many political parties, parties in their preoccupation with electoral gains and power, have not significantly concerned themselves with local level development issues in the way they should have and have belied the hopes of the citizens. Many parties do not even have grassroots cadres and women party workers have more often been used instrumentally towards the party's goals rather than allow women to raise issues of development that they think are important at the local and national levels, nor have they been given the space and encouragement to raise gender concerns. Male grassroots cadres of some political parties are even notorious for intimidating women in their local areas. Had it been otherwise it would be difficult to explain as to why the Women's Reservation Bill granting one-third seat reservation in the central and state legislatures was languishing so long, especially when the country boasts of its record of having a woman Prime Minister, a woman President, women Chief Ministers and many women elected legislators in central and state legislatures.

There are strong arguments on both sides for party and non-party contestation of Gram Panchayat elections. One argument in favour of party contestation is that it is an anomaly in the democratic structure if it does not allow for party contestation when it does so at all other levels-the Panchayat Samitis, Zilla Parishad, state and central legislatures. However a gender perspective on grassroots governance would weigh more in favour of non-party contestation at the Gram Panchayat level for it removes one more force of power that women have to negotiate with, at least until such time that most women can begin to function effectively without any fear and with self confidence.

What perhaps hinders women most is the functioning of traditional panchayats alongside the newly elected panchayats.

Traditional panchayats have overwhelmingly acted to discipline women and bind them everywhere with rigid social norms and disciplines. In north India these traditional panchayats, also including caste panchayats that cover not one village but a set of villages in a region, have on many occasions even killed young girls and couples for choosing to marry outside of the caste or from the proscribed groups. Even in states where the courts have declared traditional panchayats as illegal, as in Tamil Nadu, they still do function. The existence of traditional panchayats indicates that grassroots governance has been prevalent since time immemorial, but it has only practiced gendered exclusion and was a grassroots mechanism to ensure the systemic reproduction of social and gender hierarchies and caste domination everywhere.

The newly elected tiers of democratic panchayat governance is in fact a social and political contestation with the traditionally dominant forces that had everywhere kept women in subjugation and denied them a voice in matters concerning them, even if their actions constituted violation of human rights. In an interesting internet news report Gautham (2007) writes how the traditional panchayats also called (Katta Panchayats) practiced gendered exclusion in the distribution of post-tsunami aid in the coastal villages of Tirunelveli district in Tamil Nadu. Women by and large, especially the Dalit women, were excluded from receiving any aid because their names were omitted on the argument that males were the heads of households thereby excluding single, deserted, and divorced women and also the widows, and also on the ground that they were not boat owners and were not paying annual taxes to the traditional panchayats even when the women played numerous economic roles in supporting the fishing economy of the villages and had lost their homes and livelihoods in the tsunami. Such social and gendered exclusion had in the past forced the villagers to shun the traditional panchayats and to turn towards the Christian churches for assistance.

Women therefore have much at stake in ensuring that the democratically elected PRIs function satisfactorily in terms of the ways in which the electoral system functions, in the decision-making process in the panchayats and in service delivery. A satisfactory level of performance of the PRIs can be ensured only if women have both 'voice' and rights. Women have to be pro-active at all levels to ensure that they gain 'voice' and 'rights' to enhance their capabilities in the democratic functioning of PRIs.

Women, Voice and Rights

Women's representation in the Gram Panchayat under the 73rd Amendment was indeed meant to give women both 'Voice' and 'Rights'. But mere representation alone will not help in realizing that goal. Even if the electoral system for Gram Panchayats gets improved over time, such that the situation of proxy candidacy gets somewhat corrected, women's voice may not be articulated or heard. There should be an overall awareness of the multiple roles that different classes of women perform and especially of their crucial roles in the maintenance of household food security. It is now widely acknowledged by researchers that women's roles in subsistence among the very poor households are crucial, and vary over the year depending on the seasonal availability of different kinds of food, some even obtained through collection in fields, forests and water sources. Within each village, the arenas of women's concern have to be delineated and a consensus among women should evolve. Women's decision-making powers over issues in these arenas should be enhanced formally by restructuring the process of decision-making that give women of different classes greater say in whatever issues concern their lives. There should also be attempts to ensure that women of different classes do not work at cross-purposes because their interests vary. For instance, upper caste/class women cannot ask that restrictions be imposed on how resources in the village commons are used, or defend themselves and their male members when questioned on the illegal appropriation of the village commons, if women of lower caste/class use these resources for food, fuel, fodder and livelihood.

Dogra (2001) after observing the manner in which women elected to Gram Panchayats function in many parts of north India observed that they bring to sharp focus issues of gender bias, poor sanitation, alcoholism, wasteful expenditure and corruption. It is also widely acknowledged that women in panchayats are not sufficiently concerned and active in the areas of education, health, Self-Help Groups, watershed management, pastures, forestry and food security. In all these issues, women of all classes have indeed very high stakes as these have a direct bearing both on their own and their family's well being and survival. Not only should women in panchayats be trained to take up these issues, but also the decision-making processes too will have be reoriented at the ground level so that their voice prevails.

There is by now a well-acknowledged literature on planning for gender needs (Moser, 1989). Two sets of needs have to be cognized and planned for in development practice to empower women. These are 'practical gender needs' and 'strategic gender needs'. Practical gender needs refer to those that would advance poor women's interests on practical issues that would alleviate drudgery, oppression, domestic violence and promote well-being in everyday life. Addressing practical gender needs is important for women but that alone cannot address the problem of systemic gender exclusion. Strategic gender needs are those needs of women that would enhance their capabilities to address the issues arising out of systemic exclusion. This strategic gender needs also vary between different categories of women. While education will help women to secure better jobs than that of a casual labourer, education for empowerment such as legal literacy will help them become aware of their rights, ways and means of securing their rights and of how not to remain cowed down by the fear of police and law courts. Gender training for women in panchayats should enable them to identify the set of practical and strategic needs in their village communities through participatory research techniques.

In recent years, more and more development programmes are trying to build into the programmes both gender budgeting and social audit. Gender budgeting seeks not only financial allocation towards women in all development programmes but attempts to monitor the expenditure such that it is possible to measure the quantum of money spent towards women's benefit in every single instance at all levels. This is to ensure mainstreaming women in the development process to promote inclusive development, and to enable communities to control the performance and outcome of these programmes so that there is continuous monitoring and evaluation by the communities that are the intended beneficiaries. Coupled with power provided by the recently enacted RTI Act (Right to Information Act) it is now possible for individuals and communities to interrogate the bureaucracy and the state for negligence, corruption and other malpractices. These legal instruments and bureaucratic mechanisms to ensure transparency and accountability help to promote inclusive development and democratic decentralisation only when they are also backed up by a bundle of legally enforceable rights. The emerging discourse of rights-based development is progressively expanding the notion of universal human rights, which while it may appear to have a homogenising effect across cultures and communities also transposes social and economic rights outside the pale of national level political process into universally valid rights. As capitalist globalisation extends its predatory fangs into village communities destroying ecological balance and the livelihoods of people, non-state factors can seek to defend the exploited communities only within a well-articulated rights regime. Gender training for women in panchayats should help them to understand these issues and enable them to both demand and subject themselves to the communities' demands, for transparency and accountability in governance and participate effectively in gender budgeting at their level by demanding greater devolution of financial powers and finances as well, for a gender inclusive local development.

Building Synergy with CBOs and NGOs

Apart from the elected panchayats, there are other Community-Based Organisations (CBOs) that are run along the same lines as the panchayats with elected members. Here too, women must take an active interest and contest for decision-making positions so as to serve women's interests. For instance, many states and village communities have Joint Forest Management Committees at the village level, which has representatives from the state as well as elected community representatives. These are sometimes called "Van Panchayats." It is necessary to make it mandatory in all states to have elected women representatives in all these auxiliary CBOs as well. If there are women representatives in the Van Panchayat, they will be able to highlight, if adequate awareness is brought about through training given to them, the crucial importance of forest produce and their roles in providing family subsistence and ensure that their access to these resources are not restricted. Similarly many villages have Water Users Association, sometimes called 'Paani Panchayat" that addresses the issues of the distribution of drinking water. Here too women's representation must be made mandatory and in fact women should constitute the majority representation in these committees as the supply of drinking and home-use water is everywhere considered women's responsibility. Here too, the representation must adequately take care of caste and class issues, as it is all too well known that even upper caste women participate in reproducing systemic exclusion by prohibiting scheduled caste women from drawing water from wells and pumps used by the upper castes. Elected women in the Gram Panchayats should be trained to build a synergy with such of these CBOs, ensure women's participation in these CBOs and seek collectively to raise women voice on all matters that affect them. There are other CBOs where women are generally by-passed as these are considered 'male' domains, such as irrigation committees, marketing committees, seed procurement committee etc. All these supposedly male domains have to be critically examined and deconstructed by the community women and a place for women in all these male domains have to be secured. The elected women in Gram Panchayats should be trained along these lines as well, so that they will be able to work along with their community women in making their presence felt and voices heard on all these matters as well.

Attempts are also being made to introduce new CBOs that focus on addressing issues like health along gender lines. For instance, NIPCCD (New Delhi) has been involved in a programme of experimenting with 'Kishori Panchayats' which are (Adolescent Girls Forum) that sensitises adolescent girls on health related issues and representative members of this forum also participate in VCC (Village Coordination Committee) meetings to bring their health concerns to the fore. E-Panchayats is yet another new innovative venture to promote grassroots e-governance through the use of ICT technologies that is being tried out in some regions. Women elected members, some of whom are likely to be illiterate will be ignored from acquiring skills in the use of ICT. Care should be taken that they too are given sufficient functional and computer literacy, especially the younger women. The essence of democratic decentralization is to inculcate the democratic spirit and enable grassroots governance. Rural women should be made to understand what this spirit entails in terms of overcoming systemic exclusion and the importance of gaining rights and voice in decision- making.

It is now well known that cases of litigation in a village hang on for years, as there is no speedy settlement at the village level. Land disputes predominate among these cases. Nyaya Panchayats with women representation should be set up in all villages for speedy justice and the amicable settlement of certain disputes. Not only should women be represented in the Nyaya Panchayat and given powers of adjudication even in such purportedly 'male' matters like land disputes, there should also be a separate wing of the Nyaya Panchayat comprising of women only to function as a family court at the village level that will concern itself with family disputes including domestic violence. It is really when the Nyaya Panchayats take off, enfolding within it the all-women family courts can the dominance and disciplinary powers of the traditional panchayats be curtailed and superseded.

Self-Help Groups (SHGs) are another set of CBOs that hold remarkable potential for building synergies with PRIs for better grassroots governance. The growth of SHGs, especially among rural women to enhance their incomes and livelihood by entrepreneurial initiatives through a system of micro-credit lending has generated enthusiasm among women to become economically empowered. Such SHG initiatives facilitated by NGOs rather than through the government development programmes have in most instances a broader agenda than just income generation. They try in varied ways to encompass other aspects of social and economic empowerment. As SHGs are another avenue to promote grassroots leaders, the SHGs members by showing a greater degree of awareness on issues pertaining to exclusion and empowerment could work conjointly with the elected women members of the Gram Panchayat. But such synergies have to be conscientiously built up through various gender training programmes for women in panchayats and in the CBOs, of how to strategically create opportunities out of everyday situations to advance their gender interests in matters of grassroots governance.

Social movements are yet another community based initiative with which the elected representatives will have to work, especially as rural social movements are generally concerned with issues affecting the rural masses. Elected women panchayat members should not identify themselves solely as agents of the state and distance themselves from the social movements that engulf their communities. Social movements are increasingly taking up issues of displacement and rehabilitation arising out of development projects like dams and factories, and ecological issues. Panchayats should sensitise the community as well put pressure on the state to solve these issues. Women panchayat members should gain knowledge of these issues and encourage solving them. Social movements have done much in recent years to place the issues of public accountability and transparency in governance at the center stage. The social audit mechanisms that are now in place for the NREGS (National Rural Employment Guarantee Scheme) was conceived and experimented with by a rural NGO from Rajasthan and put forth as a demand to the state under the leadership of social activist Aruna Roy. News reports from Rajasthan itself have indicated that in some villages the panchayats were against the social audit and placed hurdles in its conduct. Such situations can occur when state-level political patronage nurtures and promotes muscle power and money power in the panchayats. Also with the deepening of the democratic spirit, people at the grassroots are increasingly going to redefine and expand the idea of grassroots governance that will likely be at variance with that designed by the state, which in the future may lead to both a struggle and restructuring of the system.

Many NGOs exist in rural areas or operate in rural areas for the welfare and up liftment of the people usually with some specific area of focus such as education, health, micro-credit, Dalit empowerment and so on. Some are specifically oriented to women's welfare and empowerment. These NGOs also serve as nurturing ground for grassroots leaders, and women often pick up experience of grassroots collective action while being associated with these NGOs. One such NGO is the Working Women's Forum (India) headquartered in Chennai and working in many areas in the three southern states of Tamil Nadu, Andhra Pradesh and Karnataka (Kalpagam and Rajagoplan, 2006). Using micro-credit as a point of entry, WWF (I) approach of group formation and group lending has promoted grassroots leadership among women who with the self confidence gained through WWF (I) association and activities have shown remarkable ability to undertake grassroots collective action. Table 1 show the grassroots initiative of WWF (I) since 2005, although in its twenty-nine years of existence, numerous such initiatives have been regularly undertaken. Many group leaders of WWF (I) have successfully contested in the elections of the Gram Panchayats as well, and have on occasions even taken the panchayats to task on various issues that concern them like pasture land, water, housing and alcoholism. Such kinds of social activism should be promoted and synergies should be built between them and the Gram Panchayats to ensure both gender-sensitive grassroots governance, and one that can effectively counter systemic gender exclusion, discrimination and oppression.

Regional variations in women's participation in panchayats are also a reflection of the effects of political mobilisation both by the women's movement and by other social and political movements. Lele (2008) shows how the rural women's movement in Maharashtra has succeeded in mobilizing and creating awareness among women elected members of the panchayats. This stresses the importance of prior political mobilization of women for the success of the panchayat representation by women. Such political mobilization could be along various trajectories and through a process of building synergies with CBOs, NGOs and social movements.

Conclusion

Gender-sensitive grassroots governance under the present system of democratic decentralisation through the PRIs can become possible and effective only if elected women members are made aware of the systemic gender exclusion and of how the process of development further marginalises them. Such an understanding has to be further bolstered by a critical mass of grassroots support by the community women who could collectively transform the nature of grassroots governance. But it is necessary to build collaborative ties and cooperative relations with CBOs, NGOs, and social movements for the process of democratic decentralisation and grassroots governance to be really effective in its transformative agendas.

Table–1

Details on Grassroots Initiatives by WWF (I)

The crisis management in WWF is handled with great care. To drive home the point an example of crisis management handled both internally and externally in WWF/ICNW is with regard to the *tsunami killer* wave that hit the Marina Coast of Chennai, the eastern coast of Tamil Nadu and few Coastal areas of Andhra Pradesh on December 26th 2004 where nearly 2000 members of WWF were worst affected in Tamil Nadu and Andhra Pradesh.
WWF/ICNW quickly volunteered to organise one-day counseling as advocacy workshop to the representatives of the fishing families who were in trauma and gave them expert advice through oceanography experts and marine engineers, assuring that the tsunami doesn't come as often but only in 50 to 60 years.

Later on 28th June 2005 a function was organised where His Excellency the Governor of Tamil Nadu, was invited as the chief guest to distribute rehabilitation measures of boats/nets and other requirements worth Rs. 1,17,57,667.00 through resources that was received from various national/international humanitarian foundations by WWF to assist tsunami victims. ***28th June 2005***

With the humanitarian assistance, the housing requirements – new houses and repairs of the damaged houses have been undertaken in not only 17 villages of eastern coastal areas of Tamil Nadu where the WWF member live but also in Chennai Marina Coast with fishing colonies. Nearly 140 houses were repaired and new houses have been constructed.

In Narsapur, Andhra Pradesh a fishing market was built for the fishing community which was inaugurated by Dr. Jaya Arunachalam President Working Women's Forum (India). ***11th September 2007***

Demanding 33 $^{1}/_{3}$ per cent reservation for the women in the Parliament, 8000 members of WWF and the President took out a rally and submitted the petition signed by 1 lakh members, to the Governor of Tamil Nadu on 5th September 2005 to protest over the delay in passing of the Women's Reservation Bill in the Parliament. The content of the petition was a message to the politicians not to find divide women on the basis of caste and religion. ***5th September 2005***

National Commission for Enterprises in the Unorganised Sector set up by Government of India as a watchdog invited President, WWF on 13th March 2006 to testify and share the experiences/achievement of WWF in enhancing socio-economic status of women-workers and to testify the same. The Commission stressed to focus on the nature of enterprises, size, scope/magnitude of unorganised labour force, constraints faced by small enterprises, lack of access to material, backward/forward linkages towards better facilitation to the unorganised poor to carry on micro enterprises. As a result a feasibility study about the weavers from Varanasi and Kanchipuram was handed to WWF. ***13th March 2006***

As a result an exchange programme between the weavers was organised from the North i.e. Varanasi and the South i.e. Kanchipuram. *29th September 2006*

A grievance petition signed by 20,000 women workers with regards to Social Security Bill not being presented in the Parliament was sent to the Prime Minister, UPA Chair Person, Central Labour Minister and Deputy Chairman, Planning Commission, Government of India. *6th June 2007*

A Petition requesting for a bore pump with a hand pumpset in the area of Thottapalayam, Pillaiyarkoil Street, Vellore was sent to the District Collector and the Municipal Commissioner. *18th October 2007*

A grievance petition from 36 women employees of TANSI Unit in Ooty who were retrenched from the services was sent to WWF which was later forwarded to the Governor of Tamil Nadu, Chief Minister of Tamil Nadu, Leader of Opposition, Local Administration Minister and Minister of Rural Industries. *3rd March 2008*

Working Women's Forum (India) Submitted a Memorandum representing views/suggestions of the members with reference to Women's Reservation Bill to the Department of Standing Committee on Personnel, Public Grievances Law and Justice–Regarding the Constitution (108) Amendment Bill 2008. *24th May 2008*

The ground work to identify pressing issues that affect poor women adversely in three districts (Dharmapuri, Bidar and Bellary) were taken up. Later, the 3-day material development workshop was organised in Chennai. *10, 11 & 12 March 2008*

The highlight of such workshop is mainly awareness and consciousness-raising where solutions are collectively found. The various events in the workshop include lectures, pictorial charts, role-play, puppet show, skit and folk song, mostly visual demonstrations.

As a follow up measure to the macro Material Development Workshop organized in Chennai on 10 to 12th March 2008. Six micro workshop were conducted from 22nd to 29th July 2008 in the backward districts of Bidar and Bellary (Karnataka) to disseminate information to the poor women on various issues lying dormant in their areas and on 31st August to 2nd

September 2008 in Dharmapuri in Tamil Nadu not only to create awareness on the most pressing issues but also to inculcate in them income generating activities, gender equality whereby enabling them to realise their potential as human beings. The workshop serves twin purposes i.e. to empower women to acquire the means and ability to participate in the main stream of economic and social development, as well as in the decision that affect their lives and those of their families. The solutions to their existing problems were conveyed through pictorial charts in vernacular. Apart from handling social problems, their economic concern too were given major emphasis. In this perspective, the food and chemical processing products were demonstrated to the poor women enabling them to prepare these products in groups and market in the local areas and neighbourhood to sustain their livelihood. ***22nd to 29th July 2008 & 31st August to 2nd September 2008***

A grievance petition signed by 50 families residing in Thiruvatravar Nagar, Perungudi for the irregular drinking water supply was sent to the Corporation Commissioner, Chennai, the President Perungudi Panchayat and the Area Engineer, X-B Chennai Metropolitan Water Supply and Sewage Board. ***19th April 2008***

Grievances of 15 members who were displaced from their hutments just because they have constructed their hutments on government (porambokku) land in Adiramapattinam was sent to the Chief Minister of Tamil Nadu, and the District Collector. ***26th May 2008***

National Union of Working Women fought several cases for the rights of women. In these five years NUWW handled 29 cases relating to dowry, 7 land dispute cases, 3 money lending cheating cases, 5 counseling cases where women who had differences with their spouse were solved, 5 cases relating to business activities and 4 cases relating to vacate the house premises. Apart from this nearly 405 families were facilitated with the drinking water supply-in Velachery (212), Kallukuttai (74) and Padi Pudhu Nagar (119) and one case relating to inter-caste marriage.

REFERENCES

Bharat Dogra, 'Women Justify Reservation Policy in Panchayats', *Good News India*, August, 2001, *http//www.goodnewsindia.com/pages/content/transitions/panwomen.html*

S. Gautham, *India Together*, 27 April, 2007, *http//www.indiatogether.org/2007/apr/soc-kattarule.html*

U. Kalpagam and Srividhya Rajagopalan, 'A Social Platform for Women Workers: The Case of Working Women's Forum (India)', in Jaya Arunachalam and U. Kalpagam (Eds.) *Development and Empowerment: Rural Women in India*, Jaipur, Rawat Publications, 2006, pp. 120-144.

Medha Kotwal Lele, 'Contesting Power in Panchayats', in U. Kalpagam and Jaya Arunachalam (Eds.) *Rural Women and Development in India*, Jaipur, Rawat Publications, 2008, pp. 219-237.

Caroline Moser, 'Gender Planning in the Third World: Meeting Practical and Strategic Gender Needs', *World Development*, Vol. 17, No. 11, November 1989.

Partha Nath Mukherji, 'Panchayat Elections and Grassroots Democracy (Comparative Study of the May 2008) Elections in West Bengal and Punjab', *Man and Development*, Vol. XXX, No. 3, September, 2008, pp. 41-54.

I am thankful to Dr. Jaya Arunachalam, Ms. Nandini and Ms. Asha for providing me information on Working Women's Forum (WWF), Chennai.

8

Women Empowerment through Reservation in Indian Legislatures: Chasing a Chimera

DR. M. KUNHAMAN

There is no dispute about the necessity and desirability of both empowering women and enhancing their representation in legislative bodies. However, the two questions, who should empower them and who should give them representation or how should they get representation merit serious attention. This is because, normally uncritical acceptance and use of conceptual categories and the influence of context-specific emotional situations can blind us to the need for objectively analyzing substantive issues.

What and How of Empowerment

The very concept of empowering somebody means that the object of empowerment is powerless and somebody else whop is powerful should empower her for the purpose of contextualizing the arguments being outlined in this chapter we take the following positions:

The plentitude of programmes and projects of empowerment not withstanding, it is our contention that no body can empower any body. Empowerment is a self-actualizing process. In this the subject role of the person/ group to be empowered is crucial.

By giving special concessions and considerations, somebody cannot be empowered. One feels empowered when one's contributions are recognized and also when one has a sense of involvement. These require entitlements in the form of equitable access to resources.

The condescension and patronizing attitude under: girding the various programmes for empowering the excluded/ marginalized sections should not be lost sight of.

Concepts such as social exclusion and marginalisation are, from an ontological point of view, obfuscating. Take the case of details as a case in point. When were they excluded? They were the providers of labour, they were always included (in material production) and exploited. The use of conceptual categories such as inclusion, empowerment, entitlement, human development etc., is indeed, thinly-veiled, attempt at ignoring exploitation and inequality, which are on the rise by the day. By harping on social exclusion, the question of economic exploitation is ignored and, thereby, the exploiter/ oppressor goes scot free. This is an ingenious project of the world ruling class now in total control of the globalised world economy. If social exclusion/marginalization is the issue, people become eligible for welfare programmes. On the other hand, if exploitation is the focal point, they may become politically empowered and wage a class struggle. The questions, who excluded them and the process by which they were excluded are never asked.

Even if we go by the trendy concepts and analytical trajectories, it has to be concede that no empowerment is possible without entitlement. And, this entitlement should not be only to populist measures like poor quality primary education and primary health care. It should be to property, i.e. land, knowledge, finance etc.

If the post deregister-postulation that government has no business is valid, the government has no business to be in development either. Nobody can develop anybody.

Who are Women?

Women are a biological rather than an economic group. In fact, from a socio-economic perspective, the term 'women' is an abstract, faceless category, defying stereotyping. It is transacts and transclass. It is a notion rather than a concrete entity.

Looked at both diachronically and synchronically, it is difficult to concede that always and in every system, women were powerless and had a subordinate position. Social systems based on the primacy of human labour accorded women an equal or sometimes even a higher social status. However, with the emergence of private property and family, subornation of women started and overtime, and entrenched. In fact, family, the most undemocratic social institution, is the primary site of the emergence and perpetuation of this subordination. From there, it spread to the larger society, polity and economy. Emancipation of women ultimately calls for the disintegration and disappearance of family. Systemically speaking, the transition from a classless to class society meant replacement of bride-price by dowry. It would, thus, appear that an understanding of the devaluation of human labour and the paradigm shift resulting in the disjunction between labour value and product price would give a better idea of this subornation.

Placing the bill, Bill yet again in Parliament on May 7, 2008 has hailed as "feminist" politics coming age "(Agnihotri 2008). According to one school of thought, "the Women's Reservation Bill (WRB)" will create the conditions for meaningful interventions by women in particular and progressive forces in general in the struggle for a more egalitarian and humane path of development" (Agnihotri, ibid).

The placing of the Bill in the Parliament was accompanied by high drama and rhetoric about women's rights and the opposition to it was "characterised by its supporters by its supporters as anti-women and patriarchal" (Menon, 2004, 170).

On the other hand, there is a dysphonic view that it is an "upper-caste project" pursed in a class-neutral, to neutral manner to thwart the rising backward class presence in parliament that is perceived as a threat to social order. The ruling elites art, thus said to be using women's movement to restore upper caste control over the social sections order. Even the prevalent women's movement is looked at skeptically by some sections whose lesser doxology to the Bill is rarely concealed. Dalit women consider it as being savarna (upper caste) while feminists of minority communities regard it as being Hindu by default. Thus, women's movement in general and WRB have entailed a rancorous socio-political fight. Besides, reservation, in general, ever an emotive issue in India, has tended to divide the country.

Women have worked shoulder to shoulder with men in many fields of social life showing savior faire. Their role in the production and reproduction of labour, which is the source of value and the cause of material progress, is beyond doubt. However, it is a fact that they have been excluded from several fields. This involves not only denial of justice but also sub-optimal utilisation of the production capabilities of women, thus entailing a social loss. Gender discrimination, like caste discrimination, limits growth and development. It may be noted, enpassant, that both women in development and women and development are relevant issues while thinking about the gender dimensions of development. In development discourses, both academic and relevant issues while and policy, there is a tendency to talk about the need for mainstreaming women. (This is also the case with regard to groups such as dailts and adivasis). The necessity for gendering development is seldom recognized or mentioned. This is because of the respectability accorded to development as a desideratum without bothering much about its nature, content direction.

Why Women Need Reservation in Legislative Bodies?

The WRB presently in the Rajya Sabha, is being widely and hotly debated. A few heckles have been raised with regard to the extent of such reservation in particular and women's movement in general. While the present writer is in favour of increasing the number of women's representatives in legislative bodies, he takes the position that some of the reasons advanced in support of the Bill call for more careful and, at times, more critical examination. That the Indian society is patriarchal in nature has never been a matter of dispute. The crucial question is how to question patriarchy.

The question of reservation for women in legislatures raises not only gender issues, whatever these may be, but also many larger and systemic and structural questions which are quintessentially socio-economic and political in nature. However, the present debates and discourses predicated mainly on concepts such as "gender revolution", "gender politics" etc. do not seem to give due attention to these questions. The present chapter intends to indicate, though in broad contours, their relevance particularly in the Indian Context.

The position taken even by prominent left leaders and writers and activists of the left persuasion betrays an ideological vacuum. Thus, one is at a loss to see how D. Raja and Com. Brinda Karat look at the reservation question, in general and women's in general and women's reservation in particular.

How are they, in the instant case, different from Sushma Swaraj, Mayawati, Jaya Lalitha and Sonia Gandhi? How do they conflate the gender question with the caste and class questions? Or are they purposefully Obtuse? Of course, gender is across-cutting category. None the less, Positing it on the highly complex social terrain of India, wherein plenteous struggles and a regular reality, calls for vision and strategy. Tackling issues in isolation, our approach hitherto, has only worsened the social situation rather than improving it.

Further, the argument that women's participation in legislatures is to ensure that women's issues are taken up properly and diligently is, it appears, warped. This argument besides being abstruse has many, even dangerous implication. It means, first of all, that women cannot and need not take up general, common issues, not to speak of issues concerning men. This is, in fact, a extrapolation of an old and retrogressive thinking. Only dailts issues. So also in the case of adivasis minorities.

One thing must be kept in mind. A dalit MP or MLA does not represent only the dailts of his constituency; he represents his constituency. Once elected, he is a representative of the people, both who did and did not vote for him.

Similarly, the argument that dailt government employees show partiality for Brahmins, and Christian employees for Christians, and so on? It is too much to expect a dailt official to be a leader committed to the up liftment of the members of his community. Often such a person may not have the knowledge and vision for that task is to do the duties entrusted to him as efficiently, honestly and impartially as possible.

Likewise, a woman M.P. does not represent only the women. Again, it is too much to expect a woman MP to have studied gender issues thoroughly and scientifically. There may be men better informed about gender issues.

Women's participation is required not ensuring gender justice (justice is not just a number game) nor for articulating women's issues (male members can also do that), not for steering debates in legislatures especially with regard to development policies (there is no guarantee that this will happen) but to make legislatures more representative.

If we insist that a woman is to represent women and take up women's issues in parliament, the question can legislatures be asked, given the socio-economic segmentation of the women folk, which women's issues she will take up?

A gain, even if women MPs are well articulate about gender issues, there can develop tendency to marginalize them from the mainstream issues. This is what has happened in the case of dalits.

Dailt politicians are fielded only in reserved constituencies. A glaring example was K.R. Narayanan, The Congress, the largest and the oldest secular party in India could field him only in reserved constituency (viz., Ottapalam in Kerala). Incidentally, it may be noted that Narayanan could rise from a humble position to the highest office in India through his hard work. Even as we accept this fact, it should not be forgotten that he never fought against the iniquities of the system. He, in fact, rose by using all the concessions that the ruling class in India has devised for the SC's.

Whereas the young Marxist (A.K. Balan) who opposed him in the Ottapalam constituency is from an even poorer situation and given to courageously fighting the iniquitous and oppressive system. Even as a starving student, he was struggling against the ruling class. If social commitment were the deciding factor, Balan should have been able to defeat Narayanan, in whose case the 'politically conscious' voters of Ottapalam considered only individual merit. So much about Indian democracy which can sustain exclusion through reservation and which can ensure individual inclusion and group exclusion. It may be noted that even left parties field SC/ ST candidates only in reserved constituencies. In fact, through reservation, the Indian ruling class is ingeniously able to prevent the exploited and oppressed groups and persons across the socio-economic spectrum from getting united and posing a threat to it.

The tendency for exclusion is ready visible in the case of women parliaments. Malini Bhattacharya, while describing her experience in parliament, maintains: "I found there was a tendency in parliament to push women in to certain corners" (Frontline p. 28). This, apart from women's minority presence in parliament, is "because of a kind of social sanction on what a woman's issue is and what is not"(ibid).

A point that Com. Brinda has made in favour of a women's reservation in legislatures merits serious attention. Reacting to the suggestion of the Election Commission of India that political parties field more women candidates, she rightly observes: "that has worked in those countries where there is proportional representation. This is known as the "List" system". In the prevailing (first-past-the-post-system) in India, the win ability of women candidates is a problem. This, she points out, more in justification of the democratic parties' refusal to field sufficient number of women candidates. By arguing for reservation for women, she is unambiguously accepting the existing electoral democratic system.

To counter the demand for specific reservation for OBC women, the question is being raised why Mulayam and Lalu, the advocates of such a demand, did not give adequate representation in party leadership and in fielding candidates.

It may justifiably be asked why women political leaders do not argue within their parties for fielding a certain number candidates in 'sure' or 'safe' seats and mobilizing all the resources of their parties for their success? After all, what is sauce for the goose is sauce for the gander. Why do not they insist on reservation in leadership positions within their parties? Is it the apprehension that in the event of raising such demands, they would be shown the door by the patriarchal leadership of their parties? Why are they opposed to charity beginning at home? And, curiously enough, by speaking about win ability (which is, by the way, equally applicable in the case of male candidates also), she is unwittingly joining the camp of Mulayam Singh Yadav and Lalu Prasad.

The contention that the question of quota will be considered once the bill is passed holds no promise, given our past experience with regard to caste-based reservation. Caste political leaders used to maintain that by organizing along caste lines the entire community will again material benefits and social respect. Caste, once an instrument for the maintenance of hierarchy is, paradoxically, seen as the vehicle for egalitarianism between castes, though not within them (Weiner, 2001, p. 209). Male preference of political leadership is true in the case of even those parties that are headed by women. What prevented Indira Gandhi from giving due representation to women at least in the party? What prevents Sonia Gandhi, Jaya Lalitha and Mayawati from during so? These leaders are, in point of fact, "female patriarchs" (Raveendran and Sherine Upot 2007).

The fact that some of the major political parties (the Congress, AIADMK and BSP) are literally under the control of women leaders should not be over-looked in any meaningful discussions on feminist politics. Unfortunately, then, these parties are the incubus of female patriarchy. Thus, female patriarchy has joined hands with male patriarchy in preventing feminisation of Indian Politics and also the spreading and deepening of feminist practice on the social transformation. "Brinda's observations in the interview referred to above gives the impression that in addition to the built-in-anti-women nature of the first-past-the-post-system, money power and the male preference of the leadership of the mainstream political parties are the hurdles in the political path of Indian women.

It must be constructed that we are implying that women are not facing problems; far from it. According to our thinking, the basic gender issue is lack of women's right to property, especially women's land rights. In fact, if property right is only through females, the existing male preference would go for ever. Then, the crucial question is, will women MPs fight for land to the landless tillers, especially, for female agricultural labourers? Will their class position permit this? Is gender question class neutral? Will women's reservation lead to the disappearance or at least weakening of the axis of caste-class-patriarchy?

A cognate point relates to participation. This much talked about term has lost its precision. Participation parse does not mean a change of direction. For instance, the dalits enjoyed participation even during the colonial period. Their participation had been broadened and deepened since Independence. However, the socio-economic developments that occurred in the country have scarcely improved their class position, let alone changing it. Will the one-third revolution sought through the WRB, lead to a total revolution? Participation of a particular group does not mean much unless that group is able to re-orient the order of priorities. Will more women MPs mean a different order of priorities in development? In favour of which class the reorientation will be sought? Have our women politicians, excepting Brinda, spoken against the disempowering and impoverishing effects of the neo-liberal economic policy? What about the women impact of the processes of actualisation and feminisation of labour brought about by labour-replacing growth under the neo-liberal strategy? What about the feminisation of poverty? Will these larger, structural questions are addressed by our women MPs whose number will and should grow? (Tandon and Ranjitha 2003: p. 12).

It is unhelpful to maintain that all basic questions cannot be solved through women's reservations. Given the continuation of historical inequalities and oppressions and the strident reactions to them from various groups of victims, what is important is to clearly understand what is political about feminism (and its potential to subvert to destabilize, not just dominate values and structures, but ourselves (Menon *op cit.*, 219). In this sense, feminist politics and more importantly, bodies through constitutional rather than political processes, let us not add more contradictions to the already existing formidable ones. Undoubtedly, since Independence, especially since 1993 with the 73rd and 74th Constitution Amendments, more women have come to leadership positions. But two questions need to be answered: *(i)* has this led to the emergence of feminist politics; and *(ii)* are we aiming at the empowerment of women representatives or that of women? Empowerment of people's representatives is not the same the empowerment of the people. The first may result, inter alia, through legal/constitutional measures while the latter calls, for relentless political struggle for overthrowing the "prevalent social structure of accumulation" predicated on the caste-patriarchy ideology (Harris, 2004, p. 198).

Legal empowerment through reservations is, in any case, less commendable than empowerment through the political process. In making this argument, however, one must be cautions. Many women got elected because of their struggle. However, it is next to possible that an adivasi leader like C.K. Janu (in Kerala) would be able to come up politically. No political party would be prepared to field her an election. This is perhaps not because she is an adivasi but because the adivasi cause she is committed to is anathema to parliamentary parties. Parenthetically, one is quite skeptical that the adivasi problem (that is the adivasi land problem) can be solved through the parliamentary process. We need adivasi women legislators not because they can get these legislative bodies to solve the adivasi problems, but because these bodies must ensure diversity and become more representative. Incidentally, the state, both, colonial and Independent, had always been anti-adivasi.

Coming back again to the local bodies, feminization of local bodies is not the same as "feminisation of political leadership at the local level" (Krishna Kumar). Nor has feminisation of local politics taken place in any significant way. Patriarchal leadership of political parties takes decisions regarding local politics. The much tom-timed democratic decentralisation of power is a blatant fraud. People who look at the PRS and euphorically call what has happened, "gender revolution" (Mani Shankar Aiyar, Frontline, *op cit.*, p. 22) seem to suffer from an optical illusion. Thus runs their argument." The person singularly responsible for this unprecedented gender revolution is

Rajiv Gandhi" (Iyer, Ibid). Sycophancy at its best! But what has changed in the countryside? Production relations? Property relations? More in favour of women? Access to resources, it seems that what has happened is decentralisation of centralisation, or in other words, centralized control of resources at the local level.

As was observed earlier, the upper caste feminism is yet to inspire and encompass the lower caste women, especially the dalit women. Also in the prevailing structure, the so called gender politics would be unrealistic, unless gender struggles are dovetailed with caste-class lines. Also, it may be noted that in India, the struggle for social justice has always been linked with caste and ethnic assertiveness (Weiner, 2001, p. 207) and this is likely to be so for a long time to come, unless our perspective shifts from caste to class.

NOTES

"Reservation policies...... generated uncertainties within the Hindu Moral order and resulted in the growth of tensions between forward and backward caste Hindus." Ornit Shani (2007): Communalism, Caste and Hindu Nationalism: The Violence in Gujarat, Cambridge University Press, p. 52. The first chapter of this book entitled "The Politics and discourse of reservations and caste" (pp. 52-76) is very instructive in our context. The first part of the chapter "unravels the processes by which reservations and communalism became inextricably linked. The second part sets the political context in which caste reservation conflicts and communalism emerged in the 1980's" (p. 52).

REFERENCES

Indu Agnihotri, 'Woman Power' *Frontline*, June 6, 2008.

Malini Bhattacharya, 'On being a Women in Parliament', *Frontline*, June 6, 2008.

Mani Shankar Aiyar, 'A Silent Revolution,' *Frontline*, June 6, 2008.

Brinda Karat, 'We have crossed the First Hurdle,' *Frontline*, June 6, 2008.

Krishna Kumar, 'Feminisation of Panchayats,' *Frontline*, June 6, 2008.

Nivedita Menon, *Recovering Subversion: Feminist Politics beyond the Law*, New York, Permanent Black, 2004.

P.P. Raveendran and Upot Sherine, 'Shasi Deshpande: An Introduction' in Shasi Despande, *Rooks and Shadows*, Hyderabad, Orient Longman Special Edition, 2007. First published in 1983.

Rajesh Tandon and Ranjitha Mohanty (Eds.), *Does Civil Society Matter? Governance in Contemporary India*, New Delhi, Sage Publications India Pvt. Ltd., 2003.

Myron Weiner, 'The Struggle for Equality: Caste in Indian Politics,' in Atul Kohli (Ed.), *The Success of India's Democracy*, Cambridge, Cambridge University Press, 2001.

Barbara Harris White, *India Working: Essays on Society and Economy*, Cambridge, Cambridge University Press, 2004.

9

Rotation Term of Reserved Seats for Women in Panchayati Raj Institutions: The Indian Experiment

DR. NUPUR TIWARI

The belief that women in decision-making is a sign of empowerment is reflected in the United Nations Gender Empowerment Measure (GEM), which tracks the percentages of women in parliament, legislators, and as senior officials and managers among professional and technical worker. Tracking women's progress through numbers is not new. There is a growing demand for increasing presence of women in political decision-making. It is argued that women need to be 'empowered' in the realm of political decision-making so as to facilitate their 'real' empowerment.

Women's Reservation Bill -which reserves 33 per cent seats for women at the national and state legislatures-has not yet got the consensus by the members of the Parliament, but the impact of the reservation of 1/3rd seats for women in the Panchayati Raj Institutions (PRIs) is certainly immense. The biggest success of Panchayati Raj is that it has made women politically and socially empowered. There are 26 lacs Panchayat representatives in our country out of which 9 lacs seventy five thousand belong to women, 8.5 lac belongs to SC & ST category. And this number is the largest is the world.

Though under Panchayati Raj System only 33 per cent reservation is made to women but Bihar took the bold step of reserving 50 per cent of the Panchayat seats for women. Currently, elected women representatives are in place in 54 per cent of seats in Bihar's panchayats. Bihar's example was followed by Sikkim, which increased their reservations for women to 40 per cent and held their elections under the new arrangement in January 2008. Chhattisgarh,

Madhya Pradesh, Rajasthan and Uttarakhand have passed laws increasing the reservations for women in Panchayats to 50 per cent. These changes will apply to the next elections to Panchayats in these States.

Bihar, Rajasthan Madhya Pradesh, Chhattisgarh, Himachal Pradesh and Uttarakhand have made 50 per cent seats available for women. This has given political and social exposures to backward, dalit, poor and illiterate.

As a result of this development more important issues like education, water, road and health have started getting more importance in the agenda of Gram Panchayats. Union Minister of Panchayati Raj, Shri Mani Shankar Aiyar views that, "the rotation term of reserved post for women should be extended upto two or three term because generally first term for women representative has proof to be a period of learning and in second and third term only women representatives started showing their real performance." There is need for an amendment in the rotation of the reserved seats for women and they should be given 10 to 15 years of continued opportunity from their seat and unless this provision of rotation is reconsidered empowerment of women representatives would be a difficult proposition. However such advocacy of reservation would definitely be opposed by the forces who are against the women reservation in our country.

The Constitution (73rd and 74th Amendment) Act, 1992 sets out in detail in Article 243D, the manner in which reservations are to be provided to women and persons belonging to the Scheduled Castes and Scheduled Tribes.

(a) Reservations to elected seats are mandated directly by the Constitution, in accordance with the following pattern:

(i) One-third of the total number of seats to be filled by direct election in every Panchayat are to be reserved for women. This is inclusive of the reservation provided for women belonging to the SCs and STs (See iii below). [See Article 243D(3)].

(ii) Within the reservation provided for persons belonging to the SCs and STs as detailed at (ii) above, not less than one-third of the total number of seats that are reserved for the respective categories in each Panchayat

concerned are to be reserved for women belonging to the SCs and STs, [See Article 243D(2)].

(b) These seats may be allotted by rotation to different constituencies within a Panchayat (Article 243D(1) and 243D(3)).

(c) The provisions for reservations to the offices of Chairpersons are nearly identical to the above provisions regarding reservations to elected seats. The additional features of reservations to the offices of Chairpersons are as follows:

(i) While providing for reservations up to a minimum level of one third in respect of women and in proportion to the population in each Panchayat for SCs and STs, the manner in which this is done is left to the legislature of a State to provide by law. [See Article 243D(4)].

(ii) Unlike in the case of rotation of reservations to elected seats, which is discretionary, the rotation of reservations to offices of Chairpersons of different Panchayats is mandatory. [See the second proviso to Article 243D(4)].

A recent survey, commissioned by the Ministry of Panchayati Raj and executed by the Nielsen Company – ORG Marg under the guidance of an academic advisory committee, provides many new insights into Social and Political empowerment of women in the new Panchayati Raj Institutions (PRIs). This is the largest-ever survey on any aspect of Panchayat functioning, covering Gram Panchayats in 23 states, with a total sample size of over 20,000, including Elected Women Representatives (EWRs), Elected Male Representatives (EMRs), ex-EWRs, official functionaries and members of the community. Nearly three-fourths of the EWRs in the sample belonged to the Scheduled Caste, Scheduled Tribe and OBC categories, and were evenly divided above and below the poverty line.

Reservation has played a significant role as four-fifths of all the representatives got elected from reserved seats. The role of reservation was also evident from the fact that it emerged as an important motivator (43%) for contesting the first election as much as its withdrawal was an important reason for not contesting the election among former women representatives (39%).

The majority of the elected representatives had contested only one election (87%) and hence the proportion of first timers in politics was also high (86%). Around 14 per cent were re-elected more than once at the Gram Panchayat level. Further analysis showed that the majority of ex-women representatives could not get re-elected because the seat from where they were elected was de-reserved in the next round.

While no gender discrimination in the Panchayat is reported by 60 per cent of elected women representatives, acceptability in Panchayat meetings and enabling them to raise issues freely was mentioned by 94 per cent. A supportive professional environment evidently motivates elected women representatives to perform better, as 60-64 per cent reported an increase in their interaction with line departments and parallel bodies. Even the participation of common women citizens in various activities such as attending Gram Sabha meeting, etc. has reportedly increased (68-78%). However, issues related to the planning for rural development works and identification of BPL families were discussed mainly by the Male Pradhans and Ward Members.

In the case of women representatives, prior association with any form of politics was low, and for most women the act of contesting the first election signaled their entry into active politics. Whatever prior association they had was of a limited nature. A significant proportion of women representatives have said that they were earlier associated with groups/committees and confirmed that this association has helped them.

While 21 per cent claimed to be self-motivated, about 22 per cent said that their spouse had inspired them, which was higher in the case of women representatives (30%). Interestingly, members of community groups (such as Mahila Mandals, Self-Help Groups, Youth Clubs, Cooperatives, etc.) seem to have played an important role, as 22 per cent of elected representatives reported how they were motivated to take the plunge in electoral politics. However, 8 per cent of the elected representatives-mainly from West Bengal, Sikkim, Tripura and Kerala-also disclosed the role of political parties in motivating them. Husbands (30%) and other family members (12%) were reported as playing an important role in motivating women representatives to contest elections the first time.

The economic status of more than half (54%) of the elected representatives was Above the Poverty Line (APL) as per the village list reported by the respondents. There were a higher proportion of

APL individuals in the case of Pradhans (72%), as compared to ward members (50%). Almost two-fifths (38%) of all EWRs were reportedly, below the poverty line, the majority of this category being ward members (41%) rather than Pradhans (24%). This indicates, overall, that the Pradhans are better off than other Panchayat Members. However, not much difference was observed between the economic status of male and female elected representatives.

One-third of elected representatives report interactions with the police, local bureaucracy and officials in the line departments to discuss scheme and participation in elections campaigns. Taking proactive initiatives in signing petitions, participating in protests, alerting media or notifying police/court about local problems was mentioned by 24-35 per cent of elected representatives.

That reservation has been critical to the representation of disadvantaged groups is confirmed by the fact that 88 per cent of them were elected on reserved seats. Approximately 85.8 per cent of all representatives surveyed were first-timers in the Panchayats, while 14.3 per cent had been elected for a second or third term. While 15 per cent of women Pradhans had been re-elected twice or more, 37 per cent of the male Pradhans had been similarly re-elected. Of the ex-EWRs interviewed, 11 per cent said they had contested but lost the election, while 39 per cent indicated that they did not contest a re-election because the seat had been de-reserved.

Now majority of women representatives are no more proxy of their male relative patrons. 58 per cent of women representatives are now taking their own decisions to contest elections. This is a big achievement. 15 per cent of women Pradhans are able to win elections second time. Women belonging to younger age groups of 21-35 years have shown better performance compared to the women belonging to the age group of 35 years and above. Women members of active committees at village level were found to be more successful at Panchayat level. Again quoting the Report, Dalits were also benefited by the whole process. Reservation has inspired and prompted them to contest elections.

Karnataka, for instance, provided, for 25 per cent reservations in their two tier Panchayati Raj System in 1987. This was replaced by the constitutionally mandated one third reservation in 1993. Along with the head start the State had in 1987, several NGOs took the lead to undertake special capacity building programmes for women elected representatives. Issues such as proxy participation and gender friendly budgets were discussed in small networks of women representatives. These small networks began to grow and share their experiences amongst each other. Today, the results of this subterranean movement are that 41210 seats of the 96090 seats in all levels of Panchayats put together are occupied by women, in spite of only 33 per cent of the seats being reserved for them. What is more remarkable than the fact that 42.89 per cent of the seats are occupied by women, is the category wise break up of L of these women. Of the 17859 SC elected representatives, 8222 are women; which is 46.04 per cent. Of the 10311 ST 5 elected to the Panchayats, 6672 are women; fully 64.71 per cent of them.

There can be no greater evidence for the fact that not only has Panchayati Raj attracted women to politics in large numbers, but also that this wish to contest for elections seems to be most keenly felt among the women belonging to the SCs and STs. In several States the practice of cyclic rotation of the reservation matrix once every five years is proposed to be slowed down, to a rotation every two or more terms. This follows the example of Tamil Nadu and gives women who are elected on a reserved seat the opportunity to stand for elections again for a second term on the same reserved seat.

There is however, big difference between representation and participation. It is easier to legislate representation, but it is rather a complex and difficult task to create conditions for participations. The proper representation does not automatically lead to proper participation. It is important that they are in a position to influence decision-making and prepare and implement the schemes for economic development and social justice.

There are many instances of EWR of the Panchayat taking a keen interest and playing a significant role in the workings of grassroots politics. EWRs have initiated work on plans of bringing in piped water in the village and also to build schools as against infrastructural development favoured by men. Results from a nationwide survey of women's participation in Panchayats suggest that a majority of the EWRs report an enhancement in their personal effectiveness and image after being elected. They also report a reduction in household responsibilities. It has often been observed that women priorities those developmental needs that seem to be more pressing from their perspective. Women are also seen to be more involved in monitoring the presence of teachers and medical staff in the school or health centre, and inspecting nutrition centres under the Integrated Child Development Scheme.

They have taken the lead in making efforts for smokeless stoves, crèches, community halls, and have taken the initiative in family and matrimonial matters, counseling abusive and/or alcoholic husbands. Sometimes, women-headed Panchayats have even experienced a dramatic increase in their revenues, sponsoring the auction of village ponds, community forests and village markets for the larger welfare of the community. (Jayal, 2006).

A Sarpanch in Dahod district in Gujarat said that she had proposed setting up a primary school in the village, but was told there was no necessity for it because there were only three children whose parents wanted it. She set about mobilising support for the school which was established, and came to be attended by 300 children. Attendance was at least partly achieved through stiff penalties for non-compliance: a fine of Rs. 600 and 6 months in prison for the parents of those children who do not attend. It is notable that until she came to the Panchayat, this woman had not stepped out of the boundaries of her home, or even been a member of any other organization.

The successful EWR, now act as kind of role models for the others. The increased proportion of the EWR has ensured the principles of justice between the sexes and this has certainly led to the fulfillment of certain interests of women, which may otherwise be neglected. It is for sure that without the system of reservation women would have had no role to play in grassroots politics in India. As statistics show, 95 per cent of women claimed they would never come to acquire positions in Panchayats, if there were no provision of reserving seats for them (Centre for Women's Development Studies 1999). Reservation has at least succeeded in bringing the womenfolk in rural India into the political forum and elected women could now imagine standing against a man in future.

It may be argued that the women members in the PRIs today are gradually learning to adjust to the new political conditions. The political knowledge of women is increasing and gradually a sense of confidence is getting instilled in them, as they are now aware of the problems being faced by their locality. By all accounts, particularly with each election round, it is clear that women have certainly made their presence in the power struggles once dominated by men. There are many instances where women have been self-motivated to fight an election. In several instances, the *Gram Sabha has* persuaded women with leadership potential to stand for elections and this has far-reaching impact on the empowerment of women.

Patriarchy is not reversed, or even significantly eroded, overnight. Nevertheless, there are, across India, many shining examples of the potential of women's leadership, and many more may join their ranks if at least the institutional conditions for their effective participation are safeguarded. Within this larger process, the debate over the reservation for women in PRIs, is extremely critical, as in most cases we see women bearing the brunt of unprogressive social practices. Thus, a change in political status may bring about a larger transformation is socio-economic processes. By extending the rotation term of reserved post for women up to two or three term, it would allow women in Panchayats the time and space to negotiate their own power relationships within them. If they are given 10 to 15 years of continued opportunity from their seat, it can perhaps nudge them in the right direction, encourage and nurture their desire to be assertive and independent. This clearly points to the need to rethink the rotation of seats reserved for women and unless this provision of rotation is reconsidered empowerment of women representative would be a difficult proposition.

REFERENCES

The State of Panchayats: 2007-08 (An Independent Assessment) Volume – One (Thematic Report), Institute of Rural Management, Anand (IRMA) with the Ministry of Panchayati Raj, Government of India, New Delhi.

Study on Elected Women Representatives in Panchayati Raj Institutions based on a Nationwide Survey, AC Nielson ORG-MARG, Ministry of Panchayati Raj, Government of India, New Delhi.

A Study in Grey, Niraja Gopal Jayal – Tuesday, April 29, 2008 *at 2320 hrs IST* posted online.

All India Mahila Adhikar Manch, *Official Information Booklet*, New Delhi, IDMAM, 2007.

Ruth Alsop, *et al.*, 'Inclusion and Local Elected Governments: The Panchayati Raj System in India', *Social Development*, Paper 37, Washington D.C., World Bank, South Asia Region, Social Development Unit, 2001.

Zenab Banu, *Tribal Women Empowerment and Gender Issues*, New Delhi, Kanishka Publishers, 2001.

Nirmala Buch, 'Women and Panchayats: Opportunities, Challenges and Support" – in L.C. Jain (ed.), *Decentralisation and Local Governance*, New Delhi, Orient Longman, 2005.

Centre for Women's Development Studies, 'From Oppression to Assertion: A Study of Panchayats and Women in M.P., Rajasthan, and U.P.', *CWDS*, New Delhi, 1999.

Abha Chauhan, 'Women's Participation in Panchayats in Scheduled Areas With Special Reference to Madhya Pradesh', *A Decade of Women's Empowerment Through Local Government in India*, Institute of Social Sciences/South Asia Partnership, New Delhi, 2003.

Alexander George and Andrew Bennett, *Case Studies and Theory Development in Social Sciences*, Boston, MIT Press, 2005.

G.K. Leiten, 'Panchayats in Western Uttar Pradesh: Nameless Member', *Economic and Political Weekly*, Vol. XXXI, No. 39, 1996, pp. 2700-2705.

Upasana Mahanta, Sinha, Samrat, 'The Political Empowerment of Minority Women through Panchayati Raj Institutions: A Critical Assessment of India's Experiment with Affirmative Action', October 2007.

George Mathew, 'Panchayati Raj Institutions and Human Rights in India', *International Council in Human Rights Policy*, 2002.

Rohini Pande, 'Can Mandated Political Representation Increase Policy Influence for Disadvantaged Minorities." *The American Economic Review*, Vol. 93 No. 4, December 2003, pp. 1132-1151.

Shirin M. Rai, 'Reserved Seats in South Asia: A Regional Perspective', *Women in Parliaments Beyond Numbers*, 2005.

Mathew Zachariah, 'Positive Discrimination in Education for India's Scheduled Castes: A Review of Problems', *Comparative Education Review*, Vol. 16 No. 1, March 1972, pp. 16-29.

10

Women Empowerment through Panchayats: An Empirical Analysis of Decision-Making at the Panchayat Level

DR. O.P. BOHRA & R. RAKSHIT

The concept of "women and development", has been recognized widely across the world. However, this truth has been repeatedly denied in the 'corridors of power', in the developed and the developing nations. The development measured in terms of human development and the gender development, India occupied lower place. It ranked 114 amongst the 128 countries, as reported by Global Gender Gap Report, 2007. The sex ratio, considered as an indicator of gender discrimination, India ranked low. The lower sex ratio in case of India is the main attributer in this case. However, in the context of political empowerment, there is wide gap, between, political opportunities available at parliament (the upper and lower house) and the state assemblies and the third tier of governance (local governments) in India. Though this chapter is mainly focused on the issues related to the political empowerment of women and the decision-making at the level of third tier of governance, particularly at the panchayat level, however, second section is devoted to the political empowerment of women at the parliament level. The status of reservation at the PRIs level is discussed in third section. The survey results with respect to the issue of decision-making at the panchayat level forms the fourth section of this chapter The concluding section discusses the findings of the survey.

Political Empowerment of Women

(a) Women in Parliament—International Scenario

Based on comparative statistics published by some international agency depicts the status of women in parliament across the countries, indicates that around the world, there is no national legislature in which women claim half of the seats. A status of women in parliament in some of the countries around the world is shown in the Figure 1. As evident from the available statistics, India ranks 119th position on Inter-Parliamentary Union's list of 182 legislatures. The developed nations are doing better in this context. Japan, a developed country, is an exception. Though the first place is occupied by Sweden, but women occupied less than half the seats. China finds its place in the upper half of the ranks.[1]

Figure: 1. National Legislative Seats held by Women (In %)

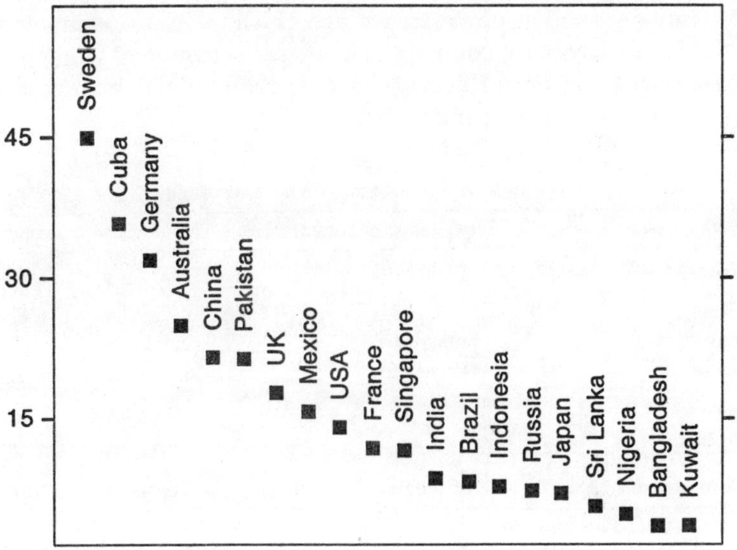

Source: Inter-Parliamentary Union, www.ipu.org

Why Reservation?

As discussed, there is no legislature mandate reservation of women in parliament. However, some of the research studies conducted in US and the University of Stockholm suggest that there is one-third participation of women in business. The same share may be extended in politics too. It has further argued that the 30 per cent representation by minorities in the decision-making at higher level could influence the decision of the majority group. Therefore, across the world a one-third reservation or quota for the women in the political decision-making considered as a significant number. The one third reservations of women in parliament could help in reducing the

1. India Together, May, 2003.

political and social gap at large, prevailing in the society. However, there is no correlation found between the development and the inequality. For instance, in the countries of France and Sweden about half of the public offices run by women where as in Japan there is evidence of greater political inequality. There is only 4 per cent seats occupied by women. In Cuba and Pakistan too, there is reservation for women. The argument for the reservation of women is generally influenced by four parameters. These are represented by: *(a)* population of women; *(b)* different social and biological experiences; *(c)* different interest between men and women; *(d)* women in position can influence and inspire more women. However, these parameters could vary across the countries. The present scenario of women in parliament—*(a)* world average and *(b)* the regional average are presented in Table 1(a) and (b) below:

Table–1*(a)*

Women in Parliament—World Average

Both Houses		*Single House or Lower House*		*Upper House or Senate*	
Total MPs	44'121	Total MPs	37'177	Total MPs	6'944
Gender breakdown known for	43'898	Gender breakdown known for	37'047	Gender breakdown known for	6'851
Men	35'893	Men	30'219	Men	5'674
Women	8'005	Women	6'828	Women	1'177
% of women	**18.20%**	**% of women**	**18.40%**	**% of women**	**17.20%**

Source: Inter-Parliamentary Union, www.ipu.org

As evident from the table, on an average, about 18.20 per cent seats are occupied by women in both the houses, together. However, in the upper house, it is little less than the lower house. The region-wise scenario is depicted in Table 1 (b). The representation of women in both the houses in Asia is lower than America and the Europe. In the Arab States, less than 10 per cent seats are occupied by women. In the case of India, it is 9 per cent (where as half of the India's population contributed by women).

(b) Women in Parliament—National Scenario

The parameters of women reservation in parliament as discussed above suggest for more than 50 per cent seats for women in Indian Parliament as this group contributes about 50 per cent in total population of the country. The issue of quota for women in parliament

Table-1(*b*)
Women in Parliament—Regional Average

	Single House or Lower House	*Upper House or Senate*	*Both Houses Combined*
Nordic Countries	41.40%	—	—
Americas	21.60%	20.00%	21.40%
Europe-OSCE member countries including Nordic countries	21.20%	18.80%	20.70%
Europe-OSCE member countries excluding Nordic countries	19.30%	18.80%	19.20%
Asia	**18.40%**	**16.60%**	**18.20%**
Sub-Saharan Africa	17.20%	20.80%	17.60%
Pacific	13.40%	31.80%	15.40%
Arab States	9.70%	7.00%	9.10%

Rank	**Country**		
106	***India***		
	LOWER OR SINGLE HOUSE		
Elections	Seats*	Women	% W
4 2004	**541**	**49**	**9.10%**
	UPPER HOUSE OR SENATE		
Elections	Seats*	Women	% W
7 2006	**243**	**24**	**9.90%**

Total Countries = 135

Source: Same as Table 1(a).

has been discussed at length on many platforms amongst the various political parties, policy makers and the scholars and experts. The Reservation Bill has been debated many times but not reached to any meaningful results. Since India being one of the largest democracies with many national and regional political parties, therefore it is very difficult to arrive at any consensus. Time and again, the issue of reservation for women in parliament has been discussed and debated without any results. However, some of the views with regard to political empowerment of women at the parliament level as expressed by the Prime Minister and the Ex-President of India are presented in the Box 1, and the discussion and views on the Reservation Bill is shown in Box 2.

Box–1
Political Empowerment of Women at Parliament Level

Women's Reservation Bill in Next Session of Parliament: Manmohan Singh

"Country needs new social reform movement for gender equality"
"Government initiatives to empower women not enough "

Prime Minister Manmohan Singh said the Government would bring forward a legislation to reserve seats for women in Parliament in the next session. Dr. Singh said such reservation at the gram panchayat level had demonstrated its efficacy in empowering women across the country. He added that those who were opposed to the legislation had been brought around. Speaking at a function Dr. Singh said a political consensus on the issue was being worked out for the past two years and it was an idea whose time had come.

"These are all legislative and administrative initiatives to empower women. These are necessary and important, but surely not enough. What we need in our country is a fundamental change in the mindset. We need a new social reform movement for gender equality and empowerment of women," he added. But when........????

[The Hindu, September 6, 2006]

President APJ Abdul Kalam' View:

With the budget session of Parliament less than two weeks away, President APJ Abdul Kalam strongly pitched for 33 per cent seats for women saying the fairer sex can do social justice. "Fifty per cent of India's one billion population is women. Women must get 33 per cent reservation. If women are there (in Parliament), they will do social justice," Kalam said during an interaction with Indian community in the Philippines at a reception organised by the Indian embassy. The Women's Reservation Bill has been hanging fire for many years with the political parties sharply divided over the quantum of reservation and the caste and tribe configurations of the reservation. Asked by a member of the audience as to what the Indian Government was doing to cut population, Kalam said priority was being given to women's education as it has been found that if women were educated it is possible to keep the size of the family small. He said a few states of India were contributing to the increase in percentage of population and what was needed is women's education.

[33% reservation for women in parliament: Kalam 3 February 2006, 2122 hrs IST, PTI]

Box–2

Some Political Views on Reservation Bill

(Excerpts of Women's Parliament in Lucknow Reproduced)

Women's Bill

The UPA Government is again dilly-dallying on the Women's Bill. The Government proposal of increasing the number of seats in Parliament to around 900 and the Assembly seats to 9000 sounds ludicrous. The UPA has finally arrived at a formula which will not only help to delay the passage of the Bill and start a fresh round of debate and controversy; the Bill may never see the light of day! To top it all, the entire thrust of the Women's Bill is diluted, with the Government trying to strike a compromise with male power, which is proving to be quite unaccommodating and headstrong. And Kudos to the CPI (M), which has no principled objection to the new formula and but seems to be just opposing it on technical grounds – that the delimitation of Parliamentary constituencies will take time. Sushmaji is most flexible this time, and has almost given a blank cheque to the Government (all is fine as long as Soniaji is not the PM). The only problem that the BJP may encounter is the on the stand of Uma Bharati on a quota within quota; she has already challenged Sushma Swaraj's statement saying she was not consulted. If the OBCs within the Congress and BJP vote according to their conscience, and the Social Justice camp keeps harping on the old tune of special quota for OBCs, Shivraj Patil's hopes for a consensus are going to be shattered. So, if after all the dilution and compromises, not to speak of extra expenditure, the Bill is going to face fresh controversies and is not going to be passed at all, isn't it better that we stick to our principles and have a vote so that those who oppose the Bill can be exposed on the floor of the house? Isn't it high time the UPA stops playing the NDA game? (Women's Parliament in Lucknow).

(c) Women Empowerment and the Third Tier of Governance (Panchayats)

(i) Constitutional Provision-243D(2). It provides that not less than one-third of the total seats reserved under Clause I (for Scheduled Castes and Scheduled Tribes) would be reserved for women belonging to the Scheduled Castes or as the case may be, the Scheduled Tribes. (3) Not less than one-third (including the number of seats reserved for women belonging to the Scheduled Castes and the Scheduled Tribes) of the total number of seats to be filled by direct election in every Panchayat shall be reserved for women and such seats may be allotted by rotation to different constituencies in a Panchayat.

Having passed this amendment, after several rounds of elections more than a million women have entered in the domain of public life. The political empowerment of women at Panchayat level has achieved success at all the three tiers of Panchayati Raj Institutions, overcoming all the barriers of caste and the class. After having completed the third round of election, some of the states have amended their Panchayats' Act and provided more than one-third reservation for women, e.g. MP and Bihar. The details of elected women representatives at Gram Panchayat, Panchayat Samiti and Zilla Parishad are shown below in Table 3. On an average all states have witnessed more than the mandate figure of seats occupied by women. Among these states, Bihar with low level of development and low female literacy, have shown encouraging results with about half of the seats occupied by women at all the three tiers of PRIs. Andhra Pradesh has occupied the lowest place among all the states with just one-third mandate seats. Graphical presentation is shown in Figure 1.

Table-3
Elected Women Representatives in PRIs (%)

	GP	*PS*	*ZP*	*TOTAL*	*Rank*
Bihar	54.6	49.2	49.9	54.1	1
Maharashtra	43.7	48.9	46.2	43.8	2
Karnataka	43.0	41.2	37.1	42.9	3
Arunachal Pradesh	39.5	35.2	33.1	38.5	4
Uttar Pradesh	38.8	37.6	41.6	38.8	5
Assam	38.3	36.8	34.6	38.1	6
Uttaranchal	37.9	35.9	33.1	37.8	7
All States	**37.5**	**37.4**	**38.2**	**37.5**	**8**
Kerala	37.3	37.3	36.9	37.3	9
West Bengal	36.6	34.8	34.2	36.3	10
Haryana	36.1	34.0	35.2	36.0	11
Orissa	35.8	35.1	34.7	35.8	12
Rajasthan	35.2	38.4	37.6	35.4	13
Punjab	35.0	33.4	32.7	35.0	14
Tripura	34.6	35.5	34.1	34.6	15
Madhya Pradesh	33.9	33.4	34.4	33.9	16
Chhattisgarh	33.7	33.8	34.0	33.7	17
Tamil Nadu	33.7	35.3	34.6	33.8	18

Contd...

	GP	*PS*	*ZP*	*TOTAL*	*Rank*
Himachal Pradesh	33.5	33.5	34.3	33.5	19
Gujarat	33.3	33.5	33.5	33.3	20
Andhra Pradesh	33.0	33.7	33.5	33.0	21

Source: GoI, MoPR (2006).

Note: GP = Gram Panchayat; PS = Panchayat Samiti; ZP = Zilla Parishad.

Elected Women Representatives in Panchayati Raj Institutions in India

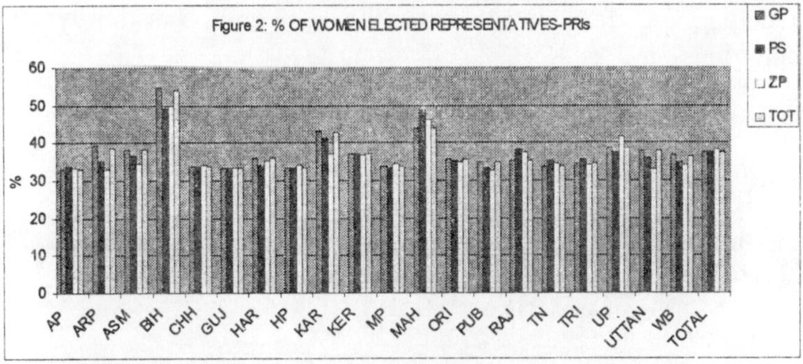

Empowering of Women at Panchayats

The historical passage of 73rd Amendment has given thrust to the democratic decentralization in the country. It has provided for the empowerment of local governments in general and the disadvantaged group (SCs/STs and the women) in particular. Once in the speech the Panchayati Raj Minister mentioned that "women members and the office-bearers in Panchayats today accounted for 42 per cent of the elected representatives."[2] While providing the constitutional recognition to the local governments institutions many developmental issues such as functional and financial devolution and the decentralised planning have also been strengthened.

Women Empowerment and the Decision-Making of Women—A Survey of Two Village of Rajasthan

For the assessment of time spent on various activities by women and the decision-making, a primary survey was carried out in two villages of Khera and Nangal Lakha in Bansur block of Alwar district

2. Excerpts from the speech of Minister of Panchayati Raj, Shri Mani Shankar Aiyar at the Conference on "Making Democratic Governments Work-Connecting Principle and Practice", Harvard University, 13th April, 2005.

in Rajasthan. About 110 and 55 households were surveyed in Khera and Nangal respectively. The households were selected from all castes in proportion to their population in the village. It was done without prejudice to their level of income and the men and women in the age group of 18-60 were interviewed. The important aspect of survey included were: *(a)* time-use survey to determine the time spent on five basic activities such as agricultural work, animal husbandry, fuel, water and household work; *(b)* a component of the survey is used to determine the average production of milk and milk products (ghee); and *(c)* A survey to determine the degree of women's participation in decision-making at the household, community and village level.

Women Participation and Time Spent in Major Activities

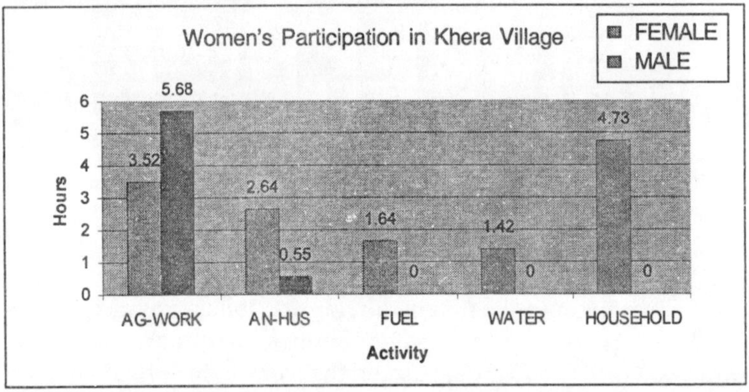

Source: Primary Survey.

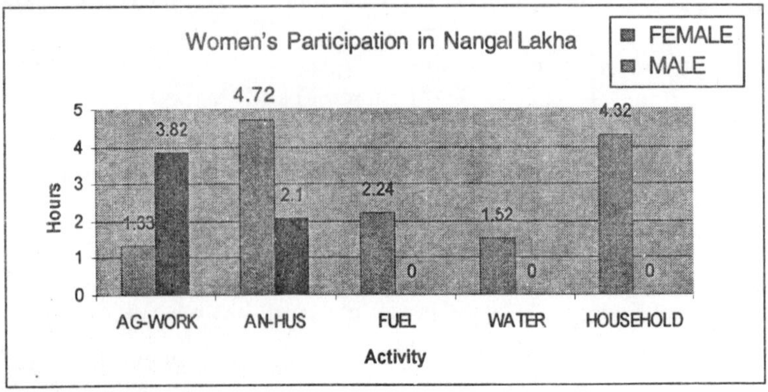

Source: Primary Survey.

The survey results (as presented in the figures above), reveal that in comparison to men women spent more time on the selected activities. In particular, men spent more time than women only on agricultural activities whereas women spent more time on all the activities (except ag. work) than men. In total, women spent about 14 hours per day on these activities where as men spent less than half. There is nil contribution of men on the activities of fuel, water and household activities which are mostly considered as female domain.

Decision-Making at Household Level

To determine the degree of women's participation in decision-making at the household level six issues such as daily expenditure, agriculture, animal husbandry, education, marriage and dowry were selected for the survey. The survey results are shown in Table 4 below:

Table-4
Decision-Making in Household Expenditure (%)

Head of Exp.	*Khera*		*Nangal*	
	Women	*Both*	*Women*	*Both*
Daily Expenditure	59.1	11.4	28.0	20.0
Agriculture	4.5	6.9	2.0	0.0
Animal Husbandry	2.5	54.5	14.0	52.0
Education	52.3	34.1	28.0	40.0
Marriage	18.2	72.7	12.0	40.0
Dowry	4.5	86.4	16.0	24.0

Source: Primary Survey.

As observed from the survey results that on the issues pertaining to daily expenditure, animal husbandry and education of children women are involved to large extent. On the contrary, on all other issues women are hardly consulted when any decisions are taken. With regard to women participation, it shows that women's participation in decision-making at household level in Nangal Lakha is much less due to low literacy level of women in that village.

It is also observed while interacting with the villagers that as the consequent of the 73rd Amendment, women participation in decision-making at the village level has improved substantially. In both the villages the Sarpanch was woman. In village Khera, there are four women representatives in the Gram Sabha, while Nangal Lakha has only one woman representative.

Women Participation and Care Economy

One of the objectives of the survey was to study the care economy to estimate the monetary value of unpaid work contributed by women in the care sector (household work). The valuation of input was estimated by using two methods, *(a)* Opportunity cost method and the *(b)* Opportunity price method. The first one is the input related method based on imputing value to labour time spent on the care economy. It is based on the wage that the person carrying out the domestic work would receive if she or he worked in the market. The output related method is based on imputing market prices of goods and services produced.

The contribution of women in the care economy based on results from the primary survey and using Opportunity Cost Method reveals as below:

Factor	*Khera*	*Nangal Lakha*
Time spent on household activities	7.79 Hrs	8.08 Hrs
Monetary Value (OCM)	Rs. 117/day	Rs. 121/day

Source: Primary Survey.

Wage rate considered Rs. 120/day = Rs. 15/hour

It is observed that when the women's contribution to the household sector is monetized using OCM, the value of household work (including time spent for collection of water and fuel) carried out by women works out to Rs. 117 per day and Rs. 121 per day for Khera and Nangal Lakha villages respectively.

Total Contribution of Women

The table below indicates the survey results pertaining to the total contribution of women in all activities based on results obtained from time-use survey, when monetized.

Activity	*Time (Hrs/Day)*		*Value*	
	Khera	*Nangal Lakha*	*Khera*	*Nangal Lakha*
Agriculture	3.52	1.33	Rs. 53/day	Rs. 20/day
Animal Husbandry	2.64	4.72	Rs. 40/day	Rs. 71/day
All Household works, including fuel, water	7.79	8.08	Rs. 117/day	Rs.121/day
Total	13.95	14.13	Rs. 209/day	Rs. 212/day

Source: Primary Survey.

Wage rate considered Rs. 120/day = Rs. 15/hour

The total contribution of women in all activities calculated on the basis of OCM and considering a wage rate of Rs. 120 per day (8 working hours) works out to Rs. 209/day and Rs. 212/day in Khera and Nangal Lakha village respectively.

Some Observations from the Survey

Traditionally, women's role in agriculture has not changed much. Women are more involved in agriculture today than the past. They are also managing the activity of animal husbandry. This activity holds a special place in women's heart as it provides crucial nutrition, fuel, manure and large proportions of family income. This activity is very important for the entire family, as it is the second important source of their livelihood. Similar to the past, women continue to be involved for long hours in household activities, despite engaged in the panchayats activities.

Obstacle to Decision-Making

It is observed that there is lack of women's participation in decision-making at household level. The women's decision-making ability is severely hampered due to socio-cultural, low literacy and skill barriers.

Conclusion

The issue of women in parliament in general and particularly in the case of India is still lying unresolved. Based on the women contribution in the population and other factors such as business and care economy, there is a need to provide at least one-third reservation for women in parliament in the country like India. The women empowered through the 73rd and 74th Amendments in India at the local (rural and urban) level showed very encouraging results. The survey results carried out in two villages of Rajasthan indicate that women participation has increased in the post 73rd Amendment era as against the pre amendment. The decision-making, though has improved, still has to a long way. The crucial obstacle of low literacy prevailing in rural areas needs to be overcome for the improvement of women participation. The exercise related to the care economy as carried through the survey indicates the substantial contribution of women in the family income as well as the enhancement of family livelihood. The women empowerment, gender budgeting and the care economy together would improve the rural development to the large extent which in tern would help in inclusive growth of economy, which India needs strongly at this crucial junction.

REFERENCES

O.P. Bohra, Women in Decentralised Democracy, *Journal of Rural Development*, Vol. 16, No. 4, October-December, 1997, pp. 673-683.

Government of India, Ministry of Panchayati Raj, *The State of the Panchayats*, New Delhi, 2006.

Government of India, Ministry of Panchayati Raj, *Study on Elected Representatives in Panchayati Raj Instiiutions*, New Delhi, 2008.

Ahooja Krishna Patel, 'Another Development with Women', *Development Dialogue*, Swedish International Development Agency (SIDA), Uppasala, Sweden, 1983.

National Institute of Public Finance and Policy, *Gender Budgeting in India*, New Delhi, 2001.

Rai, Shirin Rai, 'Class, Caste and Gender—Women in Parliament in India,' *Women in Parliament: Beyond Numbers*, Stockholm, International IDEA, 1998.

Rita Rakshit, *Role of Women in Rural Development: A Comparative Study of Two Villages*, M.A. Thesis submitted at Department of Urban and Regional Planning, School of Planning and Architecture, New Delhi, 2008.

The Constitution of India, New Delhi.

India Together website

11

Political Empowerment of Women in India: A Key for Good Governance

DR. B.S. BHARGAVA

The theme for the National Conference (AGRASRI National Conference on Women Empowerment, 19 and 20 August 2008), is *Empowerment of Women in Parliament and Local Self-Government Institutions in India: Role, Status, Participation and Decision-Making'*. It is very relevant and timely theme, to be deliberated upon. Political empowerment of women especially, and at all the three strata or levels of the political system in our country certainly assumes great significance at present.

The theme is quite large in its scope. *'Women's Empowerment'* itself has been subject to various meanings, definitions and interpretations. It has many dimensions too such as legal, political, social, economic and psychological. Spatial and temporal dimensions make the concept much more complex and complicated. It is better, therefore, to confine to its political dimension here and to share some of the thoughts in our country's contemporary context. However, one cannot neglect reference of its other dimensions in order to understand the process of empowerment.

It is widely felt that the country has been moving from *'representative democracy'* to *'participatory democracy'* and development during the last two decades, and the process continues.

Implicit in participation is empowerment or transfer of power to the people. Empowering is development of skills and abilities of people to enable them to manage better, have a say in or negotiate with existing development delivery systems. Some see it as more fundamental and as essentially concerned with enabling people to decide upon and undertake actions which they believe are essential to their development. The empowerment process, therefore, encompasses several mutually reinforcing components (economic independence, knowledge and awareness, self-image, autonomy-freedoms and rights etc.).

Ancient Indian history is the testimony of the role of women in the public sphere. Second half of the 19th century and first half of the 20th century witnessed two great movements; one having concern for the upliftment of women as a component of social reform and second, invoking participation of women under the leadership of Mahatma Gandhi for achieving independence from the yoke of the British empire. Women found political space and exposed to political process.

One theme on which Gandhiji wrote repeatedly was the need to improve the status of women. Two extracts, often quoted, from his writings are quite reflective.

> *'Woman has been suppressed under custom and law for which man was responsible and in the shaping of which she had no hand....'*
>
> *'Woman is the companion of man, gifted with equal mental capacities. She has the right to participate in every minute detail in the activities of man and she has an equal right of freedom and liberty with him..........?'*

Pandit Jawaharlal Nehru also believed in improving the status of women and involving them in the process of development.

The dawn of India's Political Independence in August 1947, and the establishment of a republican form of state in 1950, brought to women the promise of adult franchise and equality of opportunity in all spheres which included social, economic and political activities. The constitutional rights were to serve as instruments for achieving equality of status and opportunities in all spheres. Equality in all spheres is inseparable from active political participation. This means not only using the right to vote but also power-sharing, profit sharing, co-decision making and co-policy making at all levels of government. The highest law of the land, i.e., the Constitution of India pledges equality of status and opportunity, justice-social, economic and political and dignity of the individual, to men and women equally (Chapters III and IV, full with provisions related to rights, gender equality and other contextual matters).

Global consciousness about and concerns for women pointedly emerged with the charter of the United Nations; the organization should work for "*promoting and encouraging respect for human rights and fundamental freedoms for all without distinction as to race, sex, language or religion.*"

Later 1975-85 was declared as a women's development decade internationally. The fourth international conference on women development, gender issues and action plan and strategies to be adopted by nations held at Beijing in 1995.

It is worthwhile to recollect that the government in our country appointed a committee on the status of women, which undertook a comprehensive examination of all the questions relating to the rights and status of women (1977). Since then scholars and policy makers diverted their attention to the issues of women which culminated in establishing a National Commission for Women in 1992 and the National Perspective Plan for Women (1988-2000).

If we analyse the history of 60 years in regard to women's development, especially in rural areas, we find hundreds of schemes/programmes/projects have had launched and implemented under different political regimes. We have achieved a lot in different sectors. Three phases with three approaches could be discussed namely welfare, development and empowerment approach. *'Development Paradigm'* also shifted around 1991 under global thinking and forces.

Late Rajiv Gandhi took initiatives for empowering women at the grassroots (local self-government institutions). He was the spirit behind 73rd and 74th Amendments to the Constitution (1992). In addition to many progressive provisions in these amendments, the provisions relating to reservation (not less than one third of the total seats) of seats and positions of Chairpersons and Vice Chairpersons for women by rotations have to be underlined. Constitutionalisation of local self-government institutions (rural and urban) heralded a kind of silent revolution for stabilizing, strengthening these institutions and making the process of empowering of women more effective. It was assumed that political empowerment of women at the grassroots would accelerate their social and economic status. Empowerment gives women the capacity to influence decision-making process, planning, implementation and evaluation by integrating them into the political system. This implies political participation, which includes right to vote, contest, campaign, party membership and representation in political offices at all levels and effectively influence decisions thereby leading to political empowerment.

During the last 15 years (since 1993) we had 3 round of elections of rural and urban local bodies in almost all the states of the country. It is heartening to note that nearly 12 lakh women elected representatives are in position in these institutions, involved in local policy and administrative decision-making processes for the development of their geographical areas and the advancement of women in varied ways. Experiences and various studies conducted in different parts of the country on Panchayati Raj functioning and women's leaders, show positive and encouraging trends over a period of time. Success stories and best practices as reported may not be in huge number (compared to number of PRIs and elected women members). Number of women representatives is more than the quota for them; for instance, in Karnataka, women captured 43 per cent seats in Gram Panchayats, 41 per cent in Taluk Panchayats and 37 per cent in Zilla Panchayats in the last election (year: 2005).

In Bihar, 50 per cent reservation of seats for women in panchayats was given by the statute. As a consequence, they captured more than 55 per cent seats in the last election. In many panchayats women Chairpersons/Vice Chairpersons are becoming assertive because of increasing awareness about their role and rights and working of the Panchayati Raj System. Deepening of participatory democracy and broadening of its social base, and the phenomenon of '*shifting of dominance towards non-dominant castes and communities (numerically speaking) are really encouraging trends. However, in general, socio-economic background of several women, muscle and money powers in electoral process, role of local elites, lack of presence in political parties*' structures, conflict between domestic and public roles, proxy phenomenon, attitudinal aspects and unwanted behaviour of local bureaucracy are some among other factors/ constraints, coming in the way of their empowerment.

Coming to the place and role of women in National and State Legislatures, it may be mentioned that their number has been always undesirable and discouraging. "From the records available of the past 50 years, since the independence, it is seen that the strength of women in the political field as reflected in State Legislatures remained at an average of 3 per cent to 5 per cent of those elected. At the level of Parliament, the position of women members has varied between 5 per cent to 7 per cent.

"In the 14th General Elections, 2004, there were only 355 women candidates out of total of 5435 and only 45 women have been elected to the 14th Lok Sabha. And in the Rajya Sabha out of 245 members, only 28 are women." This happens after 60 years of the functioning of the Indian Constitution.

The debate began on September 12, 1996, when a bill, commonly referred to as the Women's Reservations Bill (WRB) was introduced in the Lok Sabha, seeking to reserve not less than one-third of the total number of seats in Parliament and State Assemblies for women. Till today it remains a controversial bill because of differences among political parties. It is unfortunate. Had it been through, it would have given a philip to the process of political empowerment at the higher levels i.e., above local self-governments (rural and urban). Without going into more details, certain observations are mentioned below as a concluding part of this note.

- Continuous and concerted efforts have to be made for developing consensus on Women's Reservation Bill; political parties and women's organizations (civil society) have to play a major role.
- Political empowerment of women at the grassroots, to a great extent, depends upon the empowerment of local self-governments, both rural and urban.
- In pursuance of Article 243(G) and 11th Schedule, Panchayati Raj Institutions should be armed with sufficient functions and powers, finances and functionaries, in order to make them 'institutions of self-government'. Applicable to urban local bodies also.
- Capacity building programmes for elected women in local self-governments assumes great importance. No doubt, such programmes are conducted now and then by State Governments, NGOs and some academic institutions. There is a need of a policy in this regard and such programmes should be on continuous basis for both elected members and local bureaucracy.
- Widely alleged corruption and mal practices at the

grassroots have to be contained as they, tend, to discourage women's participation. In this context, institutional mechanism is to be thought of. Social (including ethical) transformation should go side by side with political transformation.

- Now situation has come, where women have to move from 'critical mass' to 'critical action', especially at the grassroots. The government has provided suitable/enabling environment in which they themselves should enhance their status-political, economic social and legal and protect their dignity and voice in a participatory democracy mode.

12

Women in the Panchayati Raj Institutions: An Empirical Study in Kamrup District of Assam State

DR. JOGENDRA KUMAR DAS

The issue of women empowerment in India has in recent days assumed greater importance in all scholarly exercise and public discussion in the field of social sciences and humanities. In a nutshell, women empowerment refers to the process by which women acquire due recognition on par with men, to participate in the development process of the society through the political institutions as a partner with human face and dignity. (For a discussion in this regard, see. G. Palanithurai, 2001, Manikyamba 1981 and 1989). It is a process of redistribution of resources in the society in such a way that women get equal access and control over the available resources. (Also see Subha, K. and B.S. Bhargava, 2000: 74) The political empowerment of women and women leadership in PRIs is crucial not only for the development of women themselves, but also for the availability for their creative potential that is socially important and without which the country cannot hope for any sustainable development. (Smitha 2006: 38). In India men monopolize the positions of power almost absolutely. Politics, therefore, continues to be the domain of men. This is more prominent in the field of leadership. Especially, participation of women in the electoral process is far from adequate and women have been grossly underrepresented in the parliamentary politics. At the grassroots level, the participation of women was almost unknown prior to the 73rd Amendment Act, 1993. But the new dispensation has drastically changed the situation by making adequate provisions for the reservation of at least 30 per cent of seats for women in the PRIs. Reservations for women have been provided not only at the level of members, but one-third of the Chairpersons are to be women.

Since the PRIs have been charged with the responsibilities of preparing plans for economic development and social justice and implementation of these plans and schemes with regard to a fairly comprehensive list of 29 subjects, it also affords to women who are elected for an opportunity of personal growth and empowerment. (Smitha 2006: 38). Now women leaders at the grassroots level have got an opportunity to fight against the century old household bondage and disabilities that rural women have been suffered and they got an opportunity to become the partners of rural development in general and social justice for women milieu in particular. Her leadership (empowerment) has undoubtedly begun and this will logically reach its fullness and will definitely help in the abolition of inequitable and unjust laws and social practices. (Smitha 2006: 38). The 73rd Amendment Act has laid the foundation for this emergence of women leadership.

In the present chapter, an attempt has been made to understand the social background features of the women representatives in the PRIs of Kamrup district of the Indian state of Assam. The present study is based on the primary data collected from women representatives elected in 2001 in the South Kamrup area of the district of Kamrup. The data were collected during 2006-07, while conducting a UGC sponsored Minor Research Project on the *Social Base of Grassroots Politics with a Reference to the Panchayats in Kamrup District of Assam* with necessary financial assistance. Basically we have tried to understand the role of women leaders in the PRIs in terms of their social background characteristics. There were altogether 457 women representatives in the PRIs under the district of Kamrup. We have used survey technology and collected primary data from 110 women representatives including 13 Presidents from 33 Gaon Panchayats on the basis of convenient random sampling with fairly a long interview schedule. After the collection of data from our respondents, the data pertaining to women have been systematically processed, classified, quantified, checked, crosschecked and converted into Tables in simple statistical calculation and accordingly analysed. It should be noted that the data have been entirely processed on the basis of the party affiliation of the women representatives since Panchayat elections were fought completely on party lines in 2001 in Assam following the new dispensation (Aftermath of the 73rd CA Act 1992). Though women contested Panchayat elections under the banner of several regional and national political parties, most of the women were elected from the Congress (I), Assam Gana Parishad (AGP) and Dakshin Kamrup Bikash Gosthi in the name of Independents (IND).[1] The position of other parties in terms of women representation was negligible. We have drawn 45 women samples from the AGP, 54 from the Congress (I), 19 from IND, 2 from the Bharatiya Janata Party (BJP), and only 1 from the Nationalist Congress Party (NCP). The study is significant in the sense that we have generated primary data in the work for our analysis and it has tried to fill the gap of our understanding on the role of women in the grassroots bodies in an empirical setting based in Assam especially aftermath of the 73rd CA Act.

Here, it would be necessary to deal with a brief profile of Kamrup district location, which is our area of the present investigation. The present district of Kamrup was a part of the ancient Kamarupa Kingdom. The extent of the old Kamarupa Kingdom with a very crucial historical tradition varied from time to time and the present name actually derived from this old name Kamarupa. It is really the center stage of Assam history and the society as such. It has very rich historical past, as it formed passage to China during the ancient period and over and above it was the capital of the once famous *Pragjyotisaha-Kamarupa* Kingdom (See Government of Assam 1990: Preface). Today almost all the Central, State, and Quasi-Government establishments, including establishments of Multi-National Corporations, the wholesale markets of the North East India, the residences of eminent scholars and intellectuals of the state, national and international communication channels, the prominent educational institutions, all leading industrial establishments, Newspaper Houses, Head Offices of Political Parties, the Capital of Assam (Dispur), the Gauhati High Court, the NE Railway Headquarter, the Indian Institute of Technology and many more are situated in this historically enriched district of Assam. It is also the centrestage of all political activities of the state and in fact the launching pad of major social and political movements since the early British period up to the present.

According to 2001 Census, Kamrup District at present has an area of 4245 kms. The rural area comprises of 4083 km. while the urban area covers only a scanty 261 kms. The district has 2 sub-divisions and 17 rural development Blocks with 14 Revenue Circles. Moreover it has a total of 178 Gaon Panchayats and as many as 1393 villages of which 1342 are inhabited villages. At present the number of towns is 9 including Guwahati city. The total number of population is 25,22,324 of which 13,26,981 are male and the female population is 11,95,3343. The sex ratio is calculated at 901 and the density of population is estimated at 581. The number of SC population is 1,70,541 of which male population being 88,076 and female population is 82,465 (Constitutes 7% of the total population). The number of ST population is 20,2,577 of which male population is 10,2,256 and the female ST population comprises 10,032. (Constitutes 18% of the total population). The literacy rate of the district is 75 per cent, of which male literacy constitutes 82 per cent that outweighs the female literacy constituting 67 per cent according to 2001 Census.

We have conducted our present research in the South Kamrup area of the parent Kamrup district, which is located at the South bank of the river Brahmaputra. In fact there is no specific territorial division officially of the district like South Kamrup and North Kamrup. People of both parts of the district unofficially use the terms to identify themselves as belonging to North and South Kamrup respectively. South Kamrup is a vast area stretching over 200 kms along the southern bank of the river Brahmaputra covering four Assam Legislative Assembly Constituencies such as West Guwahati, Chhaygaon, Palasbari and Boko. This is predominantly a rural area and has a rich unique cultural heritage of its own. It is basically a plural society, thickly populated and the historical homeland of various castes, sub-castes, tribal ethnic groups and communities such as Brahmins, Kayastha, Kalita, Keot, Baishya, Mali, Saloi, Kumar, Hira, Mali, Nadiyal, Brittial, Namasudra, Kaiborta, Asamiya Muslim, Immigrant Muslim, Hindu Bengali, Nepali, Marwari, Bihari, Punjabi, Koch Rajbongshis, Boro, Rabha, Hazong and Garo etc. There are 5 Revenue Circles in South Kamrup such as Boko, Nagarbera, Chhaygaon, Chamaria and Palasbari and the number of Development blocks is 9, covering 66 Gaon Panchayats and only one Municipal Board that is the Palasbari Municipal Board. The South Kamrup area comprises a total of 17 Mouzas, 104 Laats and 216 Revenue Villages. The number of general villages is 669. Of the total of 17 Mouzas, 9 Mauzas are declared as severely effected by flood and erosion. The literacy rate of this area is 58 per cent at present. We have selected our empirical setting for the present research, i.e. the PRIs under the administrative jurisdiction of Chhaygaon and Palasbari Revenue Circles for our operational convenience.

Social Background of Women Representatives in Panchayati Raj Institutions

With these words we propose to study the socio-economic determinants of women leadership and their role in the PRIs of Kamrup in its southern part. In fact patriarchal culture and social structures that is dominant in India seem to inhibit women's participation in local governance through PRIs. We here try to understand whether social background characteristics have any impact and bearing in the emergence of women as leaders in the PRIs of South Kamrup District particularly after the 73rd Amendment Act. The socio-economic and political background of women members will indicate the nature of their representation and women's antecedents will have decisive impact on their political role performance but it also needs stressing that such background by itself does not effectuate effective participation of women in panchayats specifically because of their subordinate status, male ideology and extended political inexperience. (See Mandal 2003: 79). This aspect will definitely indicate the capabilities of women leaders to act as catalytic agent for general women's concerns or requirements and whether they can bridge the communication gap between development personnel and their own perception and priority (Mandal ibid. 79) Here we must note that women got adequate representation as per the reservation norms, in the PRIs under review. The social background of women representatives in the PRIs in Kamrup district has been analyzed in terms of their age, marital status, family structure, caste, community, occupation income, education, land holding pattern, industrial and business establishments along with their self assessments on the current issues and their role perception.

Age

The first determinant is the age structure of the women leaders, which is crucial for the emergence of women leadership particularly at the village level. In the tradition-bound and patriarchal Indian society, social mobility of women usually occurs very marginally and therefore entry of the young unmarried women in politics was restrictive. This contention can be supplemented everywhere from several empirical studies (See Mandal ibid. 81, Mehta ibid. 57). But the situation has been changed after the new dispensation, which inducts younger women in rural politics. This aspect can be observed in Table 1. The table demonstrates that majority of the women leaders are in the age group of 35-40 and they constitute 53 per cent followed by women leaders of the age group of 45-50 years constituting nearly 24 per cent. We have found only 8 per cent women leaders who are in the age group of between 45-60 years and the very younger blood in between 21-30 years constitute a meager 3.5 per cent. Though we do not compose the marital status separately, the age composition clearly reveals that a large majority of the women respondents are married (97%) and only 3 per cent or less are unmarried (girls). Though unmarried women are relatively free from the burdens of household chores, child care and have greater physical mobility than the married, they are less interested to come to village politics or it may be that they are hesitant to compete against matured women or may be debarred from contesting elections from the patriarchs for several reasons including social taboos.

Table-1

Age Composition of Women (In Years)

Parties/ Age Group	*AGP*	*Congress*	*IND*	*BJP*	*NCP*	*Total*
21-30	1(3)	3(7)	–			4(3.5)
30-35	7(20)	1(2)	5(19)			13(12)
35-40	18(51)	23(50)	16(61)	1(33)		58(53)
40-45	7(22)	13(28)	3(12)	1(33)	1(100)	25(23.5)
45-50	1(3)	3(8)	1(4)	1(33)		6(4.5)
50-60	1(3)	2(5)	1(4)			4(3.5)
Total	35(100)	45(100)	26(100)	3(100)	1(100)	110(100)

Source: Field data generated by the investigator. The figures in parentheses indicate percentage to total.

Most of the young women leaders are the first generation entrants to political life. Though it was once the privilege of the older people to occupy the various key positions in the villages, our observation reveals the emergence of the younger blood in rural politics. Similar results were found by several relevant studies. (Smitha 2006: 42, Rajeswari 1998: 13, Kittur 1992: 163, Babhiskar 2005: 333, Buch 2000, Mehta 2002: 57 and Mandal 2003: 80). Thus we can conclude that the new dispensation has led to the emergence of first entrants' women leadership in the PRIs.

Caste Representation

We propose to look into the caste factor of the women representatives. This aspect can be observed in Table 2.

Table–2
Caste Distribution of Women Leaders

Parties/ Castes	*AGP (35)*	*Cong. (45)*	*IND (26)*	*BJP (3)*	*NCP (1)*	*Total (110)*
Brahmin	–	2(4)	2(8)	–	–	4(3.5)
Kayastha	1(3)	–	2(8)	–	–	3(3)
Kalita	9(26)	12(26)	4(16)	–	–	26(23.5)
Keot	3(8)	1(2)	6(20)	2(68)	–	12(11)
OBC	7(20)	5(14)	4(16)	1(32)	–	17(15.5)
SC	5(14)	4(8)	4(16)	–	–	13(12)
ST	7(20)	15(33)	4(16)	–	–	26(23.5)
Baishya	2(6)	–	–	–	–	2(1)
Muslim	1(3)	6(13)	–	–	1(100)	7(6.5)

Source: Field data generated by the investigator. The figures in parentheses indicate percentage to total.

Several empirical observations reveal that high caste groups had been dominating the PRIs of the country as a whole (See Das 2008: 62). Since the introduction of the Panchayati Raj System in 1956 the rural landlords, zamindars, moneylenders and the high caste dominated the PRIs and these groups together were called as dominant caste, which controlled the rural power structure (M.N. Srinivas quoted in Mandal ibid. 84). Not only in grassroots politics, high caste groups were dominant in legislatures and parliaments. But gradually as the middle formation process has been gearing up everywhere, the intermediate castes with their middle class components started ensuring berths in the political apparatuses from top to bottom. This is especially pertinent in Assam politics (See Das 1995: 98-116 and also see for a latest picture of this aspect Das 2005: 873-900). Table 2 also supplement this standing of the non-high caste predominance in the recent grassroots political institutions. Here we find that though women belonging to the Kalita caste are the largest (23.5%), the high caste groups like Kalita, Brahmin, Kayastha and Keot together constitute 41 per cent, while the Other Backward Classes (OBC), Scheduled Castes (SC),

Scheduled Tribes (ST), Muslim and Baishya combine together constitute the majority (59%). Thus we find that discontinuing the traditional prevalence of high castes in PRI politics, the non-high caste women leader-combination now dominant the PRIs of South Kamrup. Hence, with regards to women leadership non-caste and non-high caste groups are predominant. Therefore an inference can be drawn that the leadership pattern in India, which has been institutionalized in the high caste groups, has been significantly changed due to the reservation policy and subsequently non-caste women come to the position of power at the grassroots level. An additional inference can be drawn that the non-high caste women are more interested to take up leadership responsibility in the villages than the high caste women. We also find primordial values associated with the caste norms and largely institutionalize in the socio-political interaction of women, do not debar them to come to the leadership position.

Table-3
Religious Background of Women Leaders

Parties/ Variables	*AGP 35*	*Congress 45*	*IND 26*	*BJP 3*	*NCP 1*	*Total 110*
Hinduism	32(91.5)	27(60)	26(100)	3(100)	–	88(80)
Islam	3(8.5)	16(35.5)	–	–	1(100)	20(18)
Christianity	–	2(4.4)	–	–	–	2(2)

Source: Field data generated by the investigator. The figures in parentheses indicate percentage to total.

Religion

Like the caste factor, religion has also played a very significant role in the emergence of leadership in India and the caste of Assam is also not an exception to it. Like the men, women leadership is also largely influenced by religious consideration. But in our observation we find that the Hindus, which have a direct bearing in the leadership composition, predominantly inhabit the area in which we conduct the present investigation. Table 3 highlights that the Hindu women leaders like the men exclusively dominate the PRIs that constitutes as high as 80 per cent. Though the number of Muslim women are relatively small (18%) it is not however, depressive in a predominantly Hindu inhabited area rather it is impressive that Muslim women also come to grassroots politics though marginal in composition which is reflective of their increasing interest in rural development.

Education

The leadership pattern, sharing of power and the role in decision-making significantly shaped by education. Therefore, we look into the educational background of women in question. It is important to understand whether educated women evince greater interests to participate in grassroots politics for a conscious and meaningful involvement in the rural developmental efforts. This aspect can be observed in Table 4. The Table reveals that matriculate women constituting 36 per cent dominated the PRIs. Literate and below matriculates constitute 42 per cent, while there are 6 graduate women and a significant 16 per cent are of Pre-University or Higher Secondary level. This situation can be supplemented by studies in West Bengal where over 55 per cent women Panchayat leaders were either literate or educated (See Mandal ibid. 2003: 89). But quite a reverse situation has been observed in Uttar Pradesh where over 71 per cent women PRI leaders are illiterate (See Mehta ibid. 2002: 89-90). But the overall educational qualifications of women leaders in South Kamrup of Assam are impressive and hence we can draw an inference that qualified women have come to the leadership position at the grassroots level in the state. It is observed in some studies that though women come from an economically well off group her participation would not be politically active unless she was educated that gives a sense of confidence to participate in politics. It has also been observed that due to lack of education, the women representatives in Panchayat are not able to overcome the conservative ideas that have an adverse effect in their participation in political spheres in local levels. (D'lima 1983; Vatsyana 2005; Manikyayamba 1989: 80).

Thus observing the relative advantageous position of women under review, we can infer that this group of educated women should play positive role in the Panchayat politics of the rural government in The District of Kamrup and can become the role models for our mass women folks to get themselves actively involved in grassroots politics.

Occupation

One of the important sources of leadership is one's own occupation, which yields income that consequently enables individuals to take

Table–4
Educational Background of Women Leaders

Parties/ Education	*AGP 35*	*Congress 45*	*IND 26*	*BJP 3*	*NCP 1*	*Total 110*
Literate	3(8)	11(25)	5(19)	–	1(100)	20(18)
Undermatric	15(42)	5(11)	7(27)	–	–	27(24)
Matriculation	12(31)	16(36)	7(27)	3(100)	–	38(36)
PU/HS	5(14)	9(20)	5(19)	–	–	19(16)
Graduation	1(3)	3(6)	2(8)	–	–	6(5)
PG	–	–	–	–	–	–
Illiterate	–	1(2)	–	–	–	1(1)

Source: Field data generated by the investigator. The figures in parentheses indicate percentage to total.

up a leadership position. The case of women is no exception. We intend to understand the occupational status of women leaders, which has a bearing on their leadership. This aspect can be observed in Table 5.

Table–5
Occupational Status of Women

Parties/ Occupation	*AGP 35*	*Congress 45*	*IND 26*	*BJP 3*	*NCP 1*	*Total 110*
Business	3(8.5)	4(8.8)	2(7.6)	–	–	9(8)
Teaching	1(2.8)	–	–	–	–	1(.9)
Agriculture	2(5.7)	11(25)	2(7.6)	1(33)	1(100)	17(15)
Service	–	2(44.4)	–	–	–	2(1.8)
Housewife	23(65.7)	13(28.8)	13(50)	–	–	49(45)
SPW*	4(11.5)	10(22.2)	5(19.2)	1(33)	–	20(18)
Farming	2(5.7)	3(6.6)	3(11.5)	1(33)	–	9(8)
Weaving	–	2(4.4)	1(4)	–	–	3(2.7)

Source: Field data generated by the investigator. The figures in parentheses indicate percentage.

The table reveals that the largest number of the women leaders is an unpaid housewife followed by 18 per cent who recorded themselves as Social and Political Workers. However, business, teaching and farming combine is also not negligible. It is assumed that women remain as housewives are directly or indirectly related to some basic problems like drinking water, children education, sanitation, child welfare, health problem and the like, and consequently they can focus all attention on locating the grievances of the housewives and can do something to redress these grievances by using their leadership positions in the PRIs (See Smitha 2006: 43). Even in Uttar Pradesh and in West Bengal most of the women leaders are engaged in non-economic activities like Housewives (Mehta ibid. 61 and Mandal ibid. 90). It is significant that performing all household duties including child caring, child rearing, cooking, and by doing all other domestic works regularly, the housewives could manage time to perform their public duties as PRI leaders and that their husbands also do not deter them in performing their role rather inspire them to go ahead to do their tasks sincerely, as we have obtained informations in this regard. Needless to say that the income sources of the housewives are their husbands or elder sons and virtually they are not economically independent. But economic dependence does not deter in the way of their acquiring leadership position. Now we can infer that occupation has no direct relationship with the emerging women leadership in the PRIs and this contention is supplemented by several studies. (See Ghosh 1997; Mandal, ibid. 2003).

Annual Income

Our practical observation reveals that both male and female contestants have spent a big amount of money in the Panchayat elections; though an amount is being spent by the banner political party, a considerable amount being spent by the contestants. In this connection the annual income of the women contestants needs to be reckoned with. Annual income of an individual is supplemented by occupation. But as most of the women leaders are housewives by occupation they have no income of their own and consequently they had to spent money from the sundry sources of their families. The picture of annual income can be gleaned in Table 6.

The table indicates that the average income of the women leaders is not very depressive. It is however, very difficult to get the actual income figures. Our study reveals that most of the respondents belong to the average annual income category of Rs. 10,001-50,000 that may be regarded as of an economically well-off standing of the women leaders. Even we find a relatively higher income group of

Table-6

Annual Income of the Women Leaders (In Thousands)

Parties/ Income	*AGP 35*	*Congress 45*	*IND 26*	*BJP 3*	*NCP 1*	*Total 110*
Below Rs. 9000	4(11)	3(7)	2(7)	–	–	9(8)
Rs. 9001-10,000	5(14)	3(7)	6(23)	–	–	14(13)
Rs. 10,001-15,000	8(27)	6(13)	2(7)	–	–	16(15)
Rs. 15,001-20,000	1(3)	8(18)	2(7)	–	–	11(12)
Rs. 20,001-30,000	2(6)	7(16)	5(19)	–	–	14(13)
Rs. 30,001-40,000	8(27)	5(12)	6(23)	–	–	19(17)
Rs. 40,001-50,000	5(14)	4(9)	1(4)	–	–	10(13)
Rs. 50,001-70,000	1(3)	3(7)	1(4)	1(33)	–	6(5)
Rs. 70,001-90,000	–	3(7)	–	1(33)	1(100)	5(6)
Rs. Above 1 Lakh	1(3)	3(7)	1(4)	1(33)	–	6(4)

Source: Field data generated by the investigator. The figures in parentheses indicate percentage to total.

women leaders whose annual income fall in between Rs. 50,001 and above 1 lakh and may be far more. The sound economic position of the women leaders upheld their class position and they certainly got a middle class position accordingly in the society and a section of women leaders even turned into the influential elitist position at the local level. Hence, we find that PRI women leaders are economically not weak and poor, therefore, virtually they can afford to come to the power position and their good educational status also supplement their entry into power position. Thus we can draw an inference that women leadership position in the PRIs is influenced by factors like a sound annual income that decides the opportunities to contest election for a good win and command respect from the people. So, the present women leaders are said to have emerged from an average economic strata, which significantly helped them to move up to the elitist position at the local level.

Political Experience and Training

We also intended to understand the political experiences gathered and training received, if any, by the respondents. After the statutory reservation in the 73rd CA Act, a new revolutionary era of women's political representation has ushered in. The rural women who were largely confined to their household domain, lacked information on public affairs and even were disabled to decide their own personnel issues, now asked to shoulder public responsibilities, allowed to play important role in public life and to take active part in the decision-making process at the grassroots level. Accordingly women come to the forefront of politics and public life, and political parties also figure their names into the list of their party affiliation. It is really very crucial, significant and a landmark precedent in the history of women political representation in the grassroots democracy of the country. It is commonly conceded that in undertaking political roles previous political and representative experiences helps one to understand the tangles of public roles, equips one with public information in order to set their roles in the political process. But this aspect was not relevant in case of women representation in the PRIs, because it was mandatory for women to come to rural politics as per the new dispensation and to play a desired role as representatives as well as to become parts of the rural development process. Our empirical evidence reveals that politically inexperienced women have come to grassroots politics and become the part and parcel of grassroots democracy as well as the rural development participants. This aspect can be seen in the following table.

Table–7

Previous Representative Experiences

Parties/ Variables	*AGP 35*	*Congress 45*	*IND 26*	*BJP 3*	*NCP 1*	*Total 110*
Panchayat	5(14.5)	11(24.5)	7(27)	1(33)	–	24(21.8)
MLA	–	–	–	–	–	–
No Exp.	30(85.7)	34(75.5)	19(73)	2(67)	1(100)	86(76)

Source: Field data generated by the investigator. The figures in parentheses indicate precentage to total.

As is expected and has already been found, sky high majority of the women respondents have no previous representative (political) experiences and though most of the respondents are matured and married as such, they are new entrants in public life and the accessibility in fact, given by the 73rd Constitution Amendment Act.

Political education may be corroborated by their experiences, if any, of political imprisonment. Assam has been experiencing innumerable social and political movements and ethnic upsurge, both peaceful and violent during the last thirty years, which undoubtedly provide a sort of political experiences, and training to the political aspirants including women and political imprisonment may be considered as one of the determinants of emerging leadership at the grassroots level. Table 8, has given some assumptions to us regarding the active political involvement of the women for which they had to courting arrest for an imprisonment.

Table-8
Experiences of Political Imprisonment

Parties/ Variables	*AGP 35*	*Congress 45*	*IND 26*	*BJP 3*	*NCP 1*	*Total 110*
As Student Leader	5(15)	–	1(4)	–	–	6(5.5)
Participation in Political Movement	5(1.5)	3(6.6)	1(4)	1(33)	–	10(9)
As Political Leader	–	1(1.4)	1(4)	–	–	2(1.5)
No Experience	25(70)	41(92)	23(88)	2(67)	1(100)	92(84)

Source: Field data generated by the investigator. The figures in parentheses indicate percentage to total.

The table demonstrates that only 16 per cent of the respondents have experiences of political imprisonment and the huge 84 per cent of the women leaders have no such experiences. This conforms that political imprisonment is not an important determinants of the modern emerging women leadership now a days especially at the grassroots level. But gone are the days when our old guards from top to bottom at the political level had the determinants of past representative experiences as well as they had also experiences of political imprisonment. But the compulsion of modern democratic decentralization process makes it almost mandatory for women and youth to come to the leadership position for the functional and structural necessity of our political society.

Factors of Joining Panchayats

We also intend to know the factors responsible for their joining Panchayat politics. This aspect can be observed in Table 9.

We find in the table that half of the respondents (50%) have joined the PRIs with a commitment for rural development and 15.5 per cent joined for party interest. It is interesting to note that only a very microscopic (9%) that is only one women respondent joined

Table-9
Factors Joining the Panchayats

Parties/ Factors	*AGP 35*	*Congress 45*	*IND 26*	*BJP 3*	*NCP 1*	*Total 110*
Social service	4(11.4)	8(17.7)	5(19.4)	–	–	17(15.5)
To serve women	1(2.1)	–	–	–	–	1(.9)
To serve local people	2(5.7)	5(11)	1(3.8)	–	–	8(7.2)
Rural development	10(27.5)	25(55.5)	16(61.5)	3(100)	1(100)	55(50)
Party interest	10(28.5)	5(11)	2(7.6)	–	–	17(15.5)
All	8(24.8)	2(4.5)	2(7.5)	–	–	12(10.9)

Source: Field data generated by the investigator. The figures in parentheses indicate percentage to total.

panchayat politics to serve the rural women. This is reflective of the less gender sensitiveness of the women leaders of the villages, though women reservation in the PRIs was institutionalized in the constitution only because of the broad objective of pressing women services in the grassroots governance for the welfare of the rural women. But it is impressive that majority of women leaders come to the PRIs either for rural development or for social service, which mean the same thing.

Women in the Decision-Making

After observing some important determinants of the emerging rural women leadership, it would be necessary to look into the very pertinent aspect whether or not the new women entrants have fully taken part in the decision-making process at the grassroots government. This aspect can be observed in Table 10.

The table indicates that a large majority of women (62%), according to their own perception, have been fully taking part in the decision-making process in the Panchayat bodies. It is really an impressive matter that the women leaders have got an uninterrupted accessibility to participate in the decision-making process and become the part of the developmental process for which they have been brought to the PRIs by the new dispensation. However, 12 per cent of the respondents stated that they have only partially taking part in the decision-making process, while, significantly, 12 per cent of the respondents are reportedly reluctant to actively take part in the decision-making process. A few of them stated to the investigator that observing the dominating and suppressive role of the higher echelons, coupled with certain corrupt activities, they were disappointed and loss faith in the Panchayat administration. It is pertinent to look that still male dominance prevails unabated in the PRIs as 8 per cent of our women respondents admit the fact. Though very marginal, four respondents admit that in certain cases women leaders override the male initiative in taking decisions. But the results say that majority of women leaders can take active part equally to that of male leaders.

Table–10
Women in the Decision-Making Process

Parties/ Reactions	*AGP 35*	*Congress 45*	*IND 26*	*BJP 3*	*NCP 1*	*Total 110*
Yes, taking active part in Decision-making	22(62.8)	24(53)	18(70)	3(100)	–	67(62)
Partially taking part in Decision-making	6(17.2)	5(11.5)	4(15)	–	–	15(13.5)
No/Not interested to take part in the process	4(11)	8(17.7)	2(7)	–	–	14(12)
Male dominance always prevail	1(3.3)	7(15.3)	1(4)	–	–	3(8)
Women taking leading part in the process	2(5.7)	1(2.5)	1(4)	–	–	4(3.5)

Source: Field data generated by the investigator. The figures in parentheses indicate percentage to total.

Attending the Panchayat Meetings

In addition, we have also asked to the respondents about their punctuality in attending the Panchayat meetings. Table 11 stated that barring only five women respondents (4.5%) the rest sky high number constituting nearly 96 per cent have attended the Panchayat meetings regularly, as and when the meetings have been convened. This clearly shows that women leaders are very interested in rendering their services to the rural people. It also reveals that men do not suppress the women to play the necessary role in grassroots government. This inference rejects the earlier results of an empirical study conducted by the present author during 1997 on the Panchayati Raj Institutions in Assam with a reference to the representation of women, where we found that women leaders at their first entrance in the PRIs of Assam following the 73rd CA Act, were not regularly attending the meetings rather they were very casual in the PRIs. (See for a detailed discussion Das, 1997).

Table-11

Women Attending the Panchayat Meetings

Parties/ Attendance	*AGP 35*	*Congress 45*	*IND 26*	*BJP 3*	*NCP 1*	*Total 110*
Regularly	32(92)	43(95.5)	26(100)	3(100)	1(100)	105(95.5)
Occasionally	3(8)	2(4.5)	–	–	–	5(4.5)

Source: Field data generated by the investigator. The figures in Parentheses indicate percentage to total.

Women Leaders for Women Folks

About their actual role in serving the rural women we asked as to how far they work for the betterment of rural women during their tenure. This aspect can be seen in Table 12.

Table-12

Women Leaders Working for Rural Women

Parties/ Works	*AGP 35*	*Congress 45*	*IND 26*	*BJP 3*	*NCP 1*	*Total 110*
By Self-Help Group	19(54)	23(50)	18(69)	3(100)	1(100)	64(58)
Partly	3(8.7)	5(11)	1(3.8)	–	–	4(3.6)
No work	1(2.8)	2(4.5)	1(3.8)	–	–	4(3.6)
IAY House grant*	12(34.5)	15(33)	6(23.4)	–	–	33(30.4)

Source: Field data generated by the investigator. The figures in parentheses indicate percentage to total. * IAY—Indira Awas Yojana.

We do not ask the details of working for the rural women by the women leaders. Rather we have in random, got the responses from them as to their works for the poor women during their tenure. The table thus indicates that a comfortable majority (58%) of women leaders have been successful in working for the rural poor women by organizing hundreds of women of below poverty line, into Self-Help Groups (SHGs) through which poor women could earn two-squares of meals. The organization of rural poor people into Self-Help Group is a self-employment scheme brought under the holistic programme called *Swarnajayanti Gram Swarojgar Yojana* (SGSY) along with other aspects of self-employment such as training, credit technology, infrastructure and marketing. The Central and State Government have provided fund for the execution of this programme in the ratio of 75:25 basis.

The main objective is to assist the rural poor popularly known as *swarojgaris* to come above the poverty line in three years by providing them income-generating assets through Bank Loan and Government subsidy. For the SHG (Group *swarojgaries*), the subsidy is fixed at 50 per cent of the project cost per capita subsidy of Rs. 10,000 or 1.25 lakhs whichever is less. The government has emphasized on group approach and has discouraged the sanctioning of subsidy to individual *swarojgaries* by issuing circular to have separate identity of the programme from the earlier Integrated Rural Development Programme (IRDP) and effective implementation of the programme. The government spent several thousands crores of money for the implementation of this programme and has covered thousands of individual *swarojgaries* and group *swarojgaries* (SHGs) under different economic activities in every financial year. (See for more details Government of Assam 2005-06: 40-45).

Our respondents thus stated to the investigator that they have taken up necessary initiative and give incentives to the deserving Below Poverty Line (BPL) women to organize themselves into SHG to take the opportunity of self-employment. Though four women respondents stated in the negative, a significant 31.4 per cent of the respondents positively stated that they have released several grants to the BPL women to construct dwelling houses (units) under *Indira Awaas Yojana* (IAY). It should be stated that the government has also allocated sufficient fund under this scheme for the upliftment of the rural poor.

The objectives of the IAY is primarily to build dwelling units to SC/ST, rural poor BPL by providing them grants-in-aid to the tune of Rs. 25000 for plains districts. A maximum of 40 per cent of the total IAY allocation can also be utilized for the construction of dwelling units for non-SC/ST rural BPL families. A special provision of safeguards for the women has also been made up to 40 per cent and 30 per cent of targets respectively. The respondents reportedly make spectacular achievement in this regard. But at the same time they do not hesitate to disclose that wanton misuse, mis-utilisation and corruption eat into the vitals of these glorious schemes of rural development.

Meeting the Rural People and Self-Assessment about their Leadership Quality

Two very pertinent questions relevant to the viability of their leaderships have been asked. The results have been capitulated in the following paragraphs as reflected in Table 13 and Table 14.

Table–13
Meeting the Rural People

Parties/ Times	*AGP 35*	*Congress 45*	*IND 26*	*BJP 3*	*NCP 1*	*Total 110*
Regular	10(28)	25(55.5)	20(80)	3(100)	1(100)	59(53.6)
No fixed Time	12(34.5)	10(22.5)	5(19)	–	–	27(24.4)
Meeting the women	6(17)	7(15.5)	1(1)	–	–	14(12.7)
1-3 Times	1(3)	1(2.5)	–	–	–	2(1.3)
3-4 Times	6(17)	2(4)	–	–	–	8(8)

Source: Field data generated by the investigator. The figures in Parentheses indicate percentage to total.

Table–14
Self-Assessment: Whether People Obey their Leadership

Parties/ Perception	*AGP 35*	*Congress 45*	*IND 26*	*BJP 3*	*NCP 1*	*Total 110*
Yes	15(43)	20(45)	16(61.5)	3(100)	1(100)	55(50)
Partially	12(34)	15(33)	4(15.3)	–	–	31(28)
Do not know	3(8.5)	4(9)	3(11.5)	–	–	10(9.5)
No	3(8.5)	5(11)	1(4.1)	–	–	9(8)
No comment	2(5.7)	1(2)	2(7.6)	–	–	5(4.5)

Source: Field data generated by the investigator. The figures in parentheses indicate percentage to total.

Table 13 indicate that majority of the respondents (53.6%) meet the rural people at a regular basis and try to understand their grievances and problems for quick redressal and solutions. In fact rural people always expect the Panchayat representatives at their doorsteps to hear their grievances and voices, which is easier to them than to meet the MLAs and MPs. For a significant 24.4 per cent of the respondents, there is no fixed time to meet the people. Besides, Table 14 highlights that half of the respondents (50%) have strong confidence about their popularity in the village and believe that people obey their leadership for the positive role as leaders they have been playing. This may be viewed as a great achievement of the new dispensation, which provides reservation of seats for women in the PRIs, and it can be assumed that women leadership in the PRIs would be more and more spectacular in the days to come. A significant 28 per cent of the respondents feel that they have been able to get popularity only partially while about 10 per cent respondents do not know anything about their leadership. This may be that people might loss confidence on their leadership due to their indifferent attitude towards the implementation of the available welfare schemes or their failure to achieve that primary goal.

Thus, in average, we find that women leaders meet the rural people regularly, have frequent interactions and keep contacts with them and therefore they are fully confident about their leadership image among the people. It is crucial to note that less than 13 per cent of women leaders have their specific meetings with the women folk, which once again confirm their less gender sensitiveness. Thus it remains in the dark whether women know women more, than the men and can work for the women more, than the men. On the other hand, a counter argument can be raised that the rest nearly 89 per cent of women leaders do not like to stratify rural society and the BPL poor milieu on the basis of men and women and treat them equally and remain away from a partisan feminist outlook of social upliftment. Rather emerging women leaders of grassroots politics try to do something good for both men and women who are the deserving BPL (Below Poverty Line) poor.

Concluding Observations

From our observation it appears that the experiment of women empowerment being made through the new dispensation has come out largely successful with few obvious exceptions. We find that women have found adequate representation from all social groups and communities and from every nook and corner of our rural society thereby disproving many traditional myths associated with women participation in politics. Women are elected from all the reserved seats and successfully take part in the rural decision-making process through the PRIs especially in our selected area of Kamrup district of Assam. We find that women overcome all the traditional social obstructions being imposed by patriarchy especially in the field of leadership. The Indian patriarchal culture and social structures that is dominant in the society and imposed restriction in all social interactions and discourses seem to inhibit women's participation in all political representations including local governance through the PRIs. But all these traditional theories relevant to women's political representation have been disproved in our present study.

While dealing with this aspect we have taken up variables like age, caste, education, political education, income, occupation etc. for our exercise and have tried to examine whether these could have any impact on the emerging women leadership in Kamrup district. Observing the age factor we find that majority of the women representatives are relatively younger in age, though they are married and women in between the age group of 30-40 years have dominated the PRIs. But in other states like Maharashtra, Kerala, Orissa, Punjab older aged women dominated the PRIs (Bhaskar 1992: 155). This trend cannot be found in the empirical situations in Assam and West Bengal where younger women with reasonable education have been making their ways in the PRIs (Also see Mandal 2003: 80). We infer that the new dispensation has led to the emergence of the first generation entrant's women leadership in the PRIs.

Observing caste factor, we find that non-high caste women leaders combine dominated the grassroots politics of South Kamrup discontinuing the traditional high caste dominance in the grassroots politics. But quite reverse has happened in case of Maharashtra, Karnataka and Haryana where high caste groups are still predominant in the field of local leadership (Lima 1983 and Vidya 1997). Though high caste groups individually fail to hold the sway, majority of women leaders are belonging to the Hindu fold as religious category. The Muslim representation as religious group is microscopic. The overall educational qualifications of women leaders in Kamrup district are impressive. Thus we find that qualified women have come to the leadership position at the grassroots level in the state of Assam along with an average economic standing which is certainly reflective of the emergence of a group of women rural elite who can command respectability from the village people. Occupationally, the non-paid housewives exclusively dominate the PRIs under review. Though housewives are unemployed in the economic market they are not economically weak and though dependent on their husbands they have command on the economy of the family for which they are elected as representatives and hence, economic dependence of the women on their husbands and sons does not deter in the way on their acquiring leadership position. It is impressive that despite having a heavy burden and responsibility of household works the housewives freely come out as PRI leaders to perform their public duties without any restriction being imposed by their husbands, rather as is reported, husbands are liberal and inspire a lot to their wives to sincerely perform their roles as leaders.

Thus we find that occupation has no direct relationship with the emerging women leadership in the PRIs. But interestingly the women leaders are economically not so weak and virtually, they can afford to come to the power position and their good educational status also supplement their entry into power position. Observing political background we find that political imprisonment is not an important determinant of the modern emerging women leaders, especially at the grassroots level. Most of the women leaders have entered Panchayat politics with a commitment for rural development. Empirical data reveal that majority of the women incumbents, according to their own perception, have been fully taking part in the decision-making process in the PRIs. We find that women leaders are very interested in rendering their services to the rural people and it also reveals that men do not suppress the women to play the necessary role in grassroots movement. We find that women leaders have been successful in working for the rural poor women by organizing hundreds of women of below poverty line, into Self-Help Groups through which poor women could earn two-squares of meals.

From our observation we find that women leaders have properly shouldered their responsibilities as village leaders and meeting the rural people at a regular basis and try to understand their grievances and problems for quick redresses and solutions. In fact rural people always expect the Panchayat representatives at their doorsteps to hear their voices, which is easier to them than to meet the MLAs and the MPs. This may be viewed as the great achievement of the new dispensation, which provide reservation of seats for women in the

PRIs and it can be assumed that women leadership in the PRIs would be more and more spectacular in the days to come. Thus we find that women leaders meet the rural people regularly, have frequent interactions and keep contacts with them and therefore they are fully confident about their leadership image among the people. We can thus draw up an inference that this group of first generation entrants educated, politically conscious, responsible women leaders and with an average economic standing, could play as role model to lead the vast rural women mass to become the development participants in the rural development process and could certainly take up leadership to transform the dream of rural women empowerment into reality.

Thus observing the socio-economic determinants of women leadership and their role in the PRIs we come to the conclusion that women would be certainly absolutely fit into the leadership position in our hard patriarchal social framework. Observing the various dimensions of leadership positions, we find that women are no longer lagging behind their male counterpart in this respect. Our observations reveal that in certain quarters, the women leaders even display more proficiencies than the men in the decision-making process at the grassroots level. It was formerly believed that the entry of women into the leadership position in our country would be hindered by the socio-economic profile in terms of income, education, caste religion and occupation and so on. But our study disproves all these myths associated with women leadership. Despite all odds imposed against them, the post 73rd Constitutional Amendment has shown the emerging women leadership at the grassroots level in Assam as elsewhere and we assume that in the days to come they will be more articulate to address the leading issues connected to rural development and political and economic empowerment. Their profile also reflect a wider representation across social groups and they are gradually moving ahead for more and more effective leadership at the grassroots, which should contribute much towards the successful working of our grassroots democracy. Hence, finally we submit by saying that equal political participation of both men and women in a collaborative manner at the grassroots, is definitely a condition for the successful working of democracy at the apex level which must also be equally shared by both of them.

NOTE

The Panchayats of South Kamrup area are overwhelmingly dominated by the Congress (I), The Assam Gana Parishad (AGP) and the IND. Though not stated, the IND contestants are belonging to a non-political and Non-Government Organisation (NGO) popularly known as Dakshin Kamrup Bikash Gosthi (DKBG). It was formed on 3rd May 1998 under the Presidentship of Mr. Pranab Kalita, a former Lecturer in Zoology of D.K. College, Mirza. Though initially it acted as a pressure group and later became a NGO, the DKBG was emerged as a strong political formation and assumed political popularity in the entire Dakshin Kamrup area. At present the DKBG has strength of over 1-lakh members of the relatively weaker sections of the society. The organization is basically concerned with political, social, and economic development of the area and even becomes a politically dominant organization though officially not a political party. However, its political support bases are confined to the Palasbari Legislative Assembly Constituency. Mr. Pranab Kalita, the Chairman of the DKBG is elected as MLA of the Palasbari Legislative Assembly Constituency for the last two-consecutive terms, 2001 and 2006 respectively under the banner of the organization. Mr. Kalita leads this organization in unique manner towards bringing about socio-economic and political changes in this vast area. Besides, the DKBG was able to capture a large number of Panchayat bodies in the South Kamrup area.

REFERENCES

B.S. Baviskar, Impact of Women's Participation in Local Governance in India, in L.C. Jain (ed.) *Decentralisation and Local Governance: Essays for George Mathew*, New Delhi, Orient Long Man, 2005.

M. Bhaskar, *Women in Grassroots Democracy – A Study of Kerala,*University of Kerala/ ICSSR, New Delhi, 1992.

F. Briliant, *Women in Power,* New Delhi, Lancer Publication, 1987.

Nirmala Buch, *Status of Panchayati Raj in the States and Union Territories in India,* Institute of Social Sciences, New Delhi, Concept Publishing Company, 2000.

Chandrashekher & Inbanathan, Profile and Participation of Women ZP and Mandal Members, *Journal of Rural Development.* Vol. 10, No. 6, December, 1991.

J.K. Das, *Society and Legislature: A Study of Social Background of the Eighth Assam Legislative Assembly,* Unpublished Ph.D Thesis, Gauhati University, 1995.

J.K. Das, The Panchayati Raj Institutions in Assam with Special Emphasis on The Representation of Women, *Indian Journal of Politics,* Aligarh Muslim University, Aligarh, Vol. XXXI, Nos. 3-4, December 1997.

J.K. Das, Assam: The Post-Colonial Political Developments, *The Indian Journal of Political Science,* IPSA Publication, Meerut, 2005.

J.K. Das, *Social Base of Grassroots Politics: An Empirical Study of Panchayats of*

Kamrup District of Assam, UGC Sponsored Minor Research Project Report, UGC, North East Regional Office, Guwahati, 2008. (Unpublished).

D'Lima, *Women in Local Government: A Study of Maharashtra*, Concept Publishing Company, New Delhi, 1983.

Gboyega, *Political Values and Local Government in Nigeria*, Malthous Press, Laogas, 1987.

D.K. Ghosh, Grassroots Women Leaders: Who Are They? A Study in West Bengal District, *Journal of Rural Development*, Vol. 16, No. 2, April-June,1997.

Government of India-2001, *Census of India 2001*, New Delhi, 2001.

Government of Assam, *Assam District Gazetteers*, Kamrup District, Guwahati, 1990.

Government of Assam, *Assam Panchayat Act*, Panchayat and Rural Development, Guwahati, 1994.

Government of Assam, *Economic Survey*, Directorate of Economics and Statistics, Assam, Guwahati, 2005.

Government of Assam, *Statistical Hand Book*, Directorate of Economics and Statistics, Guwahati. 2005.

Institute of Social Studies Trust, *Women in Panchayat Raj: Perspective From Different States*, New Delhi, 1995.

A.T. Kitur, Emerging Pattern of Leadership: A Study of PRIs in Dharwad District, *Journal of ISDA*, Vol. 2, April, 1992.

A. Mandal, *Women in Panchayati Raj Institutions*, Kanishka Publishers, Distributors, New Delhi, 2003.

P. Manikyamba, *Role of Women in Panchayati Raj*. A Report Submitted to ICSSR, New Delhi, 1981.

P. Manikyamba, *Women in Panchayati Raj Structures*, Gyan Publishing House, New Delhi, 1989.

Veena Mazumdar, *Role of Women in Rural Development*, Allied Publishers, Bombay, 1978.

G.S. Mehta, *Participation of Women in Panchayati Raj System*, Kanishka Publishers, Distributors, New Delhi, 2002.

G. Palanithurai, The Genre of Women Leaders in Local Bodies: Experience From Tamil Nadu, *The Indian Journal of Public Administration*, January-March, 2001.

K.C. Smitha, Socio-Economic Determinants of Women Leadership at the Grassroots: A Case Study of Andhra Pradesh, *South Asian Journal of Socio-Political Studies*, Vol. 7, No. 1, December-July, 2006.

K. Subha, *Women in Local Government*, RBSA, Jaipur, 1994.

K. Subha, & B.S. Bhargava, Feminism and Political Empowerment of Women at the Grassroots: The Karnataka Experience, *South Asian Journal of Socio-Political Studies*, Vol. 1, No. 2, December 2000.

K. Vatsyayan, *Women's Political Empowerment Day Celebration: The Journey Ahead*, Institute of Social Sciences, New Delhi, 2005.

K.C. Vidya, *Political Empowerment of Women at the Grassroots*, Kanishka Publishers, Distriubutors, New Delhi, 1997.

13

Women Empowerment and Panchayati Raj Institutions in India: A Gender Perspective in the Development Process

DR. P. ARJUN RAO & DR. BAYINENI SRINIVASULU

Empowerment is the expansion of assets and capabilities of poor people to participate in negotiate with, influence, control, and hold accountable institutions that affect their lives.

– The World Bank, 2002

Empowerment is the process of enhancing the capacity of individuals or groups to make choices and to transform those choices into desired actions and outcomes. Central to this process are actions that both build individual and collective assets, and improve the efficiency and fairness of the organizational and institutional context which govern the use of these assets. The World Bank's 2002 Empowerment Source book set out to bring together the thinking and practice of empowerment as a first step in developing a better understanding of this component of the Bank's work. It identified empowerment as 'the expansion of assets and capabilities of poor people to participate in, negotiate with, influence, control, and hold accountable institutions that affect their lives.'[1]

In India, a low caste woman currently feels empowered when she is given a fair hearing in a public meeting, which is comprised of men and women from different social and economic groups; in Brazil, in Porto Allegre, citizens–both men and women—feel empowered if they are able to engage in decisions on budget allocations; in Ethiopia, citizens and civil society groups report feeling empowered by consultations undertaken during the preparation of the poverty reduction support programme; in the USA, immigrant workers feel empowered through unionization which has allowed them to negotiate working conditions with employers; and in the UK, a battered woman feels empowered when she is freed from the threat of violence and becomes able to make decisions about her own life.

Empowerment is a cross-cutting issue. From education and health care to governance and economic policy, activities that seek to empower poor people are expected to increase development opportunities, enhance development outcomes and improve people's quality of life. Then, women's empowerment refers to the process by which women acquire due recognition on par with men, to participate in the development process of the society through the political institutions as a partner with human dignity.[2] So, why is empowerment through Panchayati Raj? According to the Document on Women's Development (1985) women's role in the political process has virtually remained unchanged since independence. Broad-based political participation of women has been severely limited due to various traditional factors such as caste, religion, feudal attitude and family status.[3] As a result, women have been left on the periphery of political life. Observing this dark picture, 73rd Constitutional Amendment Act came to provide them an opportunity to ventilate their grievances and to take active part in decision-making process in the local level.

Women Empowerment

With the passage of 73rd Amendment Act, 1992, India is at a crucial structure in the evaluation of Panchayati Raj Institutions (PRIs) – the Indian brand of rural local self-government. It has envisioned people's participation in the process of planning, decision-making, implementation and delivery system. The Panchayat Acts of State Governments have subsequently been amended to incorporate the stipulations of the Central Acts thus the constitutional mandate has heralded uniform pattern throughout Indian states. The Constitutional (73rd Amendment) Act, 1992, provides for reservation of elective posts for women. It has been provided that not less than one-third of total number of posts of Members and Chairpersons at all three tiers of PRIs (i.e. Gram Panchayat, Intermediate Panchayat and District Panchayat) shall be reserved for women. At present, there are 6,81,258 women elected to Gram Panchayats; 37,109 women to Panchayat at intermediate level and 3153 women to Panchayat at district level.

The empowerment of Rural Women is crucial for the development of the Rural Bharat. Bringing women into the mainstream of development is a major concern for the Government of India, which is why 2001 has been declared as the 'Year of Women Empowerment'. The programmes for Poverty Alleviation have a women's component to ensure flow of adequate funds to this section. The National Maternity Benefit Scheme extends financial assistance of Rs. 500 to pregnant women, who are living below the poverty line and are 19 years of age or above, up to first two live births.

Orientation training for elected representatives of PRIs is primarily the responsibility of the State Governments/Union Territory (UT) Administrations. The Constitution has placed enormous responsibility on the Panchayats to formulate and execute various programmes of economic development and social justice, and a number of Centrally Sponsored Schemes are being implemented through Panchayats. Thus, women Members and Chairpersons of Panchayats, who are basically new entrants in Panchayats, have to acquire the required skill and be given appropriate orientation to assume their rightful roles as leaders and decision makers.

Accordingly, States/UTs are organizing training programmes for elected representatives of Panchayats including women Members and Chairpersons of Panchayats. The Ministry of Rural Development also extends some financial assistance to the States/UTs with a view to improve the quality of training programmes and to catalyse capacity building initiatives for the PRI elected members and functionaries. NGOs are also involved in capacity building of women Members and Chairpersons of Panchayats. UNICEF has also funded similar capacity building initiatives in consultation with the Ministry of Rural Development in the States of Tamil Nadu, Haryana, Himachal Pradesh, Rajasthan and West Bengal. The All India Women Conference, an NGO has been provided funds by UNICEF for organizing leadership training programmes for women Members of Panchayats in Manipur and Tripura.

The Constitution of India provides that State Governments/UTs administrations shall devolve functional and financial powers upon the PRIs. Devolution of powers is an ongoing process. The States/UTs have devolved powers upon Panchayats in varying degrees. The Ministry of Rural Development has taken several steps towards greater devolution of functional and financial powers to the Panchayats. However, States/UTs have been requested to make all out efforts to create public awareness about the role of women representatives in Panchayats.

Women's Empowerment is critical to the socio-economic progress of the community and, bringing women into the mainstream of national development has, therefore, been a major concern of the government. The Ministry of Rural Development has special components for Women in its programmes and funds are earmarked as 'Women's Component' to ensure flow of adequate resources for the same.[4]

The major Schemes, having Women's Component, (implemented by the Ministry of Rural Development during the last three years) include the Swarnjayanti Gram Swarozgar Yojana (SGSY), the Jawahar Gram Samridhi Yojana (JGSY), the Indira Awas Yojana (IAY), the National Social Assistance Programme (NSAP), the Restructured Centrally Rural Sanitation Programme, the Accelerated Rural Water Supply Programme, the (erstwhile) Integrated Rural Development Programme (IRDP), the (erstwhile) Development of Women and Children in Rural Areas (DWCRA) and the Jawahar Rozgar Yojana (JRY).

Women Reservation

Women are changing governance in India. They are being elected to local councils in unprecedented numbers as a result of amendments to the Constitution that mandate the reservation of seats for women in local government. In India, we call this new system the PRIs system. The women whom PRIs has brought into politics are now governing, be it in one village, or a larger area such as 100 villages or a district. This process of restructuring the national political and administrative system started in 1994.

The sheer number of women that PRIs has brought into the political system has made a difference. By 1994, 330,000 women had entered politics as a result of PRIs and many more have been elected in the last two years. The percentages of women at various levels of political activity have shifted dramatically as a result of this constitutional change, from 4-5 per cent before PRIs to 25-40 per cent after PRIs. But the difference is also qualitative, because these women are bringing their experience in governance of civic society into governance of the State. In this way, they are making the State sensitive to issues of poverty, inequality and gender injustice.[5]

Bringing these women into politics was an act of positive discrimination. It was the pressure of law, combined with the political imperative of winning elections that changed political parties' perception of women's limited capacity for public office. But, crucially, PRI has helped to change women's perceptions of themselves. Women have gained a sense of empowerment by asserting control over resources, officials and, most of all, by challenging men. PRI has also given many women a greater understanding of the workings of politics, in particular the importance of political parties.[6] On the other hand, some women's involvement in PRI has helped them affirm their identity as women with particular and shared experiences. This self-perception arises from two sources: from women do the men impose own sense of their shared experience and from attitudes and imagery on them. It appears that gender can supersede class and party lines. Women have opened up the possibility for politics to have not only new faces but also a new quality.

But increasing the representation of women has not automatically led to a more gendered analysis of the issues confronting local government. Nor has it necessarily raised the profile of women's needs and interests in the policy agenda, given that elected women often act as proxies for men's views at the councils, being advised by their male relatives. But there is now minorities of women who are in politics because of their leadership qualities or feminist consciousness and visible changes in the articulation of ideas and leadership qualities exhibited by this minority have been noted in the different priorities and different values espoused by women in politics.

Some of the ways in which women, through PRI, are changing governance are evident in the issues they choose to tackle; water, alcohol abuse, education, health and domestic violence. Women also express different values. Women value proximity, whether it is to a drinking water source, a fuel source, a creche, a health centre, a court of justice or an office of administration. The enormous expansion of women's representation in decentralised government structures has highlighted the advantages of proximity, namely the redress of grievance and (most important of all) the ability to mobilize struggle at a local level where it is most meaningful. Thus women are helping to radicalize local government.[7]

But obstacles to the realisation of PRI's transformative potential are many. There continues to be a resistance to really devolving power and funds from centers of (male) power to the periphery. Women still face considerable handicaps to their involvement in politics; for example, inadequate education, the burden of reproductive and productive roles, a lack of self-confidence and the opposition of entrenched cultural and religious views.

Therefore, there is a need to provide women with specific kinds of support that go beyond technical training. They need support to build solidarity amongst women, through strengthening links between women's organisations and elected bodies. They need information about innovative organisations that enhance women's lives such as health providers and credit institutions. It is also necessary to strengthen women's sense of common identity by articulating the elements of a feminist consciousness and presenting it as the special quality of women's leadership. There has been insufficient elaboration of what that leadership has to offer which distinguishes it from men's leadership and which commends it as something special. Such an elaboration through feminist discourse and action is essential for this revolution to deliver the promise it holds.

There is also a need for a more enabling environment, which would allow PRIs to become a process for the empowerment of women, not to mention other social groups who have been left out of participation in representative governance. Such an environment would include legal frameworks and services as well as packages of technical support. Ironically, it is development assistance agencies that often provide vigorous examples of patriarchal obstruction to people-led development. For instance, UN agencies are often obstacles to efforts to shift power structures from the civil service to the citizens.

National Policy for the Empowerment of Women

The Constitution not only grants equality to women, but also empowers the State to adopt measures of positive discrimination in favour of women. In recent years, the empowerment of women has been recognised as the central issue in determining the status of women. The National Commission for Women was set up by an Act of Parliament in 1990 to safeguard the rights and legal entitlements of women. The 73rd and 74th Amendments (1993) to the Constitution of India have provided for reservation of seats in the local bodies of Panchayats and Municipalities for women, laying a strong foundation for their participation in decision-making at the local levels.

The goal of this policy is to bring about the advancement, development and empowerment of women. The policy will be widely disseminated so as to encourage active participation of all stakeholders for achieving its goals. Specifically, the objectives of this policy include[8]:

- Creating an environment through positive economic and social policies for full development of women to enable them to realize their full potential;
- The *de-jure* and *de-facto* enjoyment of all human rights and fundamental freedom by women on equal basis with men in all spheres – political, economic, social, cultural and civil;
- Equal access to participation and decision-making of women in social, political and economic life of the nation;
- Equal access to women to health care, quality education at all levels, career and vocational guidance, employment, equal remuneration, occupational health and safety, social security and public office etc.;
- Strengthening legal systems aimed at elimination of all forms of discrimination against women;
- Changing societal attitudes and community practices by active participation and involvement of both men and women;
- Mainstreaming a gender perspective in the development process;
- Elimination of discrimination and all forms of violence against women and the girl child; and
- Building and strengthening partnerships with civil society, particularly women's organizations.

The following are the prescriptions of National Policy for the Empowerment of Women[9]:

- *Judicial Legal Systems:* Legal-judicial system will be made more responsive and gender sensitive to women's needs, especially in cases of domestic violence and personal assault.

- *Decision-Making:* Women's equality in power sharing and active participation in decision-making, including decision-making in political process at all levels will be ensured for the achievement of the goals of empowerment.
- *Mainstreaming a Gender Perspective in the Development Process:* Policies, programmes and systems will be established to ensure mainstreaming of women's perspectives in all developmental processes, as catalysts, participants and recipients. Wherever there are gaps in policies and programmes, women specific interventions would be undertaken to bridge these.

Economic Empowerment of Women

Globalisation has presented new challenges for the realisation of the goal of women's equality, the gender impact of which has not been systematically evaluated fully. However, from the micro-level studies that were commissioned by the Department of Women and Child Development, it is evident that there is a need for re-framing policies for access to employment and quality of employment. Benefits of the growing global economy have been unevenly distributed leading to wider economic disparities, the feminisation of poverty, increased gender inequality through often deteriorating working conditions and unsafe working environment especially in the informal economy and rural areas. Strategies will be designed to enhance the capacity of women and empower them to meet the negative social and economic impacts, which may flow from the globalisation process.

Since women comprise the majority of the population below the poverty line and are very often in situations of extreme poverty, given the harsh realities of intra-household and social discrimination, macro-economic policies and poverty eradication programmes will specifically address the needs and problems of such women.[10] There will be improved implementation of programmes which are already women oriented with special targets for women. Steps will be taken for mobilisation of poor women and convergence of services, by offering them a range of economic and social options, along with necessary support measures to enhance their capabilities.

In order to enhance women's access to credit for consumption and production, the establishment of new and strengthening of existing micro-credit mechanisms and micro-finance institution will be undertaken so that the outreach of credit is enhanced. Other supportive measures would be taken to ensure adequate flow of credit through extant financial institutions and banks, so that all women below poverty line have easy access to credit.

Women's perspectives will be included in designing and implementing macro-economic and social policies by institutionalising their participation in such processes. Their contribution to socio-economic development as producers and workers will be recognised in the formal and informal sectors (including home based workers) and appropriate policies relating to employment and to her working conditions will be drawn up.[11] Such measures could include:

- *(i)* Reinterpretation and redefinition of conventional concepts of work wherever necessary e.g. in the Census records, to reflect women's contribution as producers and workers;
- *(ii)* Preparation of satellite and national accounts; and
- *(iii)* Development of appropriate methodologies for undertaking *(i)* and *(ii)* above.

Women and Agriculture

In view of the critical role of women in the agriculture and allied sectors, as producers, concentrated efforts will be made to ensure that benefits of training, extension and various programmes will reach them in proportion to their numbers. The programmes for training women in soil conservation, social forestry, dairy development and other occupations allied to agriculture like horticulture, livestock including small animal husbandry, poultry, fisheries etc. will be expanded to benefit women workers in the agriculture sector.

Women and Industry

The important role-played by women in electronics, information technology and food processing and agro industry and textiles has been crucial to the development of these sectors. They would be given comprehensive support in terms of labour legislation, social security and other support services to participate in various industrial sectors. Women at present cannot work in night shift in factories even if they wish to. Suitable measures will be taken to enable women to work on the night shift in factories. This will be accompanied with support services for security, transportation etc.

Support Services

The provision of support services for women, like child care facilities, including crèches at work places and educational institutions, homes for the aged and the disabled will be expanded and improved to create an enabling environment and to ensure their full cooperation in social, political and economic life. Women-friendly personnel policies will also be drawn up to encourage women to participate effectively in the developmental process.

Conclusion

Panchayati Raj Institution reminds us of a central truth; power is not something people give away. It has to be negotiated, and sometimes wrested from the powerful. Enshrining political change within the law has forced both the pace and direction of such change. Democratic politics is, in reality, the interplay of vested interests and PRI's great achievement has been to mandate a vested and mutual interest, between women and the political process. The lesson of PRI is clear: if the wisdom of grassroots organizations, especially the courage and clarity of women, is to become policy, it will not be through the art of intellectual persuasion but by the arrangements made within a political system for their voice to have power.

It has been the universal experience that women all over the world have been and continue to be in a disadvantaged position more so in a developing country like India. Although the Constitution of India has guaranteed equality to women in all spheres, it has been realized that women's lowly status was acting against them in utilizing the 'equality provision'. Thus, special development programmes began to be initiated to bring women into the main stream. There have been many approaches to development since independence, staring with the 'welfare' and followed by 'equity, anti-poverty, and women in development' approaches.

However, it was gradually felt that these approaches further marginalized women because the programmes were 'top-down' and did not consider the specific concerns of women. Thus, started the 'empowerment' approach, which emphasised that women should make their own choices and transform their lives through participation in decision-making.

Hence empowerment of women in politics is aimed at increasing their participation in the political institutions. Representation of women in large numbers in these institutions is intended to promote or stimulate democratisation of politics. This enlarges possibilities for women to be better integrated in the political processes. It is also expected that this power will enable them to address women's issues and influence decisions which in turn will lead to an enhancement of their status and thereby weaken patriarchy paving the way towards greater equality.

REFERENCES

1. *Empowerment Source Book 2002*, The World Bank, Washington, DC., 2002.
2. G. Palanthurai, (2001): The Genre of Women Leaders in Local Bodies: Experience from Tamil Nadu, *The Indian Journal of Public Administration*, March, 2001.
3. UN Document on Women's Development 1985.
4. Mani Shankar Aiyar, "Women in Panchayats", *Business Standard*, October 17, Hyderabad, 1996.
5. Susheela Kaushik, Women and Panchayati Raj, *Journal of Rural Development*, 1993.
6. Madhu Kishwar, Women and Politics: Beyond Quota, *Economic and Political Weekly*, October 26, 1996.
7. Sudhir Krishna, Women and Panchayati Raj: The Law, Programme and Practices, *Journal of Rural Development*, Vol. 16(4) , 1997.
8. Government of India, *National Empowerment Policy for Women*, Ministry of Human Resources Development, Department of Women and Child Welfare, New Delhi, 2001
9. Government of India, *National Empowerment Policy for Women*, Ministry of Human Resources Development, Department of Women and Child Welfare, New Delhi, 2001.
10. G. Haragopal and G. Sudarshanam, Panchayats in Andhra Pradesh, in Geroge Mathew (Ed.), *Status of Panchayati Raj in the States and Union Territories of India*, Institute of Social Sciences and Concept Publishing Company, New Delhi, 2000.
11. Leela Kasturi, Development, Patriarchy and Politics: Indian Women in the Political Process, 1947-99, in M. Valentine Moghadem (Ed.), *Patriarch and Development: Women's Position at the End of the 20th Century*, Clarendon Press, Oxford, 2000.

14

Learning Leadership in Rural India: Empowerment of Elected Women Representatives in Local Governance

DR. ALOK PANDEY

Leadership is a process whereby an individual influences a group of individuals to achieve a common goal. It is a process which catalyses change. Leadership is not restricted to a formally designated leader in a group rather it occurs in groups and directs groups of individuals to accomplish a common task or goal. In the social sector, leadership means being proactive on social issues for the larger benefit of society. Different theories and studies have thus looked at leadership around traits, qualities and attributes, behaviours and styles.

In order to facilitate citizen's participation in governance, *new leadership* also needs to be facilitated. This includes leadership of those sections, who till now have been marginalised and ignored by the society. This includes the enhancement of leadership of women, dalits, tribals and youth. The social, economic, cultural and psychological milieu prevents the emergence of leadership in these groups. Capacity building strategies to enhance their leadership, which is acquired, rather than ascribed, thus need to be developed and implemented.

Women's Leadership

In the new leadership debate, strengthening women's leadership is a necessary pre requisite for facilitating women's empowerment. The World Bank views the third Millennium Development Goal—to promote gender equality and empower women—as central to reducing poverty and stimulating economic growth. Strengthening women's leadership in the social, economic and political milieu thus becomes essential for removing gender inequality and facilitating women's empowerment.

There is a growing realisation that local self-governance systems will enable overcoming problems of centralised, top down governance mechanisms. Through the 73rd and 74th Constitution Amendment Act (CAA), 1992 the system of local self-governance has been established in India. These Acts have brought the panchayats and municipalities into existence. The PRIs (Panchayati Raj Institutions) are the constitutionally (formally) recognised third level of the government's three tier of elected bodies in rural areas, at the level of the village, block and district.

For political empowerment of women in India, provision has been made in the 73rd and 74th Constitution Amendment Acts for the reservation of one third of the seats for women. Beginning with the first round of elections to panchayats after the states passed conformity legislations in 1994, nearly three million elected women have acquired a place in local bodies. Women Elected Representatives (WER) role includes the designation of a wide spectrum of economic and social development programmes. Their responsibilities include working on an integrated approach to development, with emphasis on community participation and long term sustainability.

The affirmative action for participation in governance, however, did not get automatically translated into qualitative gains for WERs. Women's nature of political participation in PRIs across two terms reveals a distinct difference. In the first term, community was suddenly exposed to conflicting sets of expectations. As elected representatives, women lacked knowledge, skills and capacities to govern. However, in the second term, the community was more forthcoming regarding women in leadership roles. NGOs and the government were more prepared with training programmes for WERs on the functioning of the PRIs. Women were more actively involved in decision-making and implementation of schemes in their own constituencies/wards. In many instances they used their elected authority to address critical issues such as children's' education, drinking water facilities, family planning facilities, hygiene and health, and aspects of village development.

The gap between the formal recognition of the right to participate and its actualisation however still remains. A study conducted by PRIA on WERs, *Women's Leadership: Towards Gender Mainstreaming in Governance* showed that there is increased presence of women in governance, but their voices are silent. The study result shows that most of the WERs do not have previous experience in politics; have low awareness about rural and urban development/administration affairs; are dominated by Vice-Presidents, husbands, sons and male family members or others for planning and executing the powers of local self governance. The realities of gender inequality restrict the WERs' ability to exercise their leadership. The responsibilities to meet the household subsistence requirements, mobility restrictions and limited support structures restricted their social interaction and participation in local self-governance. Internalised low self-esteem has made them passive, dependent on men in matters relating to governance. Lack of awareness and low education/illiteracy would need to be tackled for raising their self-image (Pant 2007).

Other examples and cases are there those highlights factors, which obstruct WERs from playing their leadership roles effectively. This includes individual factors like low education, inexperience, low awareness, no training and lack of interest. In addition family factors (economic constraints, household chores, family interference), community factors (social customs and traditions), governance factors (rotation of seats in local bodies, the status of non-confidence motion, lack of support from male colleagues and government officials) have been identified as key hindering factors for WERs to effectively play their leadership roles. The study findings also revealed that WERs who received training were able to exercise their leadership effectively. However, systematic orientation and capacity enhancement of elected women in general had been largely ignored.

So, while there are cases where WERs are yet to find their ground, there are also a growing number of cases where WERs have been able to overcome the barriers to effectively play their roles. (Buch, 2000; Bhaskaran *et al.*, 2006; Maalan and Choudhri, 2006). Capacity building interventions, as an important strategy, can facilitate this shift towards a more and more empowered WERs playing their leadership roles effectively.

In addition to political leadership women are also playing important leadership roles in socio and economic spheres. These include leadership of women's collectives like Self-Help Groups (SHGs). The formation of SHGs has been promoted for economic and social empowerment. It has been expected that SHGs will be a means to promote income generation activities and micro credit, thereby making them economically independent. It was also expected that economic independence would also help women to be involved in the decision-making process at the household level and community level. The process of SHG formation and idea of conducting monthly meetings is also meant to discuss social and gender issues in their group and find out alternatives. There are instances and examples where women SHGs have come forward to deal with social issues like prohibition of liquor, domestic violence and reproductive rights of women.

As studies have shown that focussing only on the economic needs of women will not facilitate change in the women's social as well as political position. An integrated approach to women's empowerment thus is essential. Women leadership in the political sphere and in the socio-economic context can have a synergistic effect—each strengthening and complementing the other, thus contributing to women's empowerment, as well as effective development.

Strengthening Women's Leadership: Capacity Building Strategies

Women's representation in local government structures does not automatically result in their informed and effective participation in these structures. In addition to advocating some policy level interventions, capacity building interventions for WERs; mobilising them to network with associations/collectives; mobilising collectives to enhance their participation; and gender sensitisation can go a long way in promoting effective leadership of women. Capacity building strategies will assist translation of their acquired leadership to transformational leadership. In keeping with the perspective that *Leadership can be acquired and learnt,* capacity building strategies to strengthen women's leadership in the context of local self-governance becomes essential. It is essential so that women leaders, especially the WERs can play their designated roles more effectively.

'Capacity' can be defined as the totality of inputs needed by an factor to realise its purposes Applied to *local self-governance institutions like PRIs,* this will ensure that such institutions are able to function effectively as institutions of local self-governance in the perspective elaborated above. Capacity of such institutions can be seen in three distinct though inter-related aspects.

- *Intellectual Capacity:* This implies capacity to think, reflect and analyse reality, independently and in pursuit of self-defined purposes of local self-governance. To understand the autonomous and basic democratic nature of the Gram Panchayat as a collective decision-making body, most significant interventions have focused on preparing its collective identity. Such interventions have aimed at developing a common perspective and intellectual appreciation of the Gram Panchayat.

- *Institutional Capacity:* This implies procedures, systems, structure, staffing, decision-making, transparency and accountability, planning, implementation and monitoring. It also includes mechanisms for building linkages with other institutions and factors, and institutional mechanism to function as transparent and accountable local bodies. This includes mechanisms for conducting meetings, preparing minutes, sharing information with the gram sabha, securing participation and contribution of the gram sabha, developing participatory micro plans, procedures and systems, effective implementation and monitoring of these plans, securing and mobilising resources and maintaining transparent systems of financial management, etc.
- *Material Capacity:* This includes material resources, physical assets, funds, systems and procedures to mobilise revenues; access and control over physical and natural resources and infrastructure; systems and procedures required for adequate management of funds and such infrastructure. The capacity building intervention at this level also needs to address the question of enhancing the material base of gram panchayats, to make them financially autonomous and sustainable entities. Capacity enhancement interventions in this area are particularly focused on mobilising local resources from the village. (Tandon and Bandyopadhyaya, 2004).

Capacity Building also involves building the three ingredients of knowledge, skills, and qualities in individual learners and a group of learners i.e., enhancement of 'knowledge', which is gathered from education and life experiences; strengthening 'skills', which are learned from training and also from life experiences; and thirdly, 'attitudes' of a personal nature, which address issues of values and perceptions. Capacity building efforts address needs for enhancing capacity at the level of individual and organised collectives.

In the context of WERs, *knowledge* mainly includes creating awareness and providing information about various subjects and issues i.e., functioning of PRIs and development schemes, their roles and responsibilities as panchayat members. *Attitude* mainly deals with perspective building, more related to the sensitisation process and raising consciousness. Training on gender mainstreaming and other social issues come under this framework. The third one is *skills,* which as the name suggests deals with enhancing the capacity of a person in performing certain activities like developing micro plans, facilitating the gram sabha, developing budgets etc.

Capacity building needs change over a period of time. Capacity building is a long-term process of strengthening a local body based on the systematic learning of new knowledge, skills and attitudes. Like all learning, the factor herself must see the value of and take responsibility for that learning. This capacity building cannot be imposed from outside. Preparation of the local body to identify its particular capacity needs and motivation to take responsibility for learning those is a major part of capacity building intervention in such a framework. (Tandon, 2002).

An external intervention however also has a role in capacity building, which includes:

- Preparation of the local body in terms of external stimulation and intervention.
- Providing opportunities for systematic learning and facilitating such learning.
- Accessing and making available resources for capacity enhancement.
- Supporting on-going and sustained capacity enhancement over a long-term.

There has been the emergence of a number of *capacity-building providers* including 'support CSOs' (CSOs that specialise in providing capacity-building services to other CSOs), also government departments, businesses and private consultants. A plethora of *capacity-building tools and approaches* have been developed. Some common methods and approaches for capacity building include trainings, workshops, interface meetings, seminars, camps, dialogues, exposure visits and information dissemination channels. The application of the above approaches/methods would once again depend on the women leaders and their context and needs.

Capacity Building of WERs

In recent years the Government of India (GoI) has recognised the need for building capacity of WERs. The Tenth Plan (2003-07) also recognised that despite the move towards decentralisation through the PRIs, there is marginalisation and exclusion of people on the basis of social, caste and gender affiliation. The plan document emphasises the participation of people, especially the participation of people, especially women groups at all stages of planning, implementation and monitoring and considers this as a prerequisite for good governance.

A number of government and non-government interventions have been undertaken to facilitate capacity building of PRI members, with some focusing exclusively on strengthening the capacity of WERs.

Each implementing agency evolved capacity building strategies and tools according to their specific context. In brief:

- Strengthening Collectives of WERs
- Strengthening Women Collectives and linking them to Governance
- Structured Trainings
- Perspective Building Meetings
- Exposure Visits for WERs
- Campaigns to Create an Enabling Environment
- Information Dissemination Mechanisms

Outcomes of Capacity Building Initiatives

Any analysis of the outcomes of the initiatives on women's empowerment entails understanding *(a)* whether capacity building initiatives are instrumental in expanding spaces in women's lives and *(b)* to what extent the expanded spaces reduce gender based inequalities. This section discusses the outcomes resulting directly or indirectly from the capacity building interventions.

The multi track capacity building approaches and numerous interventions paid dividends in facilitating the leadership of WERs and functionaries. The implementation strategy varied from site to site, given the environment in which each of the state partners were working. Depending on the social environment in the respective area of work, the organisation had either directly involved WERs or other community groups. Formation of new women groups or strengthening of existing ones led to considerable increase in women's participation in public forums such as gram sabha, ward sabha, block panchayat meetings etc. It also helped in creating a synergistic relationship between women forums and WERs to raise the issues and interact with government officials. The increased participation in political and community activities may be seen as challenging deep-seated social norms and being truly transformative. WERs and collectives were able to exercise independent agency.

Some initiatives that were focused on strengthening existing networks of women in local governance and were encouraged to organise themselves into forums at block levels to address issues of social justice and participate meaningfully in local governance, it has been found that the women collectives or forums, are asserting for their rights and entitlements on different platforms at the cluster, block and district levels. They emerged as pressure groups, which strongly advocated for women rights within PRIs. They built pressure on the government to take action against the corrupt practices that they witnessed by filing complaints against them under the RTI Act. They organised gram sabha meeting for muster roll verifications under the National Rural Employment Guarantee Act (NREGA). They raised issues of gender concern like construction of women meeting halls, 10 per cent fund for women's health, ban on alcoholism etc.

Some women networks contributed in building an enabling environment for women's participation in the Mahila Gram Sabha as in Maharashtra and general gram sabha. They provided support to WERs. The WERs associated with women groups and networks, to understand the problems of other women and to collectively discuss how the panchayat could help them out. The discussion helped WERs plan the agenda for periodic panchayat meetings and in the gram sabha. In some places initiatives were taken to mobilise collective monitoring of basic services like ration shops, incentives provided by schools, payment of wages under NREGA etc. In Jharkhand, women leaders supervised and monitored construction works undertaken in the villages under different schemes. The women members of different forums have carried out surveys on many issues and shared their findings with district authorities. They have submitted petitions and memoranda for speedy actions. They are now lobbying for a change at the policy level. They successfully mobilised women's participation in the gram sabha, palli sabha, and panchayat meetings at the block and district levels.

Some interventions facilitated women to move from being passive beneficiaries to active citizens. Its impact showed three levels of empowerment: *power within*, *power to* and *power with*. At the *power within* level a key impact is the observation that women leaders have developed an awareness of one's own potential. They are confident, sensitive and informed persons. At the *power to* level the project has expanded women's control over their resources and decision-making processes. Access to networks of women outside their family and access to leadership positions have empowered them. At the *power with* level, women have intervened collectively in many institutions: family, community and PRIs. The training programmes have reinforced the collective identity among its members by building the information base and capabilities of women. Women's groups have demonstrated their newly acquired skills and confidence in dealing with people in authority. They are emerging as pressure groups, negotiating confidently with government officials, and outsiders. They are transforming the agenda of governance by ensuring that the survival needs of poor women are given priority. The fact that women are making their voice heard is an indication that there is a change in women's self-perception. The WERs who were part of the collectives were using their knowledge on PRIs to effectively address their panchayat's social development issues and in this effort they are receiving support from their women gram sabha members.

Gram Sabha's Initiative for Construction of School Building

Jaipur is a revenue village of 144 households in District Palamu of Jharkhand state. This village is 45 kilometres away from the district headquarter. Through the Sarva Shiksha Abhiyan there is a functional school in the village. Until June 2005, this school did not have a building. Women collectives had taken up the case with the block administration many times. At last, it was decided collectively during a gram sabha meeting, that relying on government aid for building the school was not a viable solution, as for the past many months the schoolteacher along with village people had struggled hard to get funds for the building, but all their efforts bore no results. The gram sabha members decided to collect contributions for the school. Women collectives did this. Some gave money and others labour (shram daan) and land was donated by one of the villagers. In this way the school building was constructed. Soon items started pouring in from other sources like sitting mats, etc. The village that has not seen a single matriculate till now is hoping for a bright future.

Women in PRIs do not necessarily wield the power that their seat and position accords to them. They still face serious problems in performing their duties. Any attempt to put the priorities of citizens and accountability issues before the panchayat is fraught with resistance and the price has to be paid physically and socially.

Usha tai Pillare is a Panch (elected representative) of the Chikhli Gram Panchayat of Kurkheda block, District Gadhchiroli, Maharashtra. She raised her voice against the local moneylender's corrupt practices and the mismanagement by an anganwadi worker. This was the first time in a panchayat that a woman elected representative raised the issue publicly. The moneylender in order to take revenge got drunk and abused and threatened her. Undeterred she lodged a complaint in the police station as a case of violence against women. She strongly objected to this incident in the panchayat and asked for a public apology from the moneylender.

The process of learning leadership has triggered off the following actions:

1. Effective functioning of elected women
2. WER forums working effectively on women issues
3. Women collectives raising women's issues
4. Awareness generation about PRIs in the community
5. Women's participation in gram sabhas enhanced
6. Women collectives monitoring service delivery
7. Women entering the political arena.

Key Challenges

The critical mass refers to the quantity needed to start an irreversible chain reaction. In the context of PRI it means that 33 per cent are needed in order to be able to effect change. However, structural (institutional) factors/individual backgrounds/cognitive experiences and circumstances also influence women's leadership. While women with inherent personality traits naturally assume leadership roles, the inexperienced can learn leadership skills. Strategies such as capacity building training of WERs to govern; mobilising them to network with associations/collectives; mobilising collectives to enhance their participation; and gender sensitisation can promote effective leadership of women.

Capability building strategies for engendering leadership need to address the history of exclusion, marginalisation and invisibility of women voices, which prevent the actual exercise of power. The project has revealed the presence of several intractable challenging areas in the training of women for leadership roles. A brief description of the challenges is as follows:

- Resistance from patriarchal forces discouraging women's leadership role.
- Although the collectivisation process led WERs to act as leaders; their role in the decision-making process is yet to be recognised.
- Women collectives are often indifferent to and aloof from political processes in panchayats. Institutional linkages between women collectives and WERs are still to be set up institutionally.
- Women elected representatives not associated with women collectives are left out.
- Insensitivity of line department officials and men from larger community.
- Absence of a holistic capacity building strategy.
- Lack of linkages with 'other parts' of government (SIRDs, women commission etc.)

It is clear that gendered identities and practices limit the capacities of women to articulate and act upon their claims and concerns. The gap between the formal recognition of right to participate and its actualisation remains large. Gender transformative training is required not just to bring about gender informed changes to societal institutions, but also changes at the personal level. Besides the need for training for personal empowerment of women, there is also a need to strengthen the spaces to resolve the issues of identity and conflicts within women in governance and other development works and build competencies of agencies facilitating their leadership. Pre-requisites to engendering governance leadership are delineated as below.

Pre-requisites to Engendering Governance Leadership

1. Gender transformative goals. The ultimate aim is the empowerment of women and conscientisation of men.
2. A process oriented training linked to actual action; emphasis on skill building and change in attitudes.
3. Sensitivity to training needs of WERs-how many times, on what issues, venue of trainings, time of training, etc.
4. A vibrant supportive mechanism at local level. For instance;
   - Establishing linkages between women collectives and

other community based organisations especially youth groups with WERs.

- Rapid addressal of the issues/grievances specific to WERs.
- Widening the outreach of institutional support structures like women commissions, gender cells of different departments etc.

5. Regular interface between WERs and government official to ease out constraints of WERs.
6. Orientations of PRI functionaries for gender sensitive and supportive roles.
7. Institutional mechanism to enable women's voices, such as mahila gram sabha and a gender sensitive budget.
8. Proactive and sensitive media partnership to educate and advocate on women's issues.
9. Sensitisation of male members and of family and panchayat functionaries at the village level.
10. Gender sensitive work environment within PRIs – creating norms, codes of conduct for ensuring safety and security of WERs.
11. Goal of education for all within the institution of local self-governance. Functional literacy component included in the training of the WERs.
12. Competency building of the implementing agencies. The functionaries of implementing civil society organisations require not only clarity on the concepts of empowerment; they also need to develop sensitivity to the needs of women leadership. The implementing agencies, in their pre-occupation with the technical success of the project, often overlook the need to strengthen the women's self-esteem, their analytical skills, competencies and consciousness and perspective of local governance. There is a need for a formal training package for implementing agencies, which comprises of a technological package (skills, technical innovations etc.), a services package (education, training,) and a public policy package (rights, decentralisation, evolution of powers to PRIs, planning implementation and monitoring of development programmes etc.). Convergence of these packages should be in such a manner that they respond to the needs of women in the village.

13. Promoting coalitions, alliances and networks of elected representatives, community based organisations such as SHGs, CSOs, media and academia to strengthen institutional basis of engendered leadership.

REFERENCES

C. Ball, and N. Jaitli, Strengthening Civil Society. In Certificate in Civil Society Building *(Course Material), New Delhi, PRIA, 2006.*

D. Bandyopadhyaya, Amitava Mukherjee, and M.S. Gavai, *Empowering Panchayats. Handbook for Master Trainers Using Participatory Approach,* Task Force on Panchayati Raj, Rajiv Gandhi Foundation, New Delhi, Concept Publishing Company, 2003.

S. Bhaskaran, S. Jayasree, and A. Vijayan, A. Women in Panchayati Raj: A Handbook on Panchayat level Women Status Study, Sakshi Women Resource Centre, 2006.

Nirmala Buch, *Women's Experience in New Panchayats: The Emerging Leadership of Rural Women,* New Delhi, Occasional Paper No. 35, Centre for Women Studies, New Delhi, 2000.

J.M. Burns, *Leadership,* New York, Harper and Row, 1978.

N. Jaitli, *Participatory Training for Empowerment,* New Delhi, PRIA, 1998.

Maalan and S.G. Choudhari, (Eds.), *Thus Spoke the Press: Select Articles on Elected Women Leadership in Village Panchayats,* New Delhi, The Hunger Project, 2006.

P.G. Northouse, *Leadership: Theory and Practice,* New Delhi, Sage Publications India Pvt. Ltd., 2007.

M. Pant, *Women's Leadership: Towards Gender Mainstreaming in Governance,* New Delhi, PRIA, 2006.

PRIA, *Women Leadership in Panchayati Raj Institutions: An Analysis of Six States,* New Delhi, PRIA, 1999.

Manoj Rai, M. Nambiar, M. and D.A. Mathew, Orientation of New Leadership in Panchayats: PRIA's Experiences of Undertaking 'PRJA'(2000-01) Participation and Governanace, *Vol. 10, No. 31, November 2004.*

Manoj Rai, *et. al., The State of Panchayats: A Participatory Perspective,* New Delhi, PRIA, 2001.

D.L. Sharma, *Women's Leadership: Towards Gender Mainstreaming Governance in Karauli District of Rajasthan* (Mimeographed).

Rajesh Tandon, Editorial, *Participation and Governance,* Vol. 10, No. 31, November 2004.

Rajesh Tandon and K.K. Bandyopadhyay, Capacity Building for Effective Democratic Local Governance: Experience from India, Participation and Governanace, *Vol. 10, No. 31, November 2004.*

APPENDICES

1

APPENDIX

Tirupati Declaration on Women Political Empowerment, 20 August, 2008

The key document that emerged from the deliberations of the National Conference on 'Empowerment of Women in Parliament and Local Self-Government Institutions in India: Role, Status, Participation and Decision-Making', organised by the Academy of Grassroots Studies and Research of India, in collaboration with the Rajiv Rural Development Foundation, during 19 and 20, 2008 at Tirupati, Andhra Pradesh, was the 'Tirupati Declaration on Women Political Empowerment'. This resolution was at the centre of the recommendations made by the delegates, academicians, researchers, participants and women elected representatives and activists of Panchayati Raj Institutions, representing the States of Gujarat, Rajasthan, Tamil Nadu, Karnataka, Andhra Pradesh,Maharashtra, Chhattisgarh, Orissa, Delhi and Assam and Union Territory of Pondicherry. The copies of the Tirupati Declaration on Women Political Empowerment is being forwarded to the policy makers at the helm of the affairs, for taking appropriate steps and initiatives in strengthening the women representation in Parliament and State Legislative Assemblies, as per the proportionate of their population in India – (Editor)

The text of the 14 point Tirupati Declaration on Women Political Empowerment is as follows:

1. Encourage the involvement of women in decision-making at all levels and achieve gender balance in the appointment of women and men, with full respect for the principle of equitable population distribution, including as judges, civil servants, ambassadors, assembly speakers, union ministers, state level ministers, chief ministers and governors, besides Members of Parliament and State Legislatures.
2. At the level of Panchayati Raj Institutions, most of the states

already cross the mark of 33 per cent seats of reservation for Women. The states of Bihar and Madhya Pradesh have already made provision of 50 per cent in their Statutes (PRIs Act). The other States should also follow the Bihar and Madhya Pradesh model immediately, in this respect.

3. There is a vacuum in the capacity building of PRIs elected representatives as well as officials, even after 15 years of enactment of the 73rd Constitution Amendment Act. It requires utmost and urgent attention for imparting Training to all the elected representatives of PRI's in a regular manner for delivering good governance at the grassroots.

4. The flow of funds from various sources towards the rural development and the poverty alleviation programmes should be linked with the performance of Panchayati Raj Institutions. The outlays and the outcome should be assessed and monitored accordingly, by the Central as well as State Governments.

5. For achieving the inclusive growth with rural development and the effective rural governance, the participation of Women and Self-Help Group Members should be encouraged by the State Governments.

6. The Panchayati Raj Institutions should be encouraged and promoted in the implementation of various developmental programmes and activities, on par with the NGO's, CBO's and SHG's.

7. Women representatives are trailing behind in decision-making in rural governance. The capacity building of these bodies needs special attention. The provision should be made for special training to the women representatives at the grassroots as well as at the State and National levels.

8. Drawing the lessons from the successful implementation of 33 per cent of reservation for Women at the level of third-tier governance through 73rd Constitution Amendment Act, it can be implemented at the State Assembly and Parliament level also in the next general elections onwards.

9. In addition to the Government Training Institutions, the NGO's and Women Training Institutions should be encouraged to involve in capacity building. The guidelines and responsibilities of these bodies on different modules for Zilla, Taluk and Gram Panchayats should be designed for imparting the training.

10. Develop national capacity to undertake policy-oriented and gender-related research and impact studies by Universities and

National Research/Training Institutes to enable gender-specific knowledge-based policy-making.

11. The decentralised planning has got momentum over the years. The participatory planning and the participatory democracy can be achieved through the active participation and involvement of women policy makers and activists at the grassroots through Panchayati Raj Institutions.
12. For an effective implementation of the National Rural Employment Guarantee Programme at all India level, the youth women and youth organisations should encourage and promote for their active participation.
13. Apply and support positive measures to give all women, particularly youth women, equal access to capacity-building and training programmes to enhance their political participation and decision-making in all fields and at all levels, as women policy makers.
14. Bring suitable Amendment in the Constitution for the provision of at least 50 per cent seats of reservation for women in Parliament and State Legislatures, as the women representatives are less corrupt, transparent and duty-minded than male representatives.

2

APPENDIX

National Policy for the Empowerment of Women in India (2001)

Introduction

The principle of gender equality is enshrined in the Indian Constitution in its Preamble, Fundamental Rights, Fundamental Duties and Directive Principles. The Constitution not only grants equality to women, but also empowers the State to adopt measures of positive discrimination in favour of women.

Within the framework of a democratic polity, our laws, development policies, Plans and programmes have aimed at women's advancement in different spheres. From the Fifth Five Year Plan (1974-78) onwards has been a marked shift in the approach to women's issues from welfare to development. In recent years, the empowerment of women has been recognized as the central issue in determining the status of women. The National Commission for Women was set up by an Act of Parliament in 1990 to safeguard the rights and legal entitlements of women. The 73rd and 74th Amendments (1993) to the Constitution of India have provided for reservation of seats in the local bodies of Panchayats and Municipalities for women, laying a strong foundation for their participation in decision-making at the local levels.

1.3 India has also ratified various international conventions and human rights instruments committing to secure equal rights of women. Key among them is the ratification of the Convention on Elimination of All Forms of Discrimination Against Women (CEDAW) in 1993.

1.4 The Mexico Plan of Action (1975), the Nairobi Forward Looking Strategies (1985), the Beijing Declaration as well as the Platform for Action (1995) and the Outcome Document adopted by the UNGA Session on Gender Equality and Development and Peace for the 21st century, titled "Further actions and initiatives to implement the Beijing Declaration and the Platform for Action" have been unreservedly endorsed by India for appropriate follow up.

1.5 The Policy also takes note of the commitments of the Ninth Five Year Plan and the other Sectoral Policies relating to empowerment of Women.

1.6 The women's movement and a wide-spread network of Non-Government Organisations which have strong grassroots presence and deep insight into women's concerns have contributed in inspiring initiatives for the empowerment of women.

1.7 However, there still exists a wide gap between the goals enunciated in the Constitution, legislation, policies, plans, programmes, and related mechanisms on the one hand and the situational reality of the status of women in India, on the other. This has been analyzed extensively in the Report of the Committee on the Status of Women in India, "Towards Equality", 1974 and highlighted in the National Perspective Plan for Women, 1988-2000, the Shramshakti Report, 1988 and the Platform for Action, Five Years After—An assessment."

1.8 Gender disparity manifests itself in various forms, the most obvious being the trend of continuously declining female ratio in the population in the last few decades. Social stereotyping and violence at the domestic and societal levels are some of the other manifestations. Discrimination against girl children, adolescent girls and women persists in parts of the country.

1.9 The underlying causes of gender inequality are related to social and economic structure, which is based on informal and formal norms, and practices.

1.10 Consequently, the access of women particularly those belonging to weaker sections including Scheduled Castes/Scheduled Tribes/Other backward Classes and minorities, majority of whom are in the rural areas and in the informal, unorganized sector—to education, health and productive resources, among others, is inadequate. Therefore, they remain largely marginalized, poor and socially excluded.

Goal and Objectives

1.11 The goal of this Policy is to bring about the advancement, development and empowerment of women. The Policy will be widely disseminated so as to encourage active participation of all stakeholders for achieving its goals. Specifically, the objectives of this Policy include:

- *(i)* Creating an environment through positive economic and social policies for full development of women to enable them to realize their full potential.
- *(ii)* The *de-jure* and *de-facto* enjoyment of all human rights and

fundamental freedom by women on equal basis with men in all spheres—political, economic, social, cultural and civil.

(iii) Equal access to participation and decision-making of women in social, political and economic life of the nation.

(iv) Equal access to women to health care, quality education at all levels, career and vocational guidance, employment, equal remuneration, occupational health and safety, social security and public office etc.

(v) Strengthening legal systems aimed at elimination of all forms of discrimination against women.

(vi) Changing societal attitudes and community practices by active participation and involvement of both men and women.

(vii) Mainstreaming a gender perspective in the development process.

(viii) Elimination of discrimination and all forms of violence against women and the girl child; and

(ix) Building and strengthening partnerships with civil society, particularly women's organizations.

Policy Prescriptions

Judicial Legal Systems

Legal-judicial system will be made more responsive and gender sensitive to women's needs, especially in cases of domestic violence and personal assault. New laws will be enacted and existing laws reviewed to ensure that justice is quick and the punishment meted out to the culprits is commensurate with the severity of the offence.

2.2 At the initiative of and with the full participation of all stakeholders including community and religious leaders, the Policy would aim to encourage changes in personal laws such as those related to marriage, divorce, maintenance and guardianship so as to eliminate discrimination against women.

2.3 The evolution of property rights in a patriarchal system has contributed to the subordinate status of women. The Policy would aim to encourage changes in laws relating to ownership of property and inheritance by evolving consensus in order to make them gender just.

Decision-Making

3.1 Women's equality in power sharing and active participation in decision-making, including decision-making in political process at all levels will be ensured for the achievement of the goals of empowerment. All measures will be taken to guarantee women equal access to and full participation in decision-making bodies at every level, including the legislative, executive, judicial, corporate, statutory bodies, as also the advisory Commissions, Committees, Boards, Trusts etc. Affirmative action such as reservations/quotas, including in higher legislative bodies, will be considered whenever necessary on a time bound basis. Women-friendly personnel policies will also be drawn up to encourage women to participate effectively in the developmental process.

Mainstreaming a Gender Perspective in the Development Process

4.1 Policies, programmes and systems will be established to ensure mainstreaming of women's perspectives in all developmental processes, as catalysts, participants and recipients. Wherever there are gaps in policies and programmes, women specific interventions would be undertaken to bridge these. Coordinating and monitoring mechanisms will also be devised to assess from time to time the progress of such mainstreaming mechanisms. Women's issues and concerns as a result will specially be addressed and reflected in all concerned laws, sectoral policies, plans and programmes of action.

Economic Empowerment of Women

Poverty Eradication

5.1 Since women comprise the majority of the population below the poverty line and are very often in situations of extreme poverty, given the harsh realities of intra-household and social discrimination, macro-economic policies and poverty eradication programmes will specifically address the needs and problems of such women. There will be improved implementation of programmes which are already women oriented with special targets for women. Steps will be taken for mobilization of poor women and convergence of services, by offering them a range of economic and social options, along with necessary support measures to enhance their capabilities.

Micro Credit

5.2 In order to enhance women's access to credit for consumption and production, the establishment of new, and strengthening of existing micro-credit mechanisms and micro-finance institution will be undertaken so that the outreach of credit is enhanced. Other supportive measures would be taken to ensure adequate flow of credit through extant financial institutions and banks, so that all women below poverty line have easy access to credit.

Women and Economy

5.3 Women's perspectives will be included in designing and implementing macro-economic and social policies by institutionalising their participation in such processes. Their contribution to socio-economic development as producers and workers will be recognized in the formal and informal sectors (including home based workers) and appropriate policies relating to employment and to her working conditions will be drawn up. Such measures could include:

Reinterpretation and redefinition of conventional concepts of work wherever necessary e.g. in the Census records, to reflect women's contribution as producers and workers.

Preparation of satellite and national accounts.

Development of appropriate methodologies for undertaking (i) and (ii) above.

Globalization

Globalization has presented new challenges for the realization of the goal of women's equality, the gender impact of which has not been systematically evaluated fully. However, from the micro-level studies that were commissioned by the Department of Women & Child Development, it is evident that there is a need for re-framing policies for access to employment and quality of employment. Benefits of the growing global economy have been unevenly distributed leading to wider economic disparities, the feminization of poverty, increased gender inequality through often deteriorating working conditions and unsafe working environment especially in the informal economy and rural areas. Strategies will be designed to enhance the capacity of women and empower them to meet the negative social and economic impacts, which may flow from the globalization process.

Women and Agriculture

5.5 In view of the critical role of women in the agriculture and allied sectors, as producers, concentrated efforts will be made to ensure that benefits of training, extension and various programmes will reach them in proportion to their numbers. The programmes for training women in soil conservation, social forestry, dairy development and other occupations allied to agriculture like horticulture, livestock including small animal husbandry, poultry, fisheries etc. will be expanded to benefit women workers in the agriculture sector.

Women and Industry

5.6 The important role played by women in electronics, information technology and food processing and agro industry and textiles has been crucial to the development of these sectors. They would be given comprehensive support in terms of labour legislation, social security and other support services to participate in various industrial sectors.

5.7 Women at present cannot work in night shift in factories even if they wish to. Suitable measures will be taken to enable women to work on the night shift in factories. This will be accompanied with support services for security, transportation etc.

Support Services

5.8 The provision of support services for women, like child care facilities, including crèches at work places and educational institutions, homes for the aged and the disabled will be expanded and improved to create an enabling environment and to ensure their full cooperation in social, political and economic life. Women-friendly personnel policies will also be drawn up to encourage women to participate effectively in the developmental process.

Social Empowerment of Women

Education

6.1 Equal access to education for women and girls will be ensured. Special measures will be taken to eliminate discrimination, universalize education, eradicate illiteracy, create a gender-sensitive educational system, increase enrolment and retention rates of girls and improve the quality of education to facilitate life-long learning as well as development of occupation/vocation/technical skills by women. Reducing the gender gap in secondary and higher education would be a focus area. Sectoral time targets in existing policies will be achieved, with a special focus on girls and women, particularly those belonging to weaker sections including the Scheduled Castes/Scheduled Tribes/Other Backward Classes/Minorities. Gender sensitive curricula would be developed at all levels of educational system in order to address sex stereotyping as one of the causes of gender discrimination.

Health

6.2 A holistic approach to women's health which includes both nutrition and health services will be adopted and special attention will be given to the needs of women and the girl at all stages of the life cycle. The reduction of infant mortality and maternal mortality, which are sensitive indicators of human development, is a priority concern. This policy reiterates the national demographic goals for Infant Mortality Rate (IMR), Maternal Mortality Rate (MMR) set out in the National Population Policy 2000. Women should have access to comprehensive, affordable and quality health care. Measures will be adopted that take into account the reproductive rights of women to enable them to exercise informed choices, their vulnerability to sexual and health problems together with endemic, infectious and communicable diseases such as malaria, TB, and water borne diseases as well as hypertension and cardio-pulmonary diseases. The social, developmental and health consequences of HIV/AIDS and other sexually transmitted diseases will be tackled from a gender perspective.

6.3 To effectively meet problems of infant and maternal mortality, and early marriage the availability of good and accurate data at micro level on deaths, birth and marriages is required. Strict implementation of registration of births and deaths would be ensured and registration of marriages would be made compulsory.

6.4 In accordance with the commitment of the National Population Policy (2000) to population stabilization, this Policy recognizes the critical need of men and women to have access to safe, effective and affordable methods of family planning of their choice and the need to suitably address the issues of early marriages and spacing of children. Interventions such as spread of education, compulsory registration of marriage and special programmes like BSY should impact on delaying the age of marriage so that by 2010 child marriages are eliminated.

6.5 Women's traditional knowledge about health care and nutrition will be recognized through proper documentation and its use will be encouraged. The use of Indian and alternative systems of medicine will be enhanced within the framework of overall health infrastructure available for women.

Nutrition

6.6 In view of the high risk of malnutrition and disease that women face at all the three critical stages viz., infancy and childhood, adolescent and reproductive phase, focussed attention would be paid to meeting the nutritional needs of women at all stages of the life cycle. This is also important in view of the critical link between the health of adolescent girls, pregnant and lactating women with the health of infant and young children. Special efforts will be made to tackle the problem of macro and micro nutrient deficiencies especially amongst pregnant and lactating women as it leads to various diseases and disabilities.

6.7 Intra-household discrimination in nutritional matters *vis-à-vis* girls and women will be sought to be ended through appropriate strategies. Widespread use of nutrition education would be made to address the issues of intra-household imbalances in nutrition and the special needs of pregnant and lactating women. Women's participation will also be ensured in the planning, superintendence and delivery of the system.

Drinking Water and Sanitation

6.8 Special attention will be given to the needs of women in the provision of safe drinking water, sewage disposal, toilet facilities and sanitation within accessible reach of households, especially in rural areas and urban slums. Women's participation will be ensured in the planning, delivery and maintenance of such services.

Housing and Shelter

6.9 Women's perspectives will be included in housing policies, planning of housing colonies and provision of shelter both in rural and urban areas. Special attention will be given for providing adequate and safe housing and accommodation for women including single women, heads of households, working women, students, apprentices and trainees.

Environment

6.10 Women will be involved and their perspectives reflected in the policies and programmes for environment, conservation and restoration. Considering the impact of environmental factors on their livelihoods, women's participation will be ensured in the conservation of the environment and control of environmental degradation. The vast majority of rural women still depend on the locally available non-commercial sources of energy such as animal dung, crop waste and fuel wood. In order to ensure the efficient use of these energy resources in an environmental friendly manner, the Policy will aim at promoting the programmes of non-conventional energy resources. Women will be involved in spreading the use of solar energy, biogas, smokeless chulahs and other rural application so as to have a visible impact of these measures in influencing eco system and in changing the life styles of rural women.

Science and Technology

6.11 Programmes will be strengthened to bring about a greater involvement of women in science and technology. These will include measures to motivate girls to take up science and technology for higher education and also ensure that development projects with scientific and technical inputs involve women fully. Efforts to develop a scientific temper and awareness will also be stepped up. Special measures would be taken for their training in areas where they have special skills like communication and information technology. Efforts to develop appropriate technologies suited to women's needs as well as to reduce their drudgery will be given a special focus too.

Women in Difficult Circumstances

6.12 In recognition of the diversity of women's situations and in acknowledgement of the needs of specially disadvantaged groups, measures and programmes will be undertaken to provide them with special assistance. These groups include women in extreme poverty, destitute women, women in conflict situations, women affected by natural calamities, women in less developed regions, the disabled widows, elderly women, single women in difficult circumstances, women heading households, those displaced from employment, migrants, women who are victims of marital violence, deserted women and prostitutes etc.

Violence Against Women

7.1 All forms of violence against women, physical and mental, whether at domestic or societal levels, including those arising from customs, traditions or accepted practices shall be dealt with effectively with a view to eliminate its incidence. Institutions and mechanisms/schemes for assistance will be created and strengthened for prevention of such violence, including sexual harassment at work place and customs like dowry; for the rehabilitation of the victims of violence and for taking effective action against the perpetrators of such violence. A special emphasis will also be laid on programmes and measures to deal with trafficking in women and girls.

Rights of the Girl Child

8.1 All forms of discrimination against the girl child and violation of her rights shall be eliminated by undertaking strong measures both preventive and punitive within and outside the family. These would relate specifically to strict enforcement of laws against prenatal sex selection and the practices of female foeticide, female infanticide, child marriage, child abuse and child prostitution etc. Removal of discrimination in the treatment of the girl child within the family and outside and projection of a positive image of the girl child will be actively fostered. There will be special emphasis on the needs of the girl child and earmarking of substantial investments in the areas relating to food and nutrition, health and education, and in vocational education. In implementing programmes for eliminating child labour, there will be a special focus on girl children.

Mass Media

9.1 Media will be used to portray images consistent with human dignity of girls and women. The Policy will specifically strive to remove demeaning, degrading and negative conventional stereotypical images of women and violence against women. Private sector partners and media networks will be involved at all levels to ensure equal access for women particularly in the area of information and communication technologies. The media would be encouraged to develop codes of conduct, professional guidelines and other self regulatory mechanisms to remove gender stereotypes and promote balanced portrayals of women and men.

Operational Strategies

Action Plans

10.1 All Central and State Ministries will draw up time bound Action Plans for translating the Policy into a set of concrete actions, through a participatory process of consultation with Centre/State Departments of Women and Child Development and National/State Commissions for Women. The Plans will specifically including the following:

- *(i)* Measurable goals to be achieved by 2010.
- *(ii)* Identification and commitment of resources.
- *(iii)* Responsibilities for implementation of action points.
- *(iv)* Structures and mechanisms to ensure efficient monitoring, review and gender impact assessment of action points and policies.
- *(v)* Introduction of a gender perspective in the budgeting process.

10.2 In order to support better planning and programme formulation and adequate allocation of resources, Gender Development Indices (GDI) will be developed by networking with specialized agencies. These could be analyzed and studied in depth. Gender auditing and development of evaluation mechanisms will also be undertaken along side.

10.3 Collection of gender disaggregated data by all primary data collecting agencies of the Central and State Governments as well as Research and Academic Institutions in the Public and Private Sectors will be undertaken. Data and information gaps in vital areas reflecting the status of women will be sought to be filled in by these immediately. All Ministries/Corporations/Banks and financial institutions etc. will be advised to collect, collate, disseminate and maintain/publish data related to programmes and benefits on a gender disaggregated basis. This will help in meaningful planning and evaluation of policies.

Institutional Mechanisms

11.1 Institutional mechanisms, to promote the advancement of women, which exist at the Central and State levels, will be strengthened. These will be through interventions as may be appropriate and will relate to, among others, provision of adequate resources, training and advocacy skills to effectively influence macro-policies, legislation, programmes etc. to achieve the empowerment of women.

11.2 National and State Councils will be formed to oversee the operationalisation of the Policy on a regular basis. The National Council will be headed by the Prime Minister and the State Councils by the Chief Ministers and be broad in composition having representatives from the concerned Departments/Ministries, National and State Commissions for Women, Social Welfare Boards, representatives of Non-Government Organizations, Women's Organisations, Corporate Sector, Trade Unions, financing institutions, academics, experts and social activists etc. These bodies will review the progress made in implementing the Policy twice a year. The National Development Council will also be informed of the progress of the programme undertaken under the policy from time to time for advice and comments.

11.3 National and State Resource Centres on women will be established with mandates for collection and dissemination of information, undertaking research work, conducting surveys, implementing training and awareness generation programmes, etc. These Centers will link up with Women's Studies Centres and other research and academic institutions through suitable information networking systems.

11.4 While institutions at the district level will be strengthened, at the grassroots, women will be helped by Government through its programmes to organize and strengthen into Self-Help Groups (SHGs) at the Anganwadi/Village/Town level. The women's groups will be helped to institutionalize themselves into registered societies and to federate at the Panchayat/Municipal level. These societies will bring about synergistic implementation of all the social and economic development programmes by drawing resources made available through Government and Non-Government channels, including banks and financial institutions and by establishing a close Interface with the Panchayats/ Municipalities.

Resource Management

12.1 Availability of adequate financial, human and market resources to implement the Policy will be managed by concerned Departments, financial credit institutions and banks, private sector, civil society and other connected institutions. This process will include:

- *(a)* Assessment of benefits flowing to women and resource allocation to the programmes relating to them through an exercise of gender budgeting. Appropriate changes in policies will be made to optimize benefits to women under these schemes.
- *(b)* Adequate resource allocation to develop and promote the policy outlined earlier based on (a) above by concerned Departments.
- *(c)* Developing synergy between personnel of Health, Rural Development, Education and Women and Child Development Department at field level and other village level functionaries.'
- *(d)* Meeting credit needs by banks and financial credit institutions through suitable policy initiatives and development of new institutions in coordination with the Department of Women and Child Development.

12.2 The strategy of Women's Component Plan adopted in the Ninth Plan of ensuring that not less than 30 per cent of benefits/funds flow to women from all Ministries and Departments will be implemented effectively so that the needs and interests of women and girls are addressed by all concerned sectors. The Department of Women and Child Development being the nodal Ministry will monitor and review the progress of the implementation of the Component Plan from time to time, in terms of both quality and quantity in collaboration with the Planning Commission.

12.3 Efforts will be made to channelize private sector investments too, to support programmes and projects for advancement of women.

Legislation

13.1 The existing legislative structure will be reviewed and additional legislative measures taken by identified departments to implement the Policy. This will also involve a review of all existing laws including personal, customary and tribal laws, subordinate legislation, related rules as well as executive and administrative regulations to eliminate all gender discriminatory references. The process will be planned over a time period 2000-03. The specific measures required would be evolved through a consultation process involving civil society, National Commission for Women and Department of Women and Child Development. In appropriate cases the consultation process would be widened to include other stakeholders too.

13.2 Effective implementation of legislation would be promoted by involving civil society and community. Appropriate changes in legislation will be undertaken, if necessary.

13.3 In addition, following other specific measures will be taken to implement the legislation effectively.

(a) Strict enforcement of all relevant legal provisions and speedy redressal of grievances will be ensured, with a special focus on violence and gender related atrocities.

(b) Measures to prevent and punish sexual harassment at the place of work, protection for women workers in the organized/unorganized sector and strict enforcement of relevant laws such as Equal Remuneration Act and Minimum Wages Act will be undertaken.

(c) Crimes against women, their incidence, prevention, investigation, detection and prosecution will be regularly reviewed at all Crime Review fora and Conferences at the Central, State and District levels. Recognised, local, voluntary organizations will be authorized to lodge Complaints and facilitate registration, investigations and legal proceedings related to violence and atrocities against girls and women.

(d) Women's Cells in Police Stations, Encourage Women Police Stations Family Courts, Mahila Courts, Counselling Centers, Legal Aid Centers and Nyaya Panchayats will be strengthened and expanded to eliminate violence and atrocities against women.

(e) Widespread dissemination of information on all aspects of legal rights, human rights and other entitlements of women, through specially designed legal literacy programmes and rights information programmes will be done.

Gender Sensitisation

14.1 Training of personnel of executive, legislative and judicial wings of the State, with a special focus on policy and programme framers, implementation and development agencies, law enforcement machinery and the judiciary, as well as non-governmental organizations will be undertaken. Other measures will include:

(*a*) Promoting societal awareness to gender issues and women's human rights.

(*b*) Review of curriculum and educational materials to include gender education and human rights issues.

(*c*) Removal of all references derogatory to the dignity of women from all public documents and legal instruments.

(*d*) Use of different forms of mass media to communicate social messages relating to women's equality and empowerment.

Panchayati Raj Institutions

15.1 The 73rd and 74th Amendments (1993) to the Indian Constitution have served as a breakthrough towards ensuring equal access and increased participation in political power structure for women. The PRIs will play a central role in the process of enhancing women's participation in public life. The PRIs and the local self-governments will be actively involved in the implementation and execution of the National Policy for Women at the grassroots level.

Partnership with the Voluntary Sector Organizations

16.1 The involvement of voluntary organizations, associations, federations, trade unions, non-governmental organizations, women's organizations, as well as institutions dealing with education, training and research will be ensured in the formulation, implementation, monitoring and review of all policies and programmes affecting women. Towards this end, they will be provided with appropriate support related to resources and capacity building and facilitated to participate actively in the process of the empowerment of women.

International Cooperation

17.1 The Policy will aim at implementation of international obligations/commitments in all sectors on empowerment of women such as the Convention on All Forms of Discrimination Against Women (CEDAW), Convention on the Rights of the Child (CRC), International Conference on Population and Development (ICPD+5) and other such instruments. International, regional and sub-regional cooperation towards the empowerment of women will continue to be encouraged through sharing of experiences, exchange of ideas and technology, networking with institutions and organizations and through bilateral and multi-lateral partnerships.

Source: National Policy for Women Empowerment, Ministry of Women and Child Development, Government of India, New Delhi, 2001.

3

APPENDIX

Women in Power and Decision-Making in India

Legislative enactments have dramatically increased women's access to decision-making structures over the last decade. The 73rd and 74th Constitutional Amendments passed in 1993 provide for reservation of 33 per cent of elected seats for women at different levels of local governance in both rural and urban local bodies. Also there would be one-third reservation for women to posts of Chairperson of these bodies. One-third of the seats are further reserved for women belonging to the SC/ST community. The *Panchayats (Extension to Schedule Areas)* Act *1996 (PESA)* made this amendment applicable to Schedule V areas. This has dramatically increased women's participation in local bodies. For 5-year tenure of local governments, about one million women get elected to panchayats and local bodies. In some states, the number of elected women exceeds the reserved one third quotas.

The Constitution provides for rotation of seats reserved for women but does not prescribe the number of terms for which seats may be served for rotation. Seats are reserved for one term, two terms or more depending upon the provisions made by the State Legislature in the State law. The option to reserve seats for more than one term is open, but it is for the State Legislature to decide the number of terms for which seats will remain reserved. Tamil Nadu has taken a positive step by freezing the reserved seats for women for two terms.

Local government institutions have not been given full financial and political powers to function independently but 29 subjects ranging from agriculture to poverty eradication have been devolved to these institutions. In theory, the Presidents of the gram panchayats, block panchayats and district panchayats are responsible for prioritising the developmental needs of the villagers and allocating the grants accordingly. In practice, the level of responsiveness and manner of functioning of the panchayats varies considerably across states. As far as women's participation is concerned however, the legislative enactments have ensured that they are represented in all states. Many of the elected women entering the public arena for the first time lack confidence, feel isolated, and have no previous political experience. They need to develop their innate leadership skills. Studies conducted in different parts of the country show that 95 per cent of the elected women representatives (EWRs) are first-timers in politics and join politics because that is what their male family/village members want.

As first timers without previous exposure to politics, many of the elected women lack the capacity to function properly in the panchayats and municipalities, and consequently are not taken seriously by their colleagues. Sustained training and networking efforts are being undertaken both by government and non-government agencies to ensure that women's capacity to participate improves. With just a few years of experience, women have emerged as articulate, motivated leaders all over the country. Gender budgeting involving grassroots elected women representatives is being used for advocacy in several places. Increased networking and formation of confederations of elected women representatives has helped to strengthen women's leadership. This approach has been especially successful in southern and western India. The formation of these networks promotes solidarity among the elected women representatives, otherwise divided by caste, religion and geographical boundaries. Thus, formation of these networks is the first step in the direction of empowering women. Their position as panchayat members adds to their ability to intervene and negotiate with the several thousand EWRs have participated in the programmes organised in the national capital as well as in state capitals. Similarly, the Hunger Project has, since 2001, focused its work on supporting and enabling EWRs with the belief that women's leadership at grassroot is essential to end hunger, poverty and injustice in India. Leadership training and building alliances are key interventions.

EWRs in some states are working in close collaboration with women's collectives and addressing issues of women's well being. Examples have been cited of women's groups in Karnataka that have played a catalytic role in bringing the issue of domestic violence into the larger forum of the panchayat for resolution, and in one case initiating counseling services for victims of abuse in collaboration with an NGO. Karnataka also boasts of the first Panchayat to computerise its administration and other aspects of governance, a unique achievement since this was an independent initiative funded by the village development committee. Interestingly, the Gram Sabha without women is not a legal entity, therefore, the traditional community forum which excluded women cannot exercise legal authority unless women also participate.

In Madhya Pradesh, the law envisages that at least one-third of members present in Gram Sabha must be women, to constitute the necessary quorum. Reservations have also meant that social biases have to give way to more inclusive forums, both in respect of gender and caste. Even in very traditional communities where previously women could not participate like those of the village assemblies, they are welcome now and are, in fact, encouraged to participate in many places. Participation in decision making as EWR has impacted on other aspects of capability development. In a study of some hundred EWRs from four districts in Haryana, it was noted that the majority were illiterate when elected to office. After two years in office, women have sought to acquire literary skills and are committed to the education of their daughters.

Supportive interventions are needed to ensure that the 73rd amendment does not lose its potential transformative edge when implemented within the reality of a feudal, patriarchal, and highly fragmented society. Thus, Maharashtra has provided for Mahila Gram Sabhas that preceded Gram Sabhas. This provides space for women's issues and concerns. Tamil Nadu has legislated two terms for its elected women representatives, keeping in mind that women need more time to be trained and then be able to make use of the training. In Karnataka, there is official recognition that a major step, needed to facilitate women's participation in political processes, is the provision of child care facilities.

While the sphere of local governance has seen significant improvement, the numbers of women in official positions remains relatively low. The representation of women in the decision-making level through the Indian Administrative Service and the Indian Police Service which stood at 5.4 per cent in 1987 increased to 7.6 per cent in 2000. Of all employees in Central, State and Local Governments, 17.47 per cent were women in 2001. An example of new role models and opportunities comes from Tamil Nadu, which has the distinction of commissioning the first all unit of Women Police Commandos in the country. These women commandos were trained on par with men in horse riding, rowing, sand running, parasailing, long distance running, winch sailing, swimming, driving, weapon handling and shooting practice of all automatic weapons, besides yoga, meditation and unarmed combat training. An exclusive 'Women Police Battalion' with a strength of 1078 Women Police personnel of all ranks has also been constituted in Tamil Nadu.

There is one woman judge in the Supreme Court out of 24 judges and 25 women judges in the High Courts across the country out of a total of 250 judges as on 13.1.2005. The challenge to ensure that *de jure* participation is also *de facto* participation continues, and this primarily calls for a range of supportive interventions. There is need to encourage and provide new opportunities and new role models in decision-making structures.

Source : Platform for Action: 10 Years after India Country Report (Chapter No. 7 on Women in Power and Decision-Making), Ministry of Women and Child Development, Government of India, New Delhi, 2006, pp. 49-54.

Table–1
Women's Presence in the Lok Sabha, 1952-2004

Year	*Seats*	*Women MPs*	*% Women MPs*
1952	499	22	4.4
1957	500	27	5.4
1962	503	34	6.8
1967	523	31	5.9
1971	521	22	4.2
1977	544	19	3.3
1980	544	28	5.2
1984	544	44	8.1
1989	517	27	5.2
1991	544	39	7.2
1996	543	39	7.2
1998	543	43	7.9
Average till 1998	**527**	**31**	**5.9**
1999	545	49	8.65
2004	539	44 (May 2004)	8.16

Note: India, Election Commission.
Source: United Nations Development Programme (2000). Women in India: How Free? How Equal? New Delhi, p. 66.

Table–2
State–Wise Number of Elected Total and Women Panchayat Representatives in the Three-Tiers in India-2002

States/Union Territories	*Gram Panchayat*		*Intermediate Panchayat*		*District Panchayat*	
	Women	*Total*	*Women*	*Total*	*Women*	*Total*
Andhra Pradesh	68736	208291	4919	14617	364	1095
Arunachal Pradesh	0	0	0	0	0	0

Contd...

States/Union Territories	Gram Panchayat		Intermediate Panchayat		District Panchayat	
	Women	Total	Women	Total	Women	Total
Assam	7851	23471	746	2148	117	390
Bihar	0	0	0	0	0	0
Chhattisgarh	41913	124211	906	2639	95	274
Delhi	0	0	0	0	0	0
Goa	457	1439	0	0	17	50
Gujarat	41180	123470	1312	3919	274	817
Haryana	18356	54646	842	2430	109	314
Himachal Pradesh	6822	18549	562	1658	87	251
Jammu & Kashmir	0	0	0	0	0	0
Jharkhand	0	0	0	0	0	0
Karnataka	35922	80073	1375	3255	339	890
Kerala	4801	13259	629	1638	105	307
Madhya Pradesh	106491	314847	2159	6456	248	734
Maharashtra	77548	232644	1407	3902	658	1951
Manipur	611	1722	0	0	22	61
Meghalaya	0	0	0	0	0	0
Mizoram	0	0	0	0	0	0
Nagaland	0	0	0	0	0	0
Orissa	31414	87547	2188	6227	296	854
Punjab	26939	75473	813	2480	89	279
Rajasthan	39450	114282	1908	5257	364	1008
Sikkim	322	873	0	0	29	92
Tamil Nadu	26181	97458	1770	6570	173	656
Tripura	1895	5686	106	299	28	82
Uttaranchal	0	0	0	0	0	0
U.P.	0	0	0	0	0	0
West Bengal	11497	51200	1923	8579	156	723

Contd...

States/Union Territories	*Gram Panchayat*		*Intermediate Panchayat*		*District Panchayat*	
	Women	*Total*	*Women*	*Total*	*Women*	*Total*
Union Territories						
Andaman & Nicobar Islands	261	759	25	67	10	30
Chandigarh	55	162	6	15	3	10
Dadra & Nagar Haveli	45	124	0	0	4	12
Daman & Diu	17	63	0	0	10	25
Lakshadweep	30	79	0	0	8	22
Pondicherry	0	0	0	0	0	0
Total	**548794**	**1630327**	**23596**	**72156**	**3605**	**10927**

Note: Ministry of Rural Areas and Employment Meghalaya, Mizoram and Nagaland are Traditional Councils. In NCT of Delhi, Panchayati Raj System is yet to be revived.

Source: India, Ministry of Statistics and Programme Implementation, Central Statistical Organisation (2003) and Women and Men in India 2002, New Delhi, p. 106.

Table–3
Representation of Women in the Indian Council of Ministers, 2002

Year	*Number of Ministers*			*Number of Women Ministers*		
	Cabinet Minister	*MOS**	*Deputy Minister*	*Cabinet Minister*	*MOS*	*Deputy Minister*
1	2	3	4	5	6	7
2002[a]	32	41	0	2	6	0

Note: MOS—Minister of State* Including Ministers of State with Independent Charge a As on January, 2002. Lok Sabha Secretariat, New Delhi.

Source: India, Ministry of Statistics and Programme Implementation, Central Statistical Organisation, 2003 and Women and Men in India 2002, New Delhi, p. 98.

Table–4
Women in Indian Bureaucracy, 2000

S.No.	States/Union Territories	Decision-making Administrative			
		I.A.S. (As on 1.6.2000) [1]		I.P.S. (As on 1.4.2000) [2]	
		Female	Male	Female	Male
1	2	3	4	5	6
	India	535 (10.4%)	4624	110 (3.3%)	3191
1.	Andhra Pradesh	33	281	11	179
2.	Arunachal Pradesh	38	194	9	147
3.	Assam	10	216	2	134
4.	Bihar	33	360	14	233
5.	Delhi	X	X	X	X
6.	Goa	X	X	X	X
7.	Gujarat	23	225	3	133
8.	Haryana	32	180	4	100
9.	Himachal Pradesh	17	109	1	73
10.	Jammu & Kashmir	3	109	1	80
11.	Karnataka	35	213	4	137
12.	Kerala	21	157	2	114
13.	Madhya Pradesh	54	342	9	273
14.	Maharashtra	40	311	6	201
15.	Manipur	5	193	3	98
16.	Meghalaya	XX	XX	XX	XX
17.	Mizoram	X	X	X	X
18.	Nagaland	1	63	1	39
19.	Orissa	17	185	7	129
20.	Punjab	28	165	6	144
21.	Rajasthan	29	231	6	141
22.	Sikkim	5	45	Nil	24
23.	Tamil Nadu	37	288	7	176

Contd...

1	2	3	4	5	6
24.	Tripura	XXX	XXX	XXX	XXX
25.	Uttar Pradesh	51	484	10	381
26.	West Bengal	23	273	4	255
Union Territories					
27.	Andaman & Nicobar Islands	X	X	X	X
28.	Chandigarh	X	X	X	X
29.	Dadra & Nagar Haveli	X	X	X	X
30.	Daman & Diu	X	X	X	X
31.	Lakshadweep	X	X	X	X
32.	Pondicherry	X	X	X	X

Note: 1. Department of Personnel and Training, Government of India, New Delhi.
2. Ministry of Home Affairs, Government of India, New Delhi.
X Included under Arunachal Pradesh.
XX Included under Assam.
XXX Included under Manipur.

Source: *India, Planning Commission, (2000). Development Indicators: A Comparative Picture of the Status of Women and Men in India: Data Sheet. New Delhi, p. 1.*

Table–5
Women Representation in Indian Judiciary
Number of Judges by Sex in Supreme Court / High Courts as on 17.01.2003

Name of the Court	*Number of Judges*		
	Female	*Male*	*Total*
1	2	3	4
Supreme Court	1	24	25
High Courts of Indian States			
Allahabad	1	69	70
Andhra Pradesh	2	32	34
Bombay	3	49	52
Calcutta	1	41	42

Contd...

1	2	3	4
Chhattisgarh	–	4	4
Delhi	1	27	28
Guwahati	–	12	12
Gujarat	1	30	31
Himachal Pradesh	1	5	6
Jammu & Kashmir	–	11	11
Jharkhand	–	12	12
Karnataka	1	31	32
Kerala	1	25	26
Madhya Pradesh	1	23	24
Madras	1	30	31
Orissa	–	12	12
Patna	1	23	24
Punjab & Haryana	1	30	31
Rajasthan	1	25	26
Sikkim	–	2	2
Uttaranchal	–	4	4
Total	**17**	**497**	**514**

Note: Department of Justice, Ministry of Law and Justice and Company Affairs, Government of India.

Source: *India, Ministry of Statistics and Programme Implementation, Central Statistical Organisation, (2003), Women and Men in India 2002, New Delhi, p. 98.*

Table–6
Progress of Indian Women: 1971-2001

Development Indicators	*Women*	*Men*	*Total*	*Women*	*Men*	*Total*
***Demography**						
–Population (in million in 1971 & 2001)	264.1	284	548.1	495.7	531.2	1027.1
–Decennial Growth (1971 & 2001)	24.9	24.4	24.6	21.7	20.9	21.34

Contd...

Development Indicators	Women	Men	Total	Women	Men	Total
***Vital Statistics**						
—Sex Ratio (1971 & 2001)	930	–	–	933	–	–
—Expectation of Life at Birth (1971 & 1996-2001)	50.2	50.5	50.9	63.4	62.4	–
—Mean Age at Marriage (1971 & 1991)	17.2	22.4	–	19.3	23.9	–
***Health and Family Welfare**						
—Birth Rate (1971 & 1998)	–	–	36.9	–	–	26.5
—Death Rate (1970 & 1998)	15.6	15.8	15.7	8.8	9.2	9.0
—Infant Mortality Rate (1978 & 1998)	131	123	127	73.5	69.8	72
—Child Mortality Rate (1970 & 1997)	55.1	51.7	–	24.5	21.8	23.1
—Maternal Mortality Rate (1980 & 1998)	468	–	–	407	–	–
***Literacy and Education**						
—Literacy Rates (1971 & 2001)	7.9	24.9	16.7	54.28	75.96	65.38
—Gross Enrolment Ratio (1990-91 & 1998-99)						
Classes I-V	85.5	113.9	100.1	82.9	100.9	92.1
Classes VI-VIII	47.8	76.6	62.1	49.1	65.3	57.6
—Drop-out Rate (1990-91 & 1998-99)						
Classes I-V	46	40.1	42.6	41.2	38.6	39.7
Classes VI-VIII	65.1	59.1	60.9	60.1	54.4	56.8
***Work and Employment**						
—Work Participation Rate (1971 & 1991)	14.2	52.8	34.3	22.3	51.6	37.7
—Organised Sector (No. in lakhs in 1971 & 1997)	19.3 (11%)	155.6	174.9	43.9 (15.9%)	231.8	275.7

Contd...

Development Indicators	*Women*	*Men*	*Total*	*Women*	*Men*	*Total*
–Public Sector (No. in lakhs in 1971 & 1997)	8.6 (8%)	98.7	107.3	26.1 (13.8%)	162.6	188.7
–Government (No. in lakhs in 1981 & 1996)	11.9 (11%)	97.1	109.0	15.0 (13.9%)	92.7	107.7
***Decision-Making**						
–Administrative						
IAS (1987 & 2000)	339 (8.1%)	3865	4204	535 (10.4%)	4624	5159
IPS (1987 & 2000)	21 (0.9%)	2397	2418	110 (3.3%)	3191	3301
–Political						
PRIs (No. in lakhs in 1995 & 1997)	3.18 (33.5%)	6.30	9.48@	8.14 (31.3%)	17.84	25.98
Legislative Assemblies (No. in 1985 & 2000)	141 (5.1%)	2632	2773	229 (5.6%)	3838	4067
Parliament (No. in 1989 & 1999)	47 (61%)	721	768	67 (8.4%)	723	790
Central Council of Ministers (1985-1999)	4 (10%)	36	40	8 (10.9%)	65	73

Notes: @ Refers to 1995 in respect of only 9 States viz. Gujarat, Haryana, Kerala, Madhya Pradesh, Punjab, Rajasthan, Tripura and West Bengal. Figure in parentheses indicate the percentage in the total and year of the data in respective columns. Data from Planning Commission.

Source: India, Ministry of Human Resource Development, Department of Women and Child Development.(2001),Working Group on Empowerment of Women: Tenth Plan (2002-07): Report, New Delhi, p. 43.

Table–7
Share of Population in Total Population, Decadal Growth Rate, 2001

India/State/Uts	*Total Population*			*Percentage Share in Total Population (Provisional)***	*% Decadal Natural Growth Rate 2001*
	Persons	*Males*	*Females*	*Females*	
INDIA*	**1028610328**	**532156772**	**496453556**	**100.00**	**21.54**
1. Andhra Pradesh	76210007	38527413	37682594	7.37	14.59
2. Arunachal Pradesh	1097968	579941	518027	0.11	27.00
3. Assam	26655528	13777037	12878491	2.59	18.92
4. Bihar	82998509	43243795	39754714	8.07	28.62
5. Chhatisgarh	20833803	10474218	10359585	2.03	18.27
6. Delhi	13850507	7607234	6243273	1.34	47.02
7. Goa	1347668	687248	660420	0.13	15.21
8. Gujarat	50671017	26385577	24285440	4.93	22.66
9. Haryana	21144564	11363953	9780611	2.05	28.43
10. Himachal Pradesh	6077900	3087940	2989960	0.59	17.54
11. Jammu & Kashmir	10143700	5360926	4782774	0.98	29.43
12. Jharkhand	26945829	13885037	13060792	2.62	23.36
13. Karnataka	52850562	26898918	25951644	5.14	17.51
14. Kerala	31841374	15468614	16372760	3.10	9.43
15. Madhya Pradesh	60348023	31443652	28904371	5.88	24.26
16. Maharashtra	96878627	50400596	46478031	9.42	22.73
17. Manipur*	2166788*	1095634*	1071154*	0.23	24.86
18. Meghalaya	2318822	1176087	1142735	0.22	30.65
19. Mizoram	888573	459109	429464	0.09	28.82

Contd...

India/State/Uts	Total Population			Percentage Share in Total Population (Provisional)**	% Decadal Natural Growth Rate 2001
	Persons	Males	Females	Females	
20. Nagaland	1990036	1047141	942895	0.19	64.53
21. Orissa	36804660	18660570	18144090	3.57	16.25
22. Punjab	24358999	12985045	11373954	2.37	20.10
23. Rajasthan	56507188	29420011	27087177	5.50	28.41
24. Sikkim	540851	288484	252367	0.05	33.06
25. Tamil Nadu	62405679	31400909	31004770	6.05	11.72
26. Tripura	3199203	1642225	1556978	0.31	16.03
27. U.P.	166197921	87565369	78632552	16.17	25.85
28. Uttaranchal	8489349	4325924	4163425	0.83	20.41
29. West Bengal	80176197	41465985	38710212	7.81	17.77
Union Territories					
30. Andaman & Nicobar Islands	356152	192972	163180	0.03	26.90
31. Chandigarh	900635	506938	393697	0.09	40.28
32. Dadra & Nagar Haveli	220490	121666	98824	0.02	59.22
33. Daman & Diu	158204	92512	65692	0.02	55.73
34. Lakshadweep	60650	31131	29519	0.01	17.30
35. Pondicherry	974345	486961	487384	0.09	20.62

Notes: *Excluding the population of Mao Maram, Paomata and Purul Sub-divisions of Senapati District of Manipur.

Source: India, Registrar General and Census Commissioner, (2004). Final Population Totals: Census of India 2001, New Delhi, pp. 1-9. India, Registrar General and Census Commissioner, (2004). Final Population Totals Datasheet: Census of India 2001. New Delhi, p. 1 **India, Registrar General and Census Commissioner, 2001. Provisional Population Totals: Census of India 2001, New Delhi, p. XII.

4

APPENDIX

Strategies for Action: Women in Local Self Governance in India

Documentation and Data Collection

1. Data should be collected on gender segregated basis, of the various local government elections in different states of India, both for Panchayat and municipal bodies. This should also include the number of total women, SC and ST contestants, socio-economic profile of the elected women, party wise figure etc., for all the three levels of both urban and rural bodies.
2. The data available with the State Election Commission should be made accessible to researchers.
3. A monitoring exercise should be undertaken to see why the number of women elected is less than the minimum stipulated figures in the various states.
4. Research with a view to analyse the impact of financial grants on the Panchayats. There is also need for more information on the functioning of PRIs.
5. Need for more data collection, dissemination and documentation on the participation and performance of women. Data on SC and ST women are singularly lacking.
6. There is a need for documenting the functioning and performance of SC women elected representatives to local bodies (both Panchayat Raj Institutions and municipal bodies) and to analyse the problems and discrimination they face.
7. Research needs to be undertaken on an all India scale on the factors that helped the women to participate in politics, as well as those that deterred or prevented them.
8. Need for a study of the utilisation of MPs and MLAs Local Area

Development Fund and the procedure adopted for identification and implementation.

Administrative and Structural Action

9. The reservation for women should be raised to 50 per cent; and the rotation should be withdrawn or at least extended to two terms.
10. Women below poverty line should be helped when they get elected to the Panchayats. There should be provision for payment of adequate honorarium to women elected representatives to Panchayati Raj Institutions and municipal bodies belonging to low income groups to compensate the man-hours lost/wages lost in performing official duties connected with the post.
11. Greater devolution of political power, authority, financial power and functions by the State Governments. Schedules 11 and 12 should be enforced and the various areas mandatorily transferred to the local governments. Needed amendments in the Acts should be undertaken (for instance changing 'may' into 'shall' in the 73rd and 74th Amendments).
12. The elections of Mayors, Municipal Chairpersons and Sarpanches should be made direct. This will eliminate the frequency of no-confidence motions, corruption and factional politics.
13. To prevent the bringing of no-confidence motion on frivolous grounds against women Sarpanches, members, etc. a fifty per cent support for tabling the no-confidence motion could be statutorily provided for.
14. The system of Mayor-in-Council should be adopted uniformly all over India, so as to enable the women Mayors and Corporations to do effective work.
15. All the State Acts should stipulate that the Executive Committees, Standing Committees, Planning Committees and quorum should have at least 50 per cent women. Women members should be included in the Planning Committees.
16. The Thirty Seventh Report of the Standing Committee on Urban and Rural Development of Parliament needs to be disseminated among the elected women, NGOs, concerned government agencies and officials.
17. Extension of infrastructural support to the Chairperson, like TA and DA for attending the meetings, working expenses and facilities like telephone etc.
18. The MPs and MLAs Local Area Development Funds needs to be

monitored and not be allowed to lapse. In planning the projects, as well as implementation the Chairpersons of the panchayat and municipal bodies of the area should be involved.

19. All schemes, information about women agencies and other relevant materials which have a concern for women, should be made accessible to the State Women's Commission, and through them to the elected women representatives.
20. The number of women among local officials like Panchayat Secretary, Panchayat Karmi should be increased. This will help in some of them being attached to women Chairpersons.

Counselling and Guidance

21. The males proxying for women has been deliberately fostered and encouraged by the bureaucrats. They hand over cheques and other papers to the males like husbands and brother in law. This should be stopped. Only the Chairperson or others occupying posts should be given the cheques and other papers.
22. Community participation in identifying and solving the local issues will be effective in quick resolution of local problems. Mechanisms like Gram Sabha and ward meeting for such participation should be strengthened.
23. There should be expert committees at the central, state and local levels, to deal with the problems faced by the elected women in local governments. The women should be able to reach the committees with their problems and get proper guidance. The NCW also could have such an expert committee.
24. Sustained, frequent and localised training programme for capacity up-gradation of women, before and after they get elected.
25. At the level of district, there should be some counselling centres for the elected women where they can learn about the legal provisions, their own powers, the ways to utilise them etc. This will remove their tensions and restore self confidence.
26. There is a need to reconsider the 2 child norm and discuss its implications as it puts enormous pressure on the women elected representatives and limits future women candidates.
27. The Reservation Bill pending in the Parliament for 33 per cent reservation to Parliament and the state assemblies should be taken up and passed immediately.
28. Political Parties should recognise the good work done by the elected women and nominate them for recontesting, even if the constituencies are opened out.

29. The political parties should take special efforts to identify the capable women in local government and nominate them for higher positions for local and State Government elections, and also utilise them in the party positions.

Training

30. There should be periodic training and capacity building activities for the elected women. They should be sustained, frequent and localised training programme for capacity upgradation of women, before and after they get elected.
31. The Government Training Institutions and NGOs should undertake such training soon after they are elected and not wait for a later date. Such training should be done at an easy distance or in the locality/village itself.
32. The training methodology should be on a practical basis and not bookish. It should be interactive, based on the experiences of the elected women and not be monologues.
33. Models need to be presented so that the women can understand and replicate them.
34. The training should include officials and male counterparts so that they understand and recognise women's rights and roles. It should be jointly for women and men.
35. There should be training workshops specially on negotiating skills. This will help in their dealing with higher authorities and powerful persons.
36. Mere training of the elected women will not be enough. There should be constant guidance. The committee suggested above should be able to help them to function better. There is also the need to discuss ways of making the committees functional.
37. Need to create an environment of social acceptance of women in local government and politics. Towards that, the need to change the pattern of social conditioning of both women and men through a process of gender sensitisation for affirmative social action by NGOs.
38. The media should be sensitised not to play up only the negative side of the elected women's functioning. There has to be a responsible reporting so that the elected women do not feel diffident. They also need to highlight the best practices and give the elected women their due credit. The media also should have some onus of building up the image of women in the political process.

Networking

39. Elected women representatives need constant guidance and support. Hence, there should be a system of networking established in each State. NGOs and State Training Institutions could be involved in building up the network.

Source: Report of the National Consultation on Women in Governance, New Delhi, Government of India, National Commission for Women, 2003.

5

APPENDIX

A World Chronology of the Recognition of Women's Rights to Vote and to Stand for Election

Unless otherwise indicated, the date signifies the year women were granted the right both to vote and to stand for election. The countries listed below currently have a Parliament or have had one at some point in their history.

1788 United States of America (to stand for election)

1893 New Zealand (to vote)

1902 Australia*

1906 Finland

1907 Norway (to stand for election)*

1913 Norway**

1915 Denmark, Iceland

1917 Canada (to vote)*, Netherlands (to stand for election)

1918 Austria, Canada (to vote)*, Estonia, Georgia1, Germany, Hungary, Ireland*, Kyrgyzstan, Latvia, Lithuania, Poland, Russian Federation, United Kingdom*

1919 Belarus, Belgium (to vote)*, Luxembourg, Netherlands (to vote), New Zealand (to stand for election), Sweden*, Ukraine

1920 Albania, Canada (to stand for election)*, Czech Republlic, Slovakia, United States of America (to vote)

1921 Armenia, Azerbaijan, Belgium (to stand for election)*, Georgia1, Sweden**

1924 Kazakhstan1, Mongolia, Saint Lucia, Tajikistan

1927 Turkmenistan

1928 Ireland**, United Kingdom**

1929 Ecuador*, Romania*

1930 South Africa (Whites), Turkey (to vote)

1931 Chile*, Portugal*, Spain, Sri Lanka

1932 Maldives, Thailand, Uruguay

1934 Brazil, Cuba, Portugal*, Turkey (to stand for election)

1935 Myanmar (to vote)

1937 Philippines

1938 Bolivia*, Uzbekistan

1939 El Salvador (to vote)

1941 Panama*

1942 Dominican Republic

1944 Bulgaria, France, Jamaica

1945 Croatia, Guyana (to stand for election), Indonesia, Italy, Japan1, Senegal, Slovenia, Togo

1946 Cameroon, D.P.R. of Korea, Djibouti (to vote), Gautemala, Liberia, Myanmar (to stand for election), Panama**, Romania**, The F.Y.R. of Macedonia, Trinidad and Tobago, Venezuela, Vietnam, Yugoslavia

1947 Argentina, Japan1, Malta, Mexico (to vote), Pakistan, Singapore

1948 Belgium**, Israel, Niger, Republic of Korea, Seychelles, Suriname

1949 Bosnia and Herzegovina, Chile**, China, Costa Rica, Syrian Arab Republic (to vote)*

1950 Barbados, Canada (to vote)**, Haiti, India

1951 Antigua and Barbuda, Dominica, Grenada, Nepal, Saint Kitts and Nevis, Saint Vincent and the Grenadines

1952 Bolivia**, CÙte dÍlvoire, Greece, Lebanon

1953 Bhutan, Guyana (to vote), Mexico (to stand for election), Syrian Arab Republic**

1954 Belize, Colombia, Ghana

1955 Cambodia, Entrea2, Ethiopia, Honduras, Nicaragua, Peru

1956 Benin, Comoros, Egypt, Gabon, Mali, Mauritius, Somalia

1957 Malaysia, Zimbabwe (to vote)**

1958 Burkina Faso, Chad, Guinea, Lap P.D.R., Nigeria (South)

1959 Madagascar, San Marino (to vote), Tunisia, United Republic of Tanzania

1960 Canada (to stand for election)**, Cyprus, Gambia, Tonga

1961 Bahamas*, Burundi, El Salvador (to stand for election), Malawi, Mauritania, Paraguay, Rwanda, Sierra Leone

1962 Algeria, Australia**, Monaco, Uganda, Zambia

1963 Afghanistan, Congo, Equatorial Guinea, Fiji, Iran (Islamic Republic of), Kenya, Morocco, Papua New Guinea (to stand for election)

1964 Bahamas**, Libyan Arab Jamahiriya, Papua New Guinea (to vote), Sudan

1965 Bostwana, Lesotho

1967 Democratic Republic of the Congo (to vote), Ecuador**, Kiribati, Tuvalu,Yemen (D.P.R.)

1968 Nauru, Swaziland

1970 Andorra (to vote), Democratic Republic of the Congo (to stand for election), Yemen (Arab Republic)

1971 Switzerland

1972 Bangladesh

1973 Andorra (to stand for election), Bahrain3, San Marino (to stand for election)

1974 Jordan, Solomon Islands

1975 Angola, Cape Verde, Mozambique, Sao Tome and Principe, Vanuatu1

1976 Portugal**

1977 Guinea Bissau

1978 Nigeria (North), Republic of Moldova1, Zimbabwe (to stand for election)

1979 Marshall Islands, Micronesia (Fed. States), Palau

1980 Iraq, Vanuatu1

1984 Liechtenstein, South Africa (Coloureds + Indians)

1986 Central African Republic, Djibouti (to stand for election)

1989 Namibia

1990 Samoa

1993 Kazakhstan1, Republic of Moldova1

1994 South Africa (Blacks)

Women in Kuwait do not yet have the right to vote or to stand for election. In the United Arab Emirates, where the Parliament is officially appointed, neither men nor women have the right to vote or to stand for election.

*Right subject to conditions or restrictions

**Restrictions or conditions lifted

1. Reference to several dates reflects the stages in the granting of rights. It is not uncommon, in countries previously under colonial rule, for women to have been granted the rights to vote and be elected by the colonial administration and to have had them confirmed at the time of accession to independence. Similarly, it is not uncommon, in countries that were formerly part of a federation and in which women were entitled to vote and be elected under the federal legislation, for women to have had these rights confirmed under the Constitution of the newly independent State.
2. In November 1955, Eritrea was part of Ethiopia. The Constitution of sovereign Eritrea adopted on 23 May 1997 stipulates that All Eritrean citizens of eighteen years of age or more, shall have the right to vote.

Source: Report of the National Consultation on Women in Governance, New Delhi, Government of India, National Commission for Women, 2003.

6

APPENDIX

Twenty-third Special Session of the General Assembly entitled 'Women 2000: Gender Equality, Development and Peace for the Twenty-first Century'

10 June 2000

Unedited final outcome document as adopted by the Plenary of the Special Session.

Further Actions and Initiatives to Implement the Beijing Declaration and the Platform for Action

I. Introduction

1. The Governments which came together at the Special Session of the General Assembly have reaffirmed their commitment to the goals and objectives contained in the Beijing Declaration and the Platform for Action adopted at the IV World Conference on Women in 1995 as contained in the report of the Conference.

   The Beijing Declaration and Platform for Action set as goals gender equality, development and peace and constituted an agenda for the empowerment of women. The Governments reviewed and appraised progress and identified obstacles and current challenges in the implementation of the Platform for Action. They recognized that the goals and commitments made in the Platform for Action have not been fully implemented and achieved and have agreed upon further actions and initiatives at local, national, regional, and international levels to accelerate its implementation and to ensure that commitments for gender equality, development and peace are fully realised.

2. The Beijing Platform for Action identified 12 critical areas for priority action to achieve the advancement and empowerment of women. The Commission on the Status of Women has reviewed progress in each of the 12 critical areas of concern and since 1996 has adopted agreed conclusions and recommendations

for accelerated implementation. The Platform for Action, together with these agreed conclusions and recommendations, forms the basis for further progress towards the achievement of gender equality, development and peace in the 21st century.

2bis. The objective of the Platform for Action, which is in full conformity with the purposes and principles of the Charter of the United Nations and international law, is the empowerment of all women. The full realization of all human rights and fundamental freedoms of all women is essential for the empowerment of women. While the significance of national and regional particularities and various historical, cultural and religious backgrounds must be borne in mind, it is the duty of States, regardless of their political, economic and cultural systems, to promote and protect all human rights and fundamental freedoms. The implementation of the Platform, as well as further actions and initiatives contained in this document, including through national laws and the formulation of strategies, policies, programmes and development priorities, is the sovereign responsibility of each State, in conformity with all human rights and fundamental freedoms, and the significance of and full respect for various religious and ethical values, cultural backgrounds and philosophical convictions of individuals and their communities should contribute to the full enjoyment by women of their human rights in order to achieve equality, development and peace.

The Platform for Action emphasises that women share common concerns that can be addressed only by working together and in partnership with men towards the common goal of gender equality around the world. It respects and values the full diversity of women's situations and conditions and recognizes that some women face particular barriers to their empowerment.

The Platform for Action recognises that women face barriers to full equality and advancement because of such factors as their race, age, language, ethnicity, culture, religion or disability, because they are indigenous women or because of other status. Many women encounter specific obstacles related to their family status, particularly as single parents; and to their socio-economic status, including their living conditions in rural, isolated or impoverished areas. Additional barriers also exist for refugee women, other displaced women, including internally displaced women as well as for immigrant women and migrant women, including women migrant workers. Many women are also particularly affected by environmental disasters, serious and infectious diseases and various forms of violence against women.

II. Achievements and Obstacles in the Implementation of the Twelve Critical Areas of the Platform for Action

Assessment of achievements and obstacles must be made in relation to the commitments made in the Beijing Platform for Action and its 12 critical areas, namely by looking into the actions taken and the results attained, as indicated in national reports as well as taking note of the reports of the Secretary-General and of the results, conclusions and agreements of the five regional meetings held in preparation for the special session of the General Assembly and other relevant sources. Such assessment shows that, even though significant positive developments can be identified, barriers remain and there is still the need to further implement the goals and commitments made in Beijing. The summary of achievements and of persistent or new obstacles can, therefore, constitute a global framework for the identification of further actions and initiatives to overcome obstacles and to achieve the full and accelerated implementation of the Platform for Action at all levels and in all areas.

A. Women and Poverty

Achievements: Considerable progress has been achieved in increasing recognition of gender dimensions of poverty and in the recognition that gender equality is one of the factors of specific importance for eradicating poverty particularly in relation to the feminization of poverty. Efforts have been made to integrate a gender perspective into poverty eradication policies and programmes by governments, in cooperation with non-governmental organisations. Multilateral, international and regional financial institutions are also giving increased attention to the incorporation of a gender perspective into their policies. Progress has been made by pursuing a two-pronged approach of promoting employment and income-generating activities for women and providing access to basic social services, including education and health care. Micro-credit and other financial instruments for women have emerged as a successful strategy for economic empowerment and have widened economic opportunities for some women living in poverty in particular in rural areas. Policy development has taken account of the particular needs of female-headed households. Research has enhanced the understanding of the differing impacts of poverty on women and men and tools have been developed to assist with this assessment.

5. *Obstacles*: Many factors have contributed to widening economic inequality between women and men including income

inequality, unemployment and deepening of poverty levels of the most vulnerable and marginalized groups. Debt burdens, excessive military spending, inconsistent with national security requirements, unilateral coercive measures not in accordance with international law and Charter of the United Nations, armed conflicts, foreign occupation, terrorism, low levels of ODA and the unfulfilled commitment to strive to fulfill the yet to be attained internationally agreed target of 0.7 per cent of the GNP of developed countries for overall official development assistance and 0.15 to 0.2 per cent for the Least Developed Countries as well as the lack of efficient use of resources, among other factors can constrain national efforts to combat poverty. In addition, gender inequalities and disparities in economic power-sharing, unequal distribution of unremunerated work between women and men, lack of technological and financial support for women's entrepreneurship, unequal access to, and control over capital, and resources, particularly land and credit and access to labour markets, as well as all harmful traditional and customary practices, have constrained women's economic empowerment and exacerbated the feminization of poverty. Fundamental economic restructuring experienced by the countries with economies in transition has led to lack of resources for poverty-eradication programmes aimed at empowerment of women.

B. Education and Training of Women

6. *Achievements*: There is an increased awareness that education is one of the most valuable means of achieving gender equality and the empowerment of women. Progress was achieved in women's and girls education and training at all levels especially where there was sufficient political commitment and resource allocation. Measures, were taken in all regions to initiate alternative education and training systems to reach women and girls in indigenous communities and other is advantaged and marginalized groups to encourage them to pursue all fields of study, in particular non-traditional fields of study, and to remove gender biases from education and training.

7. *Obstacles*: In some countries, efforts to eradicate illiteracy and strengthen literacy among women and girls and to increase their access to all levels and types of education were constrained by the lack of resources and insufficient political will and commitment to improve educational infrastructure and undertake educational reforms; persisting gender discrimination and bias including in teacher training; gender-based occupational stereotyping in schools, institutions of further education and

communities; lack of childcare facilities; persistent use of gender stereotypes in educational materials; and insufficient attention paid to the link between women's enrolment in higher educational institutions and labour market dynamics. The remote location of some communities and in some cases inadequate salaries and benefits make attracting and retaining teaching professionals difficult and can result in lower quality education. Additionally, in a number of countries, economic, social and infrastructural barriers, as well as traditional discriminatory practices have contributed to a lower enrolment and retention rates for girls. Little progress has been made in eradicating illiteracy in some developing countries, aggravating women's inequality at economic, social and political levels. In some of these countries, the inappropriate design and application of structural adjustment policies has had a particularly severe impact on the education sector, since they resulted in declining investment in education infrastructure.

C. Women and Health

8. *Achievements:* Programmes have been implemented to create awareness among policy makers and planners on the need for health programmes to cover all aspects of women's health throughout women's life cycle which have contributed to an increase in life expectancy in many countries. There is: increased attention to high mortality rates among women and girls as a result of malaria, tuberculosis, water borne diseases, communicable and diarrheal diseases and mal-nutrition; increased attention to sexual and reproductive health and reproductive rights of women as contained in para 94 and 95 of the Platform for Action, as well as in some countries increased emphasis on implementing para 96 of the Platform for Action; increased knowledge and use of family planning and contraceptive methods as well as increased awareness among men of their responsibility in family planning and contraceptive methods and their use; increased attention to sexually transmitted infections, including human immunodeficiency virus/acquired immunodeficiency syndrome (HIV/AIDS) among women and girls and methods to protect against such infections; increased attention to breast-feeding, nutrition, infants' and mothers' health; the introduction of a gender perspective in health and health related educational and physical activities, and gender-specific prevention and rehabilitation programmes on substance abuse, including tobacco, drugs and alcohol; increased attention to women's mental health, health conditions at work,

environmental considerations and recognition of the specific health needs of older women. The UN Special Session in June/ July 99 reviewed achievements and adopted key action in the field of women's health for further implementation of the ICPD Programme of Action.

9. *Obstacles:* Worldwide, the gap between and within rich and poor countries with respect to infant mortality and maternal mortality and morbidity rates, as well as with respect to measures addressing the health of women and girls given their special vulnerability regarding sexually transmitted infections including human immunodeficiency virus/acquired immunodeficiency syndrome (HIV/AIDS) and other sexual and reproductive health problems, together with endemic, infectious and communicable diseases such as malaria, tuberculosis, diarrheal and water-borne diseases and chronic non-transmissible diseases remains unacceptable. In some countries, such endemic, infectious and communicable diseases continue to take a toll on women and girls. In other countries, non-communicable diseases such as cardio/pulmonary diseases, hypertension and degenerative diseases remain among the major causes of mortality and morbidity among women. Despite progress in some countries, the rates of maternal mortality and morbidity remain unacceptably high in most countries. Investment in essential obstetric care remains insufficient in many countries. The absence of a holistic approach to health and health care for women and girls based on women's right to the enjoyment of the highest attainable standard of physical and mental health throughout the life-cycle has constrained progress. Some women continue to encounter barriers to their right to the enjoyment of the highest attainable standard of physical and mental health. The predominant focus of health care systems on treating illness rather than maintaining optimal health also prevents a holistic approach. There is, in some countries, insufficient attention to the role of social and economic determinants of health. A lack of access to clean water, adequate nutrition, safe sanitation, of gender-specific health research and technology, insufficient gender sensitivity in the provision of health information and health care and health services, including those related to environmental and occupational health hazards affect women in developing and developed countries. Poverty and the lack of development continue to affect the capacity of many developing countries to provide and expand quality health care. A shortage of financial and human resources, in particular in developing countries, as well as restructuring of the health sector and/or

the increasing trend to privatization of health care systems in some cases, has resulted in poor quality, reduced and insufficient health care services, and has also led to less attention to the health of the most vulnerable groups of women. Obstacles such as unequal power relationships between women and men where women often do not have the power to insist on safe and responsible sex practices and a lack of communication and understanding between men and women on women's health needs, inter alia, endanger women's health, particularly by increasing their susceptibility to sexually transmitted infections, including HIV/AIDS and affect women's access to health care and education, especially in relation to prevention. Adolescents, particularly adolescent girls continue to lack access to sexual and reproductive health information, education and services. Women, who are recipients of health care, are frequently not treated with respect, nor guaranteed privacy and confidentiality, and do not receive full information about options and services available. In some cases, health services and workers still do not conform to human rights and to ethical, professional and gender-sensitive standards in the delivery of women's health services nor do they ensure responsible, voluntary and informed consent. There continues to be a lack of information on availability and access to appropriate, affordable, primary health care services of high quality including sexual and reproductive health care, sufficient attention to maternal and emergency obstetric care as well as a lack of prevention, screening and treatment for breast, cervical and ovarian cancers and osteoporosis. The testing and development of male contraceptives is still insufficient. While some measures have been taken in some countries, the actions contained in paragraphs 106 j and 106 k of the Platform for Action regarding the health impact of unsafe abortion and the need to reduce the recourse to abortion have not been fully implemented. The rising incidence of tobacco use among women, particularly young women has increased their risk of cancer, and other serious diseases as well as gender-specific risks from tobacco and environmental tobacco smoke.

D. Violence Against Women

10. *Achievements*: It is widely accepted that violence against women and girls, whether occurring in public or private life, is a human rights issue. It is accepted that violence against women where perpetrated or condoned by the state or its agents constitutes a human rights violation. It is also accepted that states have an obligation to exercise due diligence to prevent investigate and

punish acts of violence whether those acts are perpetrated by the state or private persons and provide protection to victims. There is increased awareness and commitment to prevent and combat violence against women and girls, including domestic violence, which violates and impairs or nullifies the enjoyment of their human rights and fundamental freedoms through inter-alia, improved legislation, policies and programmes. Governments have initiated policy reforms and mechanisms such as interdepartmental committees, guidelines and protocols, national, multidisciplinary and co-ordinated programmes to address violence. Some Governments have also introduced or reformed laws to protect women and girls from all forms of violence and laws to prosecute the perpetrators. There is an increasing recognition at all levels that all forms of violence against women seriously affect their health. Health care providers are seen to have a significant role to play in addressing this matter. Some progress has been made in the provision of services for abused women and children, including legal services, shelters, special health services and counseling, hot lines and police units with special training. Education for law enforcement personnel, members of the judiciary, health care providers and welfare workers is being promoted. Educational materials for women and public awareness campaigns have been developed as well as research on the root causes of violence. There is increasing research and specialized studies being conducted on gender roles, in particular on men's and boys' roles, and all forms of violence against women, as well as on the situation of and impact on children growing up in families where violence occurs. Successful cooperation has been achieved between governmental and non-governmental organizations in the field of preventing violence against women. The active support of civil society in particular women's organizations and NGOs has had an important role, inter-alia in promoting awareness-raising campaigns and in the provision of support services to women victims of violence. Efforts towards the eradication of harmful traditional practices, including female genital mutilation which is a form of violence against women has received national, regional and international policy support. Many Governments have introduced educational and outreach programmes, as well as legislative measures criminalizing these practices. In addition, this support includes the appointment of a Special Ambassador for the Elimination of Female Genital Mutilation by the United Nations Population Fund (UNFPA).

11. *Obstacles*: Women continue to be victims of various forms of violence. Inadequate understanding of the root causes of all forms of violence against women and girls hinders efforts to eliminate violence against women and girls. There is a lack of comprehensive programmes dealing with the perpetrators, including programmes, where appropriate, which would enable them to solve problems without violence. Inadequate data on violence further impede informed policymaking and analysis. Socio-cultural attitudes which are discriminatory and economic inequalities reinforce women's subordinate place in society. This makes women and girls vulnerable to many forms of violence, such as physical, sexual and psychological violence occurring in the family, including battering, sexual abuse of female children in the household, dowry related violence, marital rape, female genital mutilation and other traditional practices harmful to women, non spousal violence and violence related to exploitation. In many countries, a co-ordinated multidisciplinary approach to responding to violence which includes the health system, work places, the media, the education system, as well as the justice system is still limited. Domestic violence, including sexual violence in marriage is still treated as a private matter in some countries. Insufficient awareness of the consequences of domestic violence, how to prevent it, and the rights of victims still exists. Although improving, the legal and legislative measures, especially in the criminal justice area to eliminate different forms of violence against women and children, including domestic violence and child pornography are weak in many countries. Prevention strategies also remain fragmented and reactive and there is a lack of programmes on these issues. It is also noted that in some countries problems have arisen from the use of new information and communication technologies for trafficking in women and children and for the purposes of all forms of economic and sexual exploitation.

E. Women and Armed Conflict

12. *Achievements*: There is a wider recognition that armed conflict has different destructive impacts on women and men and that a gender sensitive approach to the application of international human rights law and international humanitarian law is important. Steps have been taken at the national and international levels to address abuses against women, including increased attention to ending impunity for crimes against women in situations of armed conflict. The work of the International Criminal Tribunal for the Former Yugoslavia and the

International Criminal Tribunal for Rwanda has been an important contribution to address violence against women in the context of armed conflict. Also of historical significance is the adoption of the Rome Statute of the International Criminal Court which provides that rape, sexual slavery, enforced prostitution, forced pregnancy, enforced sterilization and other forms of sexual violence are war crimes when committed in the context of armed conflict and also under defined circumstances, crimes against humanity. Women's contribution in peace-building, peacemaking and conflict resolution is being increasingly recognized. Education and training on non-violent, conflict resolution have been introduced. Progress has been made on the dissemination and implementation of the guidelines for the protection of refugee women, and on addressing the needs of displaced women. Gender-based persecution has been accepted as a basis for refugee status in some countries. There is recognition by Governments, the international community and organizations, in particular the United Nations, that women and men experience humanitarian emergencies differently and there is a need for a more holistic support for refugee and displaced women, including those who have suffered all forms of abuse, including gender-specific abuse to ensure equal access to appropriate and adequate food and nutrition, clean water, safe sanitation, shelter, education, social and health services, including reproductive health care and maternity care. There is greater recognition of the need to integrate a gender perspective in the planning, design and implementation of humanitarian assistance and to provide adequate resources. Humanitarian relief agencies and civil society, including non-governmental organizations, have played an increasingly important role in the provision of humanitarian assistance as well as in the design where appropriate and implementation of programmes to address the needs of women and girls, including refugee and displaced women and girls in humanitarian emergencies, and in conflict and post-conflict situations.

13. *Obstacles*: Peace is inextricably linked to equality between women and men and development. Armed and other types of conflicts, wars of aggression, foreign occupation, colonial or other alien domination, as well as terrorism, continue to cause serious obstacles to the advancement of women. The targeting of civilians, including women and children, the displacement of people, and the recruitment of child soldiers in violation of national or international law, by state and/or non state factors, which occur in armed conflicts, have had a particular adverse

impact on gender equality and women's human rights. Armed conflict creates or exacerbates the high level of female-headed households, which in many cases are living in poverty. The underrepresentation, at all levels, of women from decision-making positions such as special envoys or special representatives of the Secretary-General in peacekeeping, peace-building, post-conflict reconciliation and reconstruction as well as lack of gender awareness in these areas presents serious obstacles. There has been a failure to provide sufficient resources and to adequately distribute those resources, to address the needs of increasing numbers of refugees, who are mostly women and children, particularly to developing countries hosting large numbers of refugees; international assistance has not kept pace with the increasing number of refugees. The growing number of internally displaced persons and the provision of their needs, in particular women and children, continue to represent a double burden to the affected countries and their financial resources. Inadequate training of personnel dealing with the needs of women in situations of armed conflict or as refugees such as a shortage of specific programmes that address healing of women from trauma and skills training, remains a problem.

Excessive military expenditures, including global military expenditures, trade in arms and investment for arms production taking into consideration national security requirements direct the possible allocation of funds away from social and economic development, in particular for the advancement of women. In several countries, economic sanctions have had social and humanitarian impact on the civilian population in particular women and children.

In some countries, advancement of women is adversely affected by unilateral measures not in accordance with international law and the Charter of the United Nations that create obstacles to trade relations among States, impede the full realization of social and economic development and hinder the well being of the population in the affected countries, with particular consequences for women and children.

In situations of armed conflict there are continued violations of human rights of women, which are violations of fundamental principles of international human rights law and international humanitarian law. There has been an increase of all forms of violence against women, including sexual slavery, rape, systematic rape, sexual abuse and forced pregnancies in the situations of armed conflict. Displacement compounded by loss of home and property, poverty, family disintegration and separation and other consequences of armed conflict is severely affecting population, especially women and children. Girls are also abducted or recruited in violation of international law, into situations of armed conflict including, *inter alia,* as combatants, sexual slaves or providers of domestic services.

F. Women and the Economy

14. *Achievements*: There is increased participation of women in the labour market and subsequent gain in economic autonomy. Some Governments have introduced a variety of measures, that address women's economic and social rights, equal access to and control over economic resources and equality in employment. Other measures include ratification of international labour conventions as well as enacting or strengthening legislation to make it compatible with these conventions. There is increased awareness of the need to reconcile employment and family responsibilities and the positive effect of measures such as maternity and paternity leave and also parental leave, and child and family care services and benefits. Some Governments have made provisions to address discriminatory and abusive behaviour in the workplace and to prevent unhealthy working conditions and have established funding mechanisms to promote women's roles in entrepreneurship, education and training, including scientific and technical skills and decision-making. Research has been conducted on barriers to economic empowerment faced by women including the relationship between remunerated and unremunerated work and tools are being developed to assist with this assessment.

15. *Obstacles:* The importance of a gender perspective in the development of macro-economic policy is still not widely recognised. Many women still work in the rural areas and the informal economy as subsistence producers, and in the service sector with low levels of income and little job and social security. Many women with comparable skills and experience are confronted with a gender wage gap and lag behind men in income and career mobility in the formal sector. Equal pay for women and men for equal work, or work of equal value, has not yet been fully realised. Gender discrimination in hiring and promotion and related to pregnancy including through pregnancy testing, and sexual harassment in the work place persist. In some countries, women's full and equal rights to own land and other property, including through the right to inheritance, is not recognised yet in national legislation.

Progression in the professions, in most cases, is still more difficult for women, due to the lack of structures and measures that take into account maternity and family responsibilities. In some cases, persistent gender stereotyping has led to a lower status of male workers as fathers and to an insufficient encouragement for men to reconcile professional and family responsibilities. Lack of family-friendly policies regarding the organization of work increases these difficulties. Effective implementation of legislation and practical support systems is still inadequate. The combination of remunerated work and care-giving within families, households and communities still leads to a disproportionate burden for women, as long as there is insufficient sharing of tasks and responsibilities by men. It is still also women who perform the larger part of unremunerated work.

G. Women in Power and Decision-Making

16. *Achievements:* There has been growing acceptance of the importance to society of the full participation of women in decision-making and power at all levels and in all fora, including inter-governmental, governmental, and non-governmental sectors. In some countries, women have also attained higher positions in these spheres. An increasing number of countries applied affirmative and positive action policies, including quota systems or voluntary agreements in some countries, measurable goals and targets, developed training programmes for women's leadership and introduced measures to reconcile family and work responsibilities of both women and men. National mechanisms and machineries for the advancement of women as well as national and international networks of women politicians, parliamentarians, activists and professionals in various fields have been established or upgraded and strengthened.

17. *Obstacles*: Despite general acceptance of the need for a gender balance in decision-making bodies at all levels, a gap between *de jure* and *de facto* equality has persisted. Notwithstanding substantial improvements of *de jure* equality between women and men, the actual participation of women at the highest levels of national and international decision-making has not significantly changed since Beijing 1995 and gross under-representation of women in decision-making bodies in all areas, including *inter alia* politics, conflict prevention and resolution mechanisms, the economy, the environment and the media hinders the inclusion of a gender perspective in these critical spheres of influence. Women continue to be underrepresented at

the legislative, ministerial and sub-ministerial levels, as well as at the highest levels of the corporate sector and other social and economic institutions. Traditionally assigned gender roles limit women's choices in education and careers and compel women to assume the burden for household responsibilities. Initiatives and programmes aimed at women's increased participation in decision-making were hindered by a lack of human and financial resources for training and advocacy for political careers; gender-sensitive attitudes towards women in society, awareness of women to engage in decision-making in some cases; accountability of elected officials and political parties for promoting gender equality and women's participation in public life; social awareness of the importance of balanced participation of women and men in decision-making; willingness on the part of men to share power; sufficient dialogue and co-operation with women's non-governmental organizations, along with organizational and political structures, which enable all women to participate in all spheres of political decision-making.

H. Institutional Mechanisms for the Advancement of Women

18. *Achievements*: National machineries have been instituted or strengthened and recognised as the institutional base acting as "catalysts" for promoting gender equality, gender mainstreaming and monitoring of the implementation of the Platform for Action and in many instances of the Convention on the Elimination of All Forms of Discrimination against Women. In many countries, progress has been achieved in terms of the visibility, status, outreach and coordination of activities of these machineries. Gender mainstreaming has been widely acknowledged as a strategy to enhance the impact of policies to promote gender equality. The goal of the strategy is to incorporate a gender perspective in all legislation, policies, programmes, and projects. These machineries, despite their limited financial resources, have made a significant contribution to the development of human resources in the field of gender studies and also contributed to the growing efforts for the generation and dissemination of data disaggregated by sex and age, gender-sensitive research and documentation. Within the UN system much progress has been made in the mainstreaming of a gender perspective including through the development of tools and the creation of gender focal points.

19. *Obstacles*: In a number of countries, inadequate financial and human resources and a lack of political will and commitment

are the main obstacles confronting national machineries. This is further exacerbated by insufficient understanding of gender equality and gender mainstreaming among government structures, as well as prevailing gender stereotypes, discriminatory attitudes, competing government priorities and in some countries unclear mandates, marginalized location within the national government structures, lack of data disaggregated by sex and age in many areas and insufficiently applied methods for assessing progress, in addition to paucity of authority and insufficient links to civil society. The activities of the national machineries were also hindered by structural and communication problems within and among government agencies.

I. Human Rights of Women

20. *Achievements*: Legal reforms have been undertaken to prohibit all forms of discrimination and discriminatory provisions have been eliminated in civil, penal and personal status law governing marriage and family relations, all forms of violence, women's property and ownership rights and women's political, work and employment rights. Steps have been taken to realize women's de facto enjoyment of their human rights through the creation of an enabling environment, including the adoption of policy measures, the improvement of enforcement and monitoring mechanisms and the implementation of legal literacy and awareness campaigns at all levels. The Convention on the Elimination of All Forms of Discrimination against Women has been ratified or acceded to by 165 countries and its full implementation has been promoted by the Committee on the Elimination of Discrimination against Women. The 54th session of the General Assembly adopted the Optional Protocol to the Convention allowing women claiming to be victims of a violation of any of the rights set forth in the Convention by a State party to submit their claims to the Committee on the Elimination of Discrimination against Women, to which non-governmental organizations contributed by raising awareness and generating support for its adoption. Women's NGOs have also contributed to raising awareness that women's rights are human rights. They also generated support for the inclusion of a gender perspective in the elaboration of the Rome Statute of the International Criminal Court. Progress has also been made to integrate the human rights of women and mainstream a gender perspective into the UN system, including into the work of the Office of the High Commissioner on Human Rights and of the Commission on Human Rights.

21. *Obstacles*: Gender discrimination and all other forms of discrimination, in particular racism, racial discrimination, xenophobia and related intolerance continue to cause threat to the enjoyment of women of their human rights and fundamental freedoms. In situations of armed conflict and foreign occupation, human rights of women have been extensively violated. Even though a number of countries have ratified the Convention on the Elimination of All Forms of Discrimination against Women the goal of universal ratification by the year 2000 has not been achieved, and there continues to be a large number of reservations to the Convention. While there is an increasing acceptance of gender equality, many countries have not yet implemented fully the provisions of the Convention. Discriminatory legislation as well has harmful traditional and customary practices and negative stereotyping of women and men still persist. Family, civil, penal, labour and commercial laws or codes, or administrative rules and regulations, still have not fully integrated a gender perspective. Legislative and regulatory gaps, as well as lack of implementation and enforcement of legislation and regulations, perpetuate de jure as well as de facto inequality and discrimination, and in a few cases, new laws discriminating against women have been introduced. In many countries, women have insufficient access to the law, resulting from illiteracy, lack of legal literacy, information and resources, insensitivity and gender bias, and lack of awareness of the human rights of women by law enforcement officials and the judiciary who in many cases fail to respect the human rights of women and the dignity and worth of the human person. There is insufficient recognition of women's and girls' reproductive rights, as well as barriers to their full enjoyment of those rights, which embrace certain human rights as defined in the Beijing Platform for Action, paragraph 95. Some women and girls continue to encounter barriers to justice and enjoyment of their human rights because of such factors as their race, language, ethnicity, culture, religion, disability or socio-economic class or because they are indigenous people, migrants, including women migrant worker, displaced women or refugees.

J. Women and the Media

22. *Achievements*: The establishment of local, national and international women's media networks has contributed to global information dissemination, exchange of views and support to women's groups active in media work. The development of information and communication technologies, especially the Internet, has provided

improved communication opportunities for the empowerment of women and girls which enabled an increasing number of women to contribute to knowledge sharing, networking and electronic commerce activities. The number of women's media organizations and programmes has increased, facilitating the aims of increased participation and promotion of positive portrayals of women in the media. Progress has been made to combat negative images of women by establishing professional guidelines and voluntary codes of conduct encouraging fair gender portrayal and the use of non-sexist language in media programmes.

23. *Obstacles*: Negative, violent and/or degrading images of women, including pornography, stereotyped portrayals, have increased in different forms using new communication technologies in some instances, and bias against women remains in the media. Poverty, the lack of access and opportunities, illiteracy, lack of computer literacy and language barriers, prevent some women from using the information and communication technologies, including the Internet. Development of and access to Internet infrastructure is limited especially in developing countries and particularly for women.

K. Women and the Environment

24. *Achievements*: Some national environment policies and programmes have incorporated gender perspectives. In recognition of the link between gender equality, poverty eradication, sustainable development and environmental protection, governments have included income-generating activities for women, as well as training in natural resource management and environmental protection in their development strategies. Projects have been launched to preserve and utilize women's traditional ecological knowledge, including the traditional technological knowledge of indigenous women, in the management of natural resources, and preservation of bio-diversity.

25. *Obstacles*: There is still a lack of public awareness about environmental risks faced by women and of the benefits of gender equality for promoting environmental protection. Women's limited access to technical skills, resources and information, in particular in developing countries, due to among others gender inequality, have impeded women's effective participation in decision-making, regarding the sustainable environment, including at the international level. Research, action, targeted strategies and public awareness remain limited regarding the differential impacts and implications of environmental problems

for women and men. Real solutions to environmental problems including environmental degradation need to address the root causes of these problems such as foreign occupation. Environmental policies and programmes lack a gender perspective and fail to take into account women's roles and contributions to environmental sustainability.

L. The Girl-Child

26. *Achievements:* Some progress was made in primary and, to a lesser extent, in secondary and tertiary education for girls, owing to the creation of a more gender-sensitive school environment, improved educational infrastructure, increased enrolment and retention, support mechanisms for pregnant adolescents and adolescent mothers, increased non-formal education opportunities and enhanced attendance at science and technology classes. Increased attention was given to the health of the girl child, including the sexual and reproductive health of adolescents. An increasing number of countries introduced legislation to ban female genital mutilation and imposed heavier penalties on those involved in sexual abuse, trafficking and all other forms of exploitation of the girl child, including for commercial ends. A recent achievement has been the adoption of the Optional Protocols to the Convention on the Rights of the Child on Involvement of Children in Armed Conflict and on the Sale of Children, Child Prostitution and Child Pornography by the 54th Session of the General Assembly.

27. *Obstacles*: The persistence of poverty, discriminatory attitudes towards women and girls, negative cultural attitudes and practices against girls as well as negative stereotyping of girls and boys which limit girls' potential, and inadequate awareness of the specific situation of the girl child, child labour, and the heavy burden of domestic responsibilities on girls, inadequate nutrition and access to health services, and lack of finance which often prevent her from pursuing and completing her education and training, have contributed to a lack of opportunities and possibilities for girls to become confident and self-reliant, and independent adults. Poverty, lack of parental support and guidance, lack of information and education, abuse and all forms of exploitation of, and violence against the girl child, in many cases result in unwanted pregnancies and transmission of HIV which may also lead to a restriction of educational opportunities. Programmes for the girl child were hindered by a lack of or an insufficient allocation of financial and human resources. There were few established national mechanisms to implement policies

and programmes for the girl child and, in some cases, coordination among responsible institutions was insufficient. The increased awareness of the health needs, including the sexual and reproductive health needs of adolescents has not yet resulted in sufficient provision of necessary information and services. Despite advances in legal protection, there is increased sexual abuse and sexual exploitation of the girl child. Adolescents continue to lack the education and service needed to enable them to deal in a positive and responsible way with their sexuality.

III. Current Challenges Affecting the Full Implementation of the Beijing Declaration and the Platform for Action

28. The review and appraisal of the implementation of the Beijing Declaration and the Platform for Action occurred in a rapidly changing global context. Since 1995, a number of issues have gained prominence and acquired new dimensions which pose additional challenges to the full and accelerated implementation of the Platform in order to realize gender equality, development and peace by governments, intergovernmental bodies, international organizations, the private sector, and non-governmental organizations as appropriate. Continued political commitment to gender equality, at all levels, is needed for the full implementation of the Platform for Action.

29. Globalisation has presented new challenges for the fulfillment of the commitments made and the realisation of the goals of the Beijing Conference. The globalisation process has in some countries, resulted in policy shifts in favour of more open trade and financial flows, privatisation of state-owned enterprises and in many cases lower public spending particularly on social services. This change has transformed patterns of production and accelerated technological advances in information and communication and affected the lives of women, both as workers and consumers. In a large number of countries, particularly in developing and least developed countries, these changes have also adversely impacted on the lives of women and have increased inequality. The gender impact of these changes has not been systematically evaluated. Globalisation also has cultural, political, and social impacts affecting cultural values, lifestyles and forms of communication as well as implications for the achievement of sustainable development. Benefits of the growing global economy have been unevenly distributed leading to wider economic disparities, the feminisation of poverty, increased gender inequality, including

through often deteriorating work conditions and unsafe working environments especially in the informal economy and rural areas. While globalisation has brought greater economic opportunities and autonomy to some women, many others have been marginalised, due to deepening inequalities among and within countries, by depriving them from the benefits of this process. Although in many countries the level of participation of women in the labour force has risen, in other cases, the application of certain economic policies have had a negative impact such that increases in women's employment often have not been matched by improvements in wages, promotions and working conditions. In many cases, women continue to be employed in low paid, part-time, and contract jobs marked by insecurity and by safety and health hazards. In many countries women, especially new entrants into the labour market, continue to be among the first to lose jobs and the last to be rehired.

30. Increasing disparities in the economic situation among and within countries, coupled with a growing economic interdependence and dependence of States on external factors as well as the financial crises have, in recent years, altered prospects of growth and caused economic instability in many countries, with a heavy impact on the lives of women. These have affected the ability of States to provide social protection and social security as well as funding for the implementation of the Platform for Action. Such difficulties are also reflected in the shift of the cost of social protection, social security and other welfare provisions from the public sector to the household. The decreasing levels of funding available through international cooperation has contributed to further marginalization of a large number of developing countries and countries with economies in transition within which women are amongst the poorest. The agreed target of 0.7 per cent of the gross national product of developed countries for overall official development assistance has not been achieved. These factors have contributed to the increasing feminization of poverty, which has undermined efforts to achieve gender equality. Limited funding at the state-level makes it imperative that innovative approaches to the allocation of existing resources be employed, not only by Governments but also by NGOs and the private sector. One such innovation is the gender analysis of public budgets which is emerging as an important tool for determining the differential impact of expenditures on women and men to help ensure equitable use

of existing resources. This analysis is crucial to promote gender equality.

30bis. The impact of globalisation and structural adjustment programmes, the high costs of external debt servicing and declining terms of international trade, in several developing countries, have worsened the existing obstacles to development, aggravating the feminization of poverty. Negative consequences of structural adjustment programmes, stemming from the inappropriate design and application, have continued to place a disproportionate burden on women, *inter-alia* through budget cuts in basic social services, including education and health.

30ter. There is greater acceptance that the increasing debt burden faced by most indebted developing countries is unsustainable and constitutes one of the principle obstacles to achieving progress in people-centered sustainable development and poverty eradication. For many developing countries, as well as countries with economies in transition, excessive debt servicing has severely constrained their capacity to promote social development and provide basic services and has affected full implementation of the Platform for Action.

30quinter: In countries with economies in transition women are bearing most of the hardships induced by the economic restructuring and being the first to lose jobs in times of recession. They are being squeezed out from fast growth sectors. Loss of childcare facilities due to elimination or privatization of state work places, increased need for older care without the corresponding facilities, continuing inequality of access to training for finding re-employment and to productive assets for entering or expanding businesses are current challenges facing women in these countries.

31. Science and technology, as fundamental components of development, are transforming patterns of production, contributing to the creation of jobs and new job classifications, and ways of working, and contributing to the establishment of a knowledge-based society. Technological change can bring new opportunities for all women in all fields if they have equal access, and adequate training. Women should also be actively involved in the definition, design, development, implementation and gender impact evaluation of policies related to these changes. Many women world-wide are yet to effectively use these new communications technologies for networking, advocacy, exchange of information business, education, media consultation and e-commerce initiatives. For instance, millions of the world's

poorest women and men still do not have access to and benefits from science and technologies and are currently excluded from this new field and the opportunities it presents.

32. The patterns of migratory flows of labour are changing. Women and girls are increasingly involved in internal, regional and international labour migration to pursue many occupations mainly in farm labour, domestic work and some forms of entertainment work. While this situation increases their earning opportunities and self-reliance, it also exposes them, particularly the poor, uneducated, unskilled and/or undocumented migrants to inadequate working conditions, increased health risk, the risk of trafficking, economic and sexual exploitation, racism, racial discrimination and xenophobia, and other forms of abuse, which impair their enjoyment of their human rights, and in some cases, constitute violations of human rights.

33. While recognising that governments have the primary responsibility to develop and implement policies to promote gender equality, partnerships between governments and different factors of civil society are increasingly recognized as an important mechanism to achieve this goal. Additional innovative approaches can be further developed to foster this collaboration.

36. In some countries, current demographic trends, which show that lowered fertility rates, increased life expectancy and lower mortality rates, have contributed to ageing of the population, and increase in chronic health conditions and have implications for health care systems and spending, informal care systems and research. Given the gap between male and female life expectancy, the number of widows and older single women has increased considerably, often leading to their social isolation and other social challenges. Societies have much to gain from the knowledge and life experience of older women. On the other hand, the current generation of young people is the largest in history. Adolescent girls and young women have particular needs which will require increasing attention.

37. The rapid progression of the HIV/AIDS pandemic, particularly in the developing world, has had a devastating impact on women. Responsible behaviour and gender equality are among the important prerequisites for its prevention. There is also the need for more effective strategies to empower women to have control over and decide freely and responsibly on matters related to their sexuality, to protect themselves from high risk and irresponsible behaviour leading to sexually transmitted infections including HIV/AIDS and to promote responsible, safe

and respectful behaviour by men and to also promote gender equality. HIV/AIDS is an urgent public health issue, is outstripping efforts to contain it and, in many countries, is reversing hard one gains of development. The burden of care for people living with HIV/AIDS and for children orphaned by HIV/AIDS falls particularly on women, as infrastructures are inadequate to respond to the challenges being posed. Women with HIV/AIDS often suffer from discrimination and a stigma and are often victims of violence. Issues related to prevention, mother-to-child transmission of HIV/AIDS, breastfeeding, information and education in particular of youth, curbing high risks behaviour, intravenous drug users, support groups, counseling and voluntary testing, partner notification, and provision and high costs of essential drugs have not been sufficiently addressed. There are positive signs in the fight against HIV/AIDS in some countries that behavoural changes have occurred among young people and experience shows that educational programmes for young people can lead to a more positive view on gender relations and gender equality, delayed sexual initiation and reduced risks of sexually transmitted infections.

37bis. Growing drug and substance abuse among young women and girls, both in developed and developing countries, has raised the need for increased efforts towards demand reduction and fight against illicit production, supply and trafficking of narcotic drugs, and psychotropic substances.

38. The increase in casualties and damage caused by natural disasters has raised awareness of the inefficiencies and inadequacies in the existing approaches and intervention methods in responding to such emergency situations, in which women, more often than men, are burdened with the responsibility of meeting the immediate daily needs of their families. This situation has raised awareness that a gender perspective must be incorporated whenever disaster prevention, mitigation and recovery strategies are being developed and implemented.

41. The changing context of gender relations, as well as the discussion on gender equality has led to increased reassessment of gender roles. This has further encouraged a discussion on the roles and responsibilities of women and men working together towards gender equality and the need for changing those stereotypical and traditional roles that limit women's full potential. There is a need for balanced participation between women and men in remunerated and unremunerated work.

Failure to recognize and measure in quantitative terms unremunerated work of women which is often not valued in national accounts has meant that women's full contribution to social and economic development remains underestimated and undervalued. As long as there is insufficient sharing of tasks and responsibilities with men, the combination of remunerated work and care-giving will lead to the continued disproportionate burden for women in comparison to men.

IV. Actions and Initiatives to Overcome Obstacles and to Achieve the Full and Accelerated Implementation of the Beijing Platform for Action

42. In view of the evaluation of progress made five years since the Beijing Conference in implementing the Beijing Declaration and Platform for Action, contained in Chapter II, as well as the current challenges affecting its full realization, outlined in Chapter III, Governments now recommit themselves to the Beijing Declaration and Platform for Action and also commit to further actions and initiatives to overcome the obstacles and address the challenges. Governments, in taking continued and additional steps to achieve the goals of the Platform, recognize that the full enjoyment of all human rights—civil, cultural, economic, political and social, including the right to development—are universal, indivisible, interdependent and interrelated, and are essential for realizing gender equality, development and peace in the twenty-first century.

43. Organisations of the United Nations system and the Bretton Woods institutions, as well as the World Trade Organization, other international and regional intergovernmental bodies, parliaments, civil society, including the private sector and NGOs, trade unions and other stakeholders are called upon to support government efforts and, where appropriate, develop complementary programmes of their own to achieve full and effective implementation of the Platform for Action.

43bis. Governments and intergovernmental organizations recognize the contribution and complementary role of NGOs, with full respect for their autonomy, in ensuring the effective implementation of the Platform for Action and should continue to strengthen partnerships with NGOs, particularly women's organizations in contributing to the effective implementation and follow-up of the Platform for Action.

43ter. Experience has shown that the goal of gender equality can be fully achieved only in the context of renewed relations among different stakeholders at all levels. The full effective participation of women on the basis of equality in all spheres of society is necessary to contribute to this goal.

44. Achieving gender equality and empowerment of women requires redressing inequalities between women and men and girls and boys and ensuring their equal rights, responsibilities, opportunities, and possibilities. Gender equality implies that women's as well as men's needs, interests, concerns, experiences and priorities are an integral dimension of the design, implementation, national monitoring, and follow-up and evaluation, including at the international level, of all actions in all areas.

46. By adopting the Platform for Action governments and the international community agreed to a common development agenda with gender equality and women's empowerment as underlying principles. The efforts towards ensuring women's participation in development have expanded and need to combine a focus on women's conditions and basic needs with an holistic approach based on equal rights and partnerships, promotion and protection of all human rights and fundamental freedoms. Policies and programmes should be formulated to achieve the goal of people-centered sustainable development, secure livelihoods and adequate social protection measures, including safety nets, strengthened support systems for families equal access to and control over financial and economic resources, and eliminate increasing and disproportionate poverty among women. All economic policies, institutions and resource allocation should adopt a gender perspective to ensure that development dividends are shared on equal grounds.

46bis. Increased efforts are needed to provide equal access to education, health, and social services and to ensure women's and girls' rights to education and the enjoyment of the highest attainable standard of physical and mental health and well-being throughout the life cycle, as well as adequate, affordable and universally accessible health care and services including sexual and reproductive health, particularly in the face of the HIV/AIDS pandemic; they are also necessary with regard to the growing proportion of older women.

47. Given that a majority of the world's women are subsistence producers and users of environmental resources, there is a need to recognise and integrate women's knowledge and priorities in the conservation and management of such resources to ensure their sustainability. Programmes and infrastructures that are

gender-sensitive are needed in order to effectively respond to disaster and emergency situations that threaten the environment, livelihood security, as well as the management of the basic requirements of daily life.

47bis. Sustaining the livelihoods of populations in States with limited or scarce resources, including Small Island Developing States is critically dependent on the preservation and protection of the environment. Women's customary knowledge, management and sustainable use of biodiversity should be recognised.

48bis. Continue to design efforts for the promotion of respect for cultural diversity and dialogue among and within civilizations in a manner which contributes to the implementation of the Platform for Action, which aims at the empowerment of women and the full realization of all human rights and fundamental freedoms for all women and in a manner which ensures that gender equality and the full enjoyment of all human rights by women are not undermined;

Note: ***To be Moved to Section IV, Action to be Taken at National and International Level***

49. Political will and commitment at all levels are crucial to ensure mainstreaming of a gender perspective in the adoption and implementation of comprehensive and action oriented policies in all areas. Policy commitments are essential for further developing the necessary framework which ensures women's equal access to and control over economic and financial resources, training, services and institutions as well as their participation in decision-making and management. Policy making processes require the partnership of women and men at all levels. Men and boys should also be actively involved and encouraged in all efforts to achieve the goals of the Platform for Action and its implementation.

51. Violence against women and girls is a major obstacle to the achievement of the objectives of gender equality, development and peace. Violence against women both violates and impairs or nullifies the enjoyment by women of their human rights and fundamental freedoms. Gender based violence, such as battering and other domestic violence, sexual abuse, sexual slavery and exploitation, and international trafficking in women and children, forced prostitution and sexual harassment, as well as violence against women, resulting from cultural prejudice, racism and racial discrimination, xenophobia, pornography, ethnic cleansing, armed conflict, foreign occupation, religious

and anti-religious extremism and terrorism are incompatible with the dignity and worth of the human person and must be combated and eliminated.

51ter. Women play a critical role in the family. The family is the basic unit of society and is a strong force for social cohesion and integration and as such should be strengthened. The inadequate support to women and insufficient protection and support to their respective families affect society as a whole and undermines efforts to achieve gender equality. In different cultural, political and social systems, various forms of the family exist and the rights, capabilities and responsibilities of family members must be respected. Women's social and economic contributions to the welfare of the family and the social significance of maternity and paternity continue to be inadequately addressed. Motherhood and fatherhood and the role of parents and legal guardians in the family and in the upbringing of children and the importance of all family members to the family's well-being is also acknowledged and must not be a basis for discrimination. Women also continue to bear a disproportionate share of the household responsibilities and the care of children, the sick and the elderly. Such imbalance needs to be consistently addressed through appropriate policies and programmes, in particular those geared towards education and through legislation where appropriate. In order to achieve full partnership, both in public and private spheres, both women and men must be enabled to reconcile and share equally work responsibilities and family responsibilities.

52. Strong national machineries for the advancement of women and promotion of gender equality require political commitment at the highest level and all necessary, human and financial resources to initiate, recommend and facilitate the development, adoption and monitoring of policies, legislation, programmes and capacity-building for the empowerment of women and to act as catalysts for open public dialogue on gender equality as a societal goal. This would enable them to promote the advancement of women and mainstreaming a gender perspective in policy and programmes in all areas, to play an advocacy role, and to ensure equal access to all institutions and resources, as well as enhanced capacity building for women in all sectors. Reforms to meet the challenges of the changing world are essential to ensure women's equal access to institutions and organizations. Institutional and conceptual changes are a strategic and important aspect of creating an enabling environment for the implementation of the Platform for Action.

53. Programme support to enhance women's opportunities, potentials and activities need to have a dual focus: one the one hand, programmes aimed at meeting the basic as well as the specific needs of women for capacity building, organizational development and empowerment; and on the other, gender mainstreaming in all programme formulation and implementation activities. It is particularly important to expand into new areas of programming to advance gender equality in response to current challenges.

53bis. Girls and women of all ages with any form of disability are generally among the more vulnerable and marginalised of society. There is therefore need to take into account and to address their concerns in all policy making and programming. Special measures are needed at all levels to integrate them into the mainstream of development.

54. Effective and coordinated plans and programmes for the full implementation of the Platform for Action require a clear knowledge on the situation of women and girls, a clear research-based knowledge and data disaggregated by sex, short and long-term time-bound targets and measurable goals and follow-up mechanisms to assess progress. Efforts are needed to ensure capacity building for all the factors involved in the achievement of these goals. Efforts are also needed at the national level, to increase transparency and accountability.

55. The realisation of the goals of gender equality, development and peace at the national and international level needs to be supported by the allocation of necessary human and financial resources for specific and targeted activities to ensure gender equality at the local, national, regional and international level as well as by enhanced and increased international cooperation. The explicit attention to these goals in budgetary processes at the national, regional and international level is essential.

55bis. Recognising the persistent and increasing burden of poverty on women in many countries, particularly in developing countries, it is essential to continue from a gender perspective to review, modify and implement integrated macro-economic and social policies and programmes, including, *inter alia,* those related to structural adjustment and external debt problems, to ensure universal and equitable access to social services, in particular to education, and affordable quality health care services and equal access to and control over economic resources.

Note: To be Moved between Paras 46 and 46 bis

Actions to be Taken at the National Level

Actions to be taken by Governments

100 a. Set and encourage the use of explicit short and long-term time bound targets or measurable goals, including where appropriate, quotas, to promote progress towards gender balance, including women's equal access to and full participation on a basis of equality with men in all areas and at all levels of public life, especially in decision and policy making positions, in political parties and political activities, in all government ministries and at key policy-making institutions, as well as in local development bodies and authorities;

100 e. Address the barriers faced by women, particularly by indigenous and other marginalized women, in accessing and participating in politics and decision-making, including lack of training, women's double burden of paid and unpaid work, negative societal attitudes and stereotypes;

101 a. Ensure policies that guarantee equal access to education and elimination of gender disparities in education, including vocational training, science and technology and completion of basic education for girls, especially for those living in rural and deprived areas, and opportunities for continuing education at all levels for all women and girls;

101 b. Support the implementation of plans and programmes of action to ensure quality education and improved enrolment retention rates for boys and girls and the elimination of gender discrimination as well as gender stereotypes in educational curricula and education material, as well as in the process of education;

101 d. Accelerate action and strengthen political commitment to close the gender gap in primary and secondary education by 2005 and to ensure free compulsory and universal primary education for both girls and boys by 2015 as advocated by several global conferences and eliminate policies which have been proven to worsen and perpetuate the gap;

101 e. Develop gender sensitive curricula from kindergarten to elementary schools to vocational training and universities in order to address gender stereotyping as one of the root causes of segregation in working life;

102 a. Design and implement policies that promote and protect women's enjoyment of all human rights and fundamental freedoms and create an environment that does not tolerate violations of the rights of women and girls;

102 b. Create and maintain, a non-discriminatory, as well as a gender sensitive legal environment by reviewing legislation with the view to striving to remove discriminatory provisions as soon as possible, preferably by 2005, and eliminating legislative gaps that leave women and girls without protection of their rights and without effective recourse against gender-based discrimination;

102 d. Ratify the Convention on the Elimination of All Forms of Discrimination against Women, limit the extent of any reservations to it and withdraw reservations which are contrary to the object and purpose of the Convention or otherwise incompatible with international treaty law;

102 g. Consider signing and ratifying the Optional Protocol to the Convention on the Elimination of All Forms of Discrimination against Women;

102 h. Develop, review and implement laws, procedures to prohibit and eliminate all forms of discrimination against women and girls;

102 i. Take measures, including programmes and policies, to ensure that maternity, motherhood, parenting and the role of women in procreation are not used as a basis for discrimination nor restrict the full participation of women in society;

102 k. Ensure that national legislative and administrative reform processes, including those linked to land reform, decentralization and reorientation of the economy to promote women's rights, particularly those of rural women and women living in poverty, and take measures to promote and implement those rights through women's equal access to and control over economic resources, including land, property rights, right to inheritance, credit and traditional saving schemes, such as women's banks and cooperatives;

102 l. Mainstream a gender perspective into national immigration and asylum policies, regulations and practices, as appropriate, in order to promote and protect the rights of all women, including the consideration of steps to recognize gender-related persecution and violence when assessing grounds for granting refugee status and asylum;

102 m. Take all appropriate measures to eliminate discrimination and violence against women and girls by any person, organization or enterprise;

102 n. Take necessary measures for the private sector and for educational establishments to facilitate and strengthen compliance with non-discriminatory legislation;

103 a. As a matter of priority, review and revise, where appropriate, legislation, with a view to introducing effective legislation including on violence against women, and take other necessary measures to ensure all women and girls are protected against all forms of physical, psychological, and sexual violence, and are provided recourse to justice;

103 b. Treat all forms of violence against women and girls of all ages as a criminal offence punishable by law including violence based on all forms of discrimination;

103 c. Establish legislation and/or strengthen appropriate mechanisms to handle criminal matters relating to all forms of domestic violence, including marital rape and sexual abuse of women and girls, and ensure that such cases are brought to justice swiftly;

103 d. Develop, adopt and fully implement laws and other measures as appropriate, such as policies and educational programmes, to eradicate harmful customary or traditional practices including female genital mutilation, early and forced marriage, and so-called honour crimes that are violations of the human rights of women and girls, obstacles to the full enjoyment by women of their human rights and fundamental freedoms and to intensify efforts, in cooperation with local women's groups, to raise collective and individual awareness on how these harmful traditional or customary practices violate women's human rights;

103 e. Continue to undertake research to develop a better understanding of the root causes of all forms of violence against women in order to design programmes and take measures towards eliminating these forms of violence;

103 f. Take measures to address through policies and programmes, racism and racially motivated violence against women and girls;

103 g. Take concrete steps, as a priority and with their full voluntary participation, to address the impact of violence on indigenous women, in order to implement appropriate, effective programmes and services to eliminate all forms of violence;

103 h. Promote women's and girls' mental well being, integrate mental health services into primary health-care systems, develop gender-sensitive supportive programmes and train health workers to recognize gender-based violence and care for girls and women of all ages who have experienced any form of violence;

103 i. Adopt and promote a holistic approach to respond to all forms of violence and abuse against girls and women of all ages,

including girls and women with disabilities, as well as vulnerable and marginalized women and girls in order to address their diverse needs including education, provision of appropriate health care and services and basic social services;

103 i.bis. Approve and promote a holistic approach to combat violence against women during all their life cycle and circumstances;

104 a. Take appropriate measures to address the root factors, including external factors, that encourage trafficking in women and girls for prostitution and other forms of commercialised sex, forced marriages and forced labour in order to eliminate trafficking in women, including by strengthening existing legislation with a view to providing better protection of the rights of women and girls and to punishing the perpetrators, through both criminal and civil measures;

104 b. Devise, enforce, and strengthen effective measures to combat and eliminate all forms of trafficking in women and girls through a comprehensive anti-trafficking strategy consisting of, *inter alia*, legislative measures, prevention campaigns, exchange of information, assistance and protection for and reintegration of the victims and prosecution of all the offenders involved, including intermediaries;

104 c. Consider preventing, within the leading framework and in accordance with national policies, victims of trafficking, particularly women and girls, from being prosecuted for their illegal entry or residence, taking into account that they are victims of exploitation;

104 d. Consider setting up or strengthening a national coordinating mechanism, for example, a national rapporteur or an inter-agency body, with participation of the civil society including NGOs, to encourage the exchange of information and to report on data, root causes, factors and trends in violence against women, in particular trafficking;

104 e. Provide protection and support to women and their respective families and develop and strengthen policies to support family security;

106 a. Consider adopting, where appropriate, national legislation consistent with the Convention on Biological Diversity to protect the knowledge, innovations and practices of women in indigenous and local communities relating to traditional medicines, biodiversity and indigenous technologies;

106 b. Adapt environmental and agricultural policies and mechanisms,

when necessary, to incorporate a gender perspective, and in cooperation with civil society, support farmers, particularly women farmers and those living in rural areas, with education and training programmes;

107 a. Adopt policies and implement measures to address, on a prioritised basis, the gender aspects of emerging and continued health challenges, such as malaria, tuberculosis, HIV/AIDS and other diseases having a disproportionate impact on women's health, including those resulting in the highest mortality and morbidity rates;

107 a. bis. Ensure that the reduction of maternal morbidity and mortality is a health sector priority and that women have ready access to essential obstetric care, well-equipped and adequately staffed maternal health-care services, skilled attendance at delivery, emergency obstetric care, effective referral and transport to higher levels of care when necessary, post-partum care and family planning in order to, *inter alia,* promote safe motherhood, and give priority attention to measures to prevent, detect and treat breast, cervical and ovarian cancer and osteoporosis, and sexually transmitted infections, including HIV/AIDS;

107 a. ter. Take measures to meet the unmet needs in good quality family planning services and in contraception, namely regarding the existing gap in services, supplies and use;

107 b. Collect and disseminate up-dated and reliable data on women's health, including mortality and morbidity of women, and conduct further research regarding how social and economic factors affect the health of girls and women of all ages as well as research about the provision of health care services to girls and women and the patterns of their use of such services and the value of disease prevention and health promotion programmes for women;

107 d. Ensure universal and equal access for women and men throughout the life-cycle, to social services related to health care, including education, clean water and safe sanitation, nutrition, food security and health education programmes;

107 d. bis. Ensure the provision of safe working conditions for health care workers;

107 g. Adopt, enact, review and revise, where necessary or appropriate, and implement health legislation, policies and programmes in consultation with women's organizations and other factors of civil society, and allocate the necessary budgetary resources to ensure the highest attainable standard of physical and mental

health, so that all women have full and equal access to comprehensive, high quality and affordable health care, information, education and services throughout their life cycle; to reflect the new demands for service and care by women and girls as a result of the HIV/AIDS pandemic and new knowledge about women's needs for specific mental and occupation health programmes and for the ageing process; to protect and promote human rights by ensuring that all health services and workers conform to ethical, professional and gender-sensitive standards in the delivery of women's health services, including by establishing or strengthening, as appropriate, regulatory and enforcement mechanisms;

107 g. bis. Eliminate discrimination against all women and girls in access to health information, education, and health care and health services;

107 g. ter. Reproductive health is a state of complete physical, mental and social well-being and not merely the absence of disease or infirmity, in all matters relating to the reproductive system and to its functions and processes. Reproductive health therefore implies that people are able to have a satisfying and safe sex life and that they have the capability to reproduce and the freedom to decide if, when and how often to do so. Implicit in this last condition are the right of men and women to be informed and to have access to safe, effective, affordable and acceptable methods of family planning of their choice, as well as other methods of their choice for regulation of fertility which are not against the law, and the right of access to appropriate health-care services that will enable women to go safely through pregnancy and childbirth and provide couples with the best chance of having a healthy infant. In line with the above definition of reproductive health, reproductive health care is defined as the constellation of methods, techniques and services that contribute to reproductive health and well-being by preventing and solving reproductive health problems. It also includes sexual health, the purpose of which is the enhancement of life and personal relations, and not merely counselling and care related to reproduction and sexually transmitted diseases.

Bearing in mind the above definition, reproductive rights embrace certain human rights that are already recognized in national laws, international human rights documents and other consensus documents. These rights rest on the recognition of the basic right of all couples and individuals to decide freely and responsibly the number, spacing and timing of their children and to have the information and means to do so, and the right to attain the highest standard of sexual and reproductive health. It also includes their right to make decisions concerning reproduction free of discrimination, coercion and violence, as expressed in human rights documents. In the exercise of this right, they should take into account the needs of their living and future children and their responsibilities towards the community. The promotion of the responsible exercise of these rights for all people should be the fundamental basis for government- and community-supported policies and programmes in the area of reproductive health, including family planning. As part of their commitment, full attention should be given to the promotion of mutually respectful and equitable gender relations and particularly to meeting the educational and service needs of adolescents to enable them to deal in a positive and responsible way with their sexuality. Reproductive health eludes many of the world's people because of such factors as: inadequate levels of knowledge about human sexuality and inappropriate or poor-quality reproductive health information and services; the prevalence of high-risk sexual behaviour; discriminatory social practices; negative attitudes towards women and girls; and the limited power many women and girls have over their sexual and reproductive lives. Adolescents are particularly vulnerable because of their lack of information and access to relevant services in most countries. Older women and men have distinct reproductive and sexual health issues which are often inadequately addressed.

The human rights of women include their right to have control over and decide freely and responsibly on matters related to their sexuality, including sexual and reproductive health, free of coercion, discrimination and violence. Equal relationships between women and men in matters of sexual relations and reproduction, including full respect for the integrity of the person, require mutual respect, consent and shared responsibility for sexual behaviour and its consequences.

107 g. quarter. Design, and implement programmes to encourage and enable men to adopt safe and responsible sexual and reproductive behaviour, and to effectively use methods to prevent unwanted pregnancies and sexually transmitted infections, including HIV/AIDS;

107 g. quinter. Take all appropriate measures to eliminate harmful, medically unnecessary or coercive medical interventions as well as inappropriate medication and overmedication of women and

ensure that all women are properly informed of their options, including likely benefits and potential side effects, by properly trained personnel;

107 h. Adopt measures to ensure non-discrimination against and respect for the privacy of those living with HIV/AIDS and sexually transmitted infections, including women and young people, so that they are not denied the information needed to prevent further transmission of HIV/AIDS and sexually transmitted infections and are able to access treatment and care services without fear of stigmatization, discrimination or violence;

107 i. In the light of paragraph 8.25 of the Programme of Action of the International Conference on Population and Development, which states: "In no case should abortion be promoted as a method of family planning. All Governments and relevant intergovernmental and non-governmental organizations are urged to strengthen their commitment to women's health, to deal with the health impact of unsafe abortion[1] as a major public health concern and to reduce the recourse to abortion through expanded and improved family-planning services.

Prevention of unwanted pregnancies must always be given the highest priority and every attempt should be made to eliminate the need for abortion. Women who have unwanted pregnancies should have ready access to reliable information and compassionate counselling. Any measures or changes related to abortion within the health system can only be determined at the national or local level according to the national legislative process. In circumstances where abortion is not against the law, such abortion should be safe. In all cases, women should have access to quality services for the management of complications arising from abortion. Post-abortion counselling, education and family-planning services should be offered promptly, which will also help to avoid repeat abortions", consider reviewing laws containing punitive measures against women who have undergone illegal abortions;

107 j. Promote and improve comprehensive gender-specific tobacco prevention and control strategies for all women, particularly

---

1. *Unsafe abortion is defined as a procedure for terminating an unwanted pregnancy either by persons lacking the necessary skills or in an environment lacking the minimal medical standards or both (based on World Health Organization, The Prevention and Management of Unsafe Abortion, Report of a Technical Working Group, Geneva, April 1992 (WHO/MSM/92.5).*

adolescent girls and pregnant women, which would include, *inter alia*, education, prevention and cessation programmes and services, and the reduction of people's exposure to environmental tobacco smoke and support the development of the World Health Organization's Framework Convention on Tobacco Control;

107 j. bis. Promote or improve information programmes and measures including treatment for the elimination of the increasing substance abuse among women and adolescent girls, including information campaigns about the risks to health and other consequences and its impact on families;

109 aa. Mainstream a gender perspective into key macro economic and social development policies and national development programmes;

109 a. Incorporate a gender perspective into the design, development, adoption and execution of all budgetary processes, as appropriate, in order to promote equitable, effective and appropriate resource allocation and establish adequate budgetary allocations to support gender equality and development programmes which enhance women's empowerment and develop the necessary analytical and methodological tools and mechanisms for monitoring and evaluation;

109 b. Increase as appropriate and effectively utilize financial and other resources in the social sector, particularly in education and health, to achieve gender equality and women's empowerment as a central strategy for addressing development and poverty eradication;

109 c. bis. Strive to reduce the disproportionate presence of women living in poverty particularly rural women by implementing national poverty eradication programmes with a focus on a gender perspective and the empowerment of women, including short and long-term goals;

110 a.bis. Undertake socio-economic policies that promote sustainable development and support and ensure poverty eradication programmes, especially for women, by inter alia, providing skills training, equal access to and control over resources, finance, credit, including micro-credit, information, technology, and equal access to markets to benefit women of all ages, in particular those living in poverty and marginalized women, including rural women, indigenous women, and female headed households;

110 a. Create and ensure equal access to social protection systems, taking into account the specific needs of all women living in poverty, demographic changes and changes in society, to provide

safeguards against the uncertainties and changes in conditions of work associated with globalization and strive to ensure that new, flexible and emerging forms of work are adequately covered by social protection;

111 a. Facilitate employment for women through *inter alia* promotion of adequate social protection, simplification of administrative procedures, removal of fiscal obstacles, where appropriate, and other measures, such as access to risk capital, credit schemes, micro credit and other funding, facilitating the establishment of micro enterprises and small and medium enterprises;

112 a. Establish or reinforce existing institutional mechanisms at all levels to work with national machineries to strengthen societal support for gender equality, in cooperation with civil society, particularly women's NGOs;

112 b. Take action at the highest levels for the continued advancement of women particularly by strengthening national machineries to mainstream the gender perspective to accelerate the empowerment of women in all areas and ensure commitment to gender equality policies;

112 c. Provide national machineries with the necessary human and financial resources, including through exploring innovative funding schemes so that gender mainstreaming is integrated in all policies, programmes and projects;

112 d. Consider establishing effective commissions or other institutions to promote equal opportunities;

112 e. Strengthen efforts to fully implement national action plans developed for the implementation of the Beijing Platform for Action and, when necessary, adjust or develop national plans for the future;

112 f. Ensure that the design of all government information policies and strategies is gender-sensitive;

113 a. Provide national statistical offices with institutional and financial support in order to collect, compile and disseminate data disaggregated by sex, age, and other factors as appropriate, in formats that are accessible to the public and to policy-makers for *inter alia* gender-based analysis, monitoring and impact assessment, and support new work to develop statistics and indicators, especially in areas where information is particularly lacking;

113 b. Develop national capacity to undertake policy-oriented and

gender-related research and impact studies by universities and national research/training institutes to enable gender-specific knowledge-based policy-making;

Actions to be Taken at National Level

By Governments, the Private Sector, Non-Governmental Organisations and other Factors of Civil Society:

114 a. Encourage the creation of training and legal literacy programmes, which build and support the capacities of women's organizations to advocate for women's and girls' human rights and fundamental freedoms;

114 b. Encourage collaboration and, where appropriate, among various levels of Governments, NGOs, grassroots organizations, traditional and community leaders for the promotion and protection of all human rights and fundamental freedoms of women and girls and the dignity and worth of the human person and equal rights for women and men;

115 a. Adopt a holistic approach to women's physical and mental health throughout the life cycle, take further measures to redesign health information, services and training for health workers in order to make them gender-sensitive, promote gender balance at all levels of the health care system, and reflect women's perspective and right to privacy, confidentiality, voluntary and informed consent;

115 a. bis Reinforce efforts to ensure universal access to high quality primary health care, throughout the life cycle, including sexual and reproductive health care, not later than 2015;

115 a. ter. Review and revise national policies, programmes and legislation to implement the "Key actions for the further implementation of the Programme of Action of the International Conference on Population and Development" adopted by the twenty-first special session of the General Assembly[2], paying particular attention to achieving the specific benchmarks to reduce maternal mortality, to increase the proportion of births assisted by skilled attendants, to provide the widest achievable range of safe and effective family planning and contraceptive methods and reduce young people's risk of HIV/AIDS;

115 c. Strengthen measures to improve the nutritional status of all girls and women, recognizing the effects of severe and moderate malnutrition, the life-long implications of nutrition and the link between mother and child health, by promoting and enhancing

2. *General Assembly Resolution S-21/2, Annex.*

support for programmes to reduce malnutrition, such as school meal programmes mother-child-nutrition programmes and micro-nutrient supplementation, giving special attention to bridging the gender gap in nutrition;

115 d. Review, with the full participation of women, and monitor the impact of health sector reform initiatives on women's health and their enjoyment of human rights, in particular with regard to rural and urban health service delivery to women living in poverty, and ensure that reforms secure full and equal access to available, affordable and high quality health care and services for all women, taking into account the diverse needs of women;

115 f. bis. Design and implement programmes with the full involvement of adolescents as appropriate, to provide them with education, information and appropriate, specific, user-friendly and accessible services without discrimination to address effectively their reproductive and sexual health needs taking into account their right to privacy, confidentiality, respect and informed consent and the responsibilities, rights and duties of parents and legal guardians to provide in a manner consistent with the evolving capacities of the child appropriate direction and guidance in the exercise by the child of the rights recognised in the Convention on the Rights of the Child and in conformity with CEDAW and ensuring that in all actions concerning children, the best interests of the child are a primary consideration. These programmes should, *inter alia,* build adolescent girls' self esteem and help them take responsibility for their own lives; promote gender equality and responsible sexual behaviour; raise awareness about, prevent and treat sexually transmitted infections, including HIV/AIDS and sexual violence and abuse; counsel adolescents on avoiding unwanted and early pregnancies;

115 g. Design and implement programmes to provide social services and support to pregnant adolescents and adolescent mothers, in particular to enable them to continue and complete their education;

115 h. Give particular attention to developing and improving access to improved and new technologies and to safe and affordable drugs and treatments to meet women's health needs, including, *inter alia,* cardio/pulmonary diseases, hypertension, osteoporosis, breast-, cervical-and ovarian cancer and family planning and contraceptive methods, for both women and men;

116 a. Develop and use frameworks, guidelines and other practical tools and indicators to accelerate gender mainstreaming, including

gender-based research, analytical tools and methodologies, training, case studies, statistics and information;

117 a. Provide equal opportunities and favourable conditions for women of all ages and backgrounds on equal terms with men by encouraging their entry into politics and their participation at all levels;

117 a. bis. Encourage the nomination of more women candidates, including, *inter alia*, through political parties, quotas or measurable goals, or other appropriate means for election to parliaments and other legislative structures, to increase their share and contribution in the formulation of public policy;

118 b. Promote and protect the rights of women workers and take action to remove structural and legal barriers as well as stereotypical attitudes to gender equality at work, addressing *inter alia*: gender bias in recruitment; working conditions; occupational segregation and harassment; discrimination in social protection benefits; women's occupational health and safety; unequal career opportunities and inadequate sharing, by men, of family responsibilities;

118 b. bis. Promote programmes to enable women and men to reconcile their work and family responsibilities, and to encourage men to share equally with women household and childcare responsibilities;

118 b. ter. Develop or strengthen policies and programmes to support the multiple roles of women in contributing to the welfare of the family in its various forms, which acknowledge the social significance of maternity and motherhood, parenting, the role of parents and legal guardians in the upbringing of children and caring for other family members. Such policies and programmes should also promote shared responsibility of parents, women and men and society as a whole in this regard;

118 f. Design, implement and promote family friendly policies and services, including affordable, accessible and quality care services for children and other dependents, parental and other leave schemes, campaigns to sensitize public opinion and other relevant factors on equal sharing of employment and family responsibilities between women and men;

118 j. Develop policies and programmes to enhance the employability of women and their access to quality jobs, through improving access to formal, non-formal and vocational training, life long learning and retraining, long-distance education, including in information and communications technology and entre-preneurial

skills, particularly in developing countries, to support women's empowerment in the different stages of their lives;

118 c. Take action to increase women's participation and to bring about a balanced representation of women and men in all sectors and occupations in the labour market, among others by encouraging the creation or expansion of institutional networks to support the career development and promotion of women;

118 d. Develop and/or strengthen programmes and policies to support women entrepreneurs, including those engaged in new enterprises, through access to information, training, including vocational training, new technologies, networks, credit and financial services;

118 e. Initiate positive steps to promote equal pay for equal work or work of equal value and to diminish differentials in incomes between women and men;

118 i. Encourage and support the education of girls in science, mathematics, new technologies including information technologies, and technical subjects and encourage women, including through career advising to seek employment in high growth and high wage sectors and jobs;

118 k. Analyse and respond, as necessary, to the major reasons why men and women may be affected differently by the process of job creation and retrenchment associated with economic transition and structural transformation of the economy, including globalization;

Actions to be Taken at the International Level

By the United Nations System, International and Regional Organisations, as Appropriate:

120 a. Assist Governments, at their request, to build institutional capacity and develop national action plans, or further implement existing action plans, for the implementation of the Platform for Action;

120 b. Support non-governmental organizations, especially women's organisations, to build their capacity to advocate for, implement, assess, and follow up the Platform for Action;

120 b. bis. Strengthen or establish where appropriate, national collaborative and regular reporting mechanisms, with the participation of NGOs, especially women's organisations, to monitor progress on the implementation of national policies, programmes and benchmarks for achieving gender equality;

Note: To be Moved to National Level

120 c. Allocate sufficient resources to regional and national programmes to implement the Platform for Action in its twelve critical areas;

120 d. Assist Governments in countries with economies in transition to further develop and implement plans and programmes aimed at economic and political empowerment of women;

120 e. Encourage the Economic and Social Council to request the Regional Commissions within their respective mandates and resources, to build up a data base to be updated regularly, in which all programmes and projects carried out in their respective regions by agencies or organisations of the United Nations system are listed, to facilitate their dissemination, as well as the evaluation of their impact on the empowerment of women through the implementation of the Platform for Action;

121 a. Continue to implement and evaluate and follow up the mandated work of the UN agencies, drawing on the full range of expertise available within the UN system, as well as ECOSOC Agreed Conclusions and other programmes and initiatives to mainstream a gender perspective into all policies, programmes and planning of the UN system, including through the integrated and coordinated follow-up to all major UN conferences and summits, as well as to ensure the allocation of sufficient resources and maintenance of gender units and focal points to achieve this end;

121 a. bis. Support national efforts, particularly in developing countries, for enlarged access to new information technology as part of the efforts to develop collaborative research, training and information dissemination, including through the Gender Awareness Internet Networking System (GAINS) being developed by the International Research and Training Institute for the Advancement of Women (INSTRAW), while at the same time supporting traditional methods of information dissemination, research and training;

121 b. Ensure that all UN personnel and officials at headquarters and in the field, especially in field operations, receive training in order to mainstream a gender perspective in their work, including gender impact analysis, and ensure appropriate follow-up to such training;

121 e. Support the Commission on the Status of Women, within its mandate, in assessing and advancing the implementation of the Beijing Platform for Action and its follow-up;

121 f. Assist governments, upon their request, to incorporate a gender

perspective as a key dimension of development into national development planning;

121 g. Assist States Parties, upon their request, in building capacity to implement the Convention on the Elimination of All Forms of Discrimination against Women, and in this regard encourages States Parties to pay attention to the concluding comments as well as the general recommendations of the Committee;

122 a. Assist Governments, upon request, in developing gender-sensitive strategies for the delivery of assistance and, where appropriate, responses to humanitarian crises resulting from armed conflict and natural disasters;

122 a. bis. Invite the United Nations High Commissioner for Refugees, other relevant United Nations Agencies, within their respective mandates, and other relevant humanitarian organizations as well as Governments to continue to provide adequate support to countries hosting large numbers of refugees and those with displaced persons, in their efforts to provide protection and assistance, paying particular attention to the needs of refugee and other displaced women and children;

Note: To be Moved to National and International Level

122 b. Ensure and support the full participation of women at all levels of decision-making and implementation in development activities and peace processes, including conflict prevention and resolution, post-conflict reconstruction, peace-making, peace-keeping and peace-building and in this regard, support the involvement of women's organizations, community based organizations and NGOs;

122 b. bis. Encourage the involvement of women in decision-making at all levels and achieve gender balance in the appointment of women and men, with full respect for the principle of equitable geographical distribution, including as special envoys and special representatives and to pursue good offices on behalf of the Secretary-General, *inter alia* in matters relating to peace-keeping, peace-building, and in operational activities, including resident coordinators;

122 b. ter. Take further effective measures to remove the obstacles for the realisation of the right of peoples to self-determination, in particular peoples living under colonial and foreign occupation, that continue to adversely affect their economic and social development;

123 a. Support activities aimed at the elimination of all forms of

violence against women and girls, including providing support for the activities of women's networks and organizations within the United Nations system;

123 b. Consider launching an international "zero tolerance" campaign on violence against women;

124 a. Encourage implementation of measures designed to achieve the goal of 50/50 gender balance in all posts including at the professional level and above, in particular at the higher levels in their secretariats including in peacekeeping missions and peace negotiations and in all activities and report thereon as appropriate, and enhancing management accountability mechanisms;

125 B. Take measures, with the full participation of women, to create, at all levels, an enabling environment conducive to the achievement and maintenance of world peace, for democracy and peaceful settlement of disputes with the full respect for the principles of sovereignty, territorial integrity and political independence of states and non-intervention in matters which are essentially within the jurisdiction of any state, in accordance with the Charter of the United Nations and international law, as well as, the promotion and protection of all human rights, including the right to development, and fundamental freedoms;

Actions to be Taken at the National and International Level

By Governments, Regional and International Organisations, Including the United Nations System and International Financial Institutions and other Factors, as Appropriate:

125 E. Take steps with a view to the avoidance of, and refrain from any unilateral measure, not in accordance with international law and the Charter of the United Nations, that impedes the full achievement of economic and social development by the population of the affected countries, in particular women and children, that hinders their well-being and that creates obstacles to the full enjoyment of their human rights, including the right of everyone to a standard of living adequate for their health and well-being and their right to food, medical care and the necessary social services. Ensure that food and medicine are not used as tools for political pressure;

125 E. bis. Take urgent and effective measures in accordance with international law with a view to alleviating the negative impact of economic sanctions on women and children.

125 H. Create an enabling environment as well as design and implement

policies that promote and protect the enjoyment of all human rights—civil, cultural, economic, political and social rights, including the right to development—and fundamental freedoms, as part of the efforts to achieve gender equality, development and peace;

Note: To be Moved to 135

125 I. Continue to review, modify and implement macro-economic and social policies and programmes, including *inter alia,* through an analysis from a gender perspective of those related to structural adjustment, external debt problems, in order to ensure women's equal access to resources and universal access to basic social services;

Note: To be Moved to National Level

125 (a) Promote international cooperation to support regional and national efforts in the development and use of gender-related analysis and statistics by, *inter alia,* providing national statistical offices, upon their request, with institutional and financial support in order to enable them to respond to requests for data disaggregated by sex and age for use by national governments in the formulation of gender-sensitive statistical indicators for monitoring and policy and programme impact assessments, as well as to undertake regular strategic surveys;

125 b. Assist countries, upon their request, in developing methods for, and compiling statistics on the contributions of women and men to society and the economy, and the socio-economic situation of women and men, in particular in relation to poverty, and paid and unpaid work in all sectors;

Note: To be Moved to International Level (following 121 a)

125 g. Regularly compile and publish crime statistics and map trends in law enforcement concerning violations of the rights of women and girls to increase awareness in order to develop more effective policies;

Note: To be Moved to National Level

125 h. Develop with the full participation of all countries an international consensus on indicators and ways to measure violence against women and consider establishing a readily accessible database on statistics, legislation, training models, good practices, lessons learned and other resources with regard to all forms of violence against women, including women migrant workers;

125 i. In partnership, as appropriate, with relevant institutions promote, improve, systemize and fund the collection of data disaggregated by sex, age and other appropriate factors, on health and access to health services, including comprehensive information on the impact of HIV/AIDS on women, throughout the life-cycle;

125 i. bis. Eliminate gender biases in bio-medical, clinical and social research, including by conducting voluntary clinical trials involving women, with due regard for their human rights and in strict conformity with internationally accepted legal, ethical, medical, safety, and scientific standards and gather, analyze and make available to appropriate institutions and to end-users, gender-specific information about dosage, side-effects and effectiveness of drugs, including contraceptives and methods that protect against sexually transmitted infections;

126 a. Develop and support the capacity of universities, national research and training institutes and other relevant research institutes to undertake gender related and policy oriented research in order to inform policy makers and to promote full implementation of the Platform for Action and its follow-up;

126 a. bis. Develop a South-South cooperation programme with a view to assisting in the capacity building of national machineries on women through, among others, the sharing of expertise, experiences and knowledge of national machineries on women's empowerment, gender issues and gender mainstreaming methodologies and approaches on the 12 critical areas of the Platform for Action;

126 b. Support Governments in their efforts to institute action-oriented programmes and measures to accelerate the full implementation of the Platform for Action, with time-bound targets and/or measurable goals and evaluation methods, including gender impact assessments, with full participation of women for measuring and analysing progress;

126 d. bis. Undertake appropriate data collection and research on indigenous women, with their full participation, in order to foster accessible, culturally and linguistically appropriate policies, programmes and services;

126 e. Continue research on all current trends that may be creating new gender disparities in order to provide a basis for policy action;

127 a. Take measures to develop and implement gender sensitive programmes aimed at stimulating women's entrepreneurship

and private initiative and assist women-owned business to participate in and benefit from, *inter alia,* international trade, technological innovation and investment;

127 b. Respect, promote and realize the principles contained in the ILO Declaration on Fundamental Principles and Rights at Work and its follow-up and strongly consider ratification and full implementation of ILO Conventions which are particularly relevant to ensure women's rights at work;

127 e. bis. Encourage the strengthening of existing and emerging micro-credit institutions and their capacity, including through the support of international financial institutions, so that credit and related services for self-employment and income generating activities may be made available to an increasing number of people living in poverty, in particular women and to further develop, where appropriate, other micro-finance instruments;

127 g. Reaffirm commitment to gender-sensitive development and support women's role in sustainable and ecologically sound consumption and production patterns and approaches to natural resource management;

127 h. Adopt measures to ensure that the work of rural women, who continue to play a vital role in providing food security and nutrition, and are engaged in agricultural production, and enterprises related to farming, fishing and resource management, and home-based work, especially in the informal sector, is recognized and valued in order to enhance their economic security, their access to and control over resources and credit schemes, services and benefits, and their empowerment;

128 a. Encourage and implement curriculum changes in training for public officials to make them fully gender-sensitive;

128 b. Develop policies and implement programmes including education programmes, particularly for men and boys, on changing stereotypical attitudes and behaviours concerning gender roles and responsibilities to promote gender equality and positive attitudes and behaviours;

Note: To be Moved to National Level–118 i. bis

128 c. Strengthen and promote programmes to support the participation of young women in youth organisations and encourage dialogue among youth between and among developed and developing countries;

128 d. Support national efforts to promote formal and non-formal education and mentoring programmes for women and girls, in

order to enable them to acquire knowledge, develop self-esteem and skills in leadership, advocacy and conflict resolution;

128 d. bis. Undertake comprehensive actions to provide skills training for women and girls at all levels, in order to eradicate poverty, in particular the feminization of poverty, through national and international efforts;

128 e. Strengthen gender-awareness campaigns and gender equality training among women and men, girls and boys to eliminate the persistence of harmful stereotypes;

Note: To be Moved to National Level

128 h. With the full voluntary participation of indigenous women, develop and implement educational and training programmes that respect their history, culture, spirituality, languages and aspirations and ensure their access to all levels of formal and non-formal education, including higher education;

128 i. Continue to support and strengthen national, regional and international adult literacy programmes with international cooperation in order to achieve a 50 per cent improvement in levels of adult literacy by 2015, especially for women, and equitable access to basic and continuing education for all adults;

128 j. Continue to examine the decline in enrollment rates and the increase in the drop-out rates of girls and boys at the primary and secondary education levels in some countries, and with international cooperation, design appropriate national programmes to eliminate the root causes and support lifelong learning for women and girls, with a view to ensuring achievement of relevant international targets on education set by the relevant international conferences;

128 l. Ensure equal opportunities for women and girls in cultural, recreational and sports activities, as well as in participation in athletics and physical activities at national, regional and international levels, such as access, training, competition, remuneration and prizes;

128 O. Design and implement policies and programmes, to fully address specific needs of women and girls with disabilities, to ensure their equal access to education at all levels, including technical and vocational training and adequate rehabilitation programmes, to health care and services and employment opportunities, to protect and promote their human rights and, where appropriate, eliminate existing inequalities between women and men with disabilities;

Note: To be Moved to National Level

129 b. Develop and maintain consultative processes and mechanisms, in partnership with women's organizations including NGOs and community groups, to ensure that all women, with attention to those who face particular barriers to their participation in public life, are fully involved in and informed about decisions which impact their lives;

Note:* *To be Moved to National Level

129 d. Apply and support positive measures to give all women, particularly indigenous women, equal access to capacity-building and training programmes to enhance their participation in decision-making in all fields and at all levels;

130 a. Increase cooperation, policy responses, effective implementation of national legislation and other protective and preventive measures aimed at the elimination of violence against women and girls, especially all forms of commercial sexual exploitation, as well as economic exploitation, including *inter alia,* trafficking in women and children, female infanticide, crimes committed in the name of honour, crimes committed in the name of passion, racially motivated crimes, abduction and sale of children, dowry related violence and deaths, acid attacks and harmful traditional or customary practices such as FGM, early and forced marriages;

130 c. Increase awareness and knowledge of the Rome Statute of the ICC which affirms that rape, sexual slavery, enforced prostitution, forced pregnancy, enforced sterilization and other forms of sexual violence constitute war crimes and, in defined circumstances, crimes against humanity, with the aim of preventing such crimes from occurring and take measures to support prosecution of all persons responsible for such crimes and provide avenues for redress to victims; also increase awareness of the extent to which such crimes are used as a weapon of war;

130 d. Provide support to NGOs, in collaboration with the UN system, *inter alia* through regional and international cooperation, including women's organizations, and community groups in addressing all forms of violence against women and girls, including for programmes to combat race and ethnic-based violence against women and girls;

130 e. Prosecute the perpetrators of all forms of violence against women and girls and sentence them appropriately and introduce actions aimed at helping and motivating perpetrators to break the cycle of violence and take measures to provide avenues for redress to victims;

Note: To be Moved to National Level, 103 a bis

130 f. Provide gender sensitive training to all factors, as appropriate, in peacekeeping missions in dealing with victims of violence, particularly women and girls, including sexual violence;

Note: To be Moved to International Level

130 f. bis Provide gender sensitive training to all factors, including police, prosecutors and the judiciary in dealing with victims of violence, particularly women and girls, including sexual violence;

Note: To be Moved to National Level

130 g. Encourage and support public campaigns, as appropriate, to enhance public awareness of the unacceptability and social costs of violence against women and undertake prevention activities to promote healthy and balanced relationships based on gender equality;

131 a. Intensify cooperation between states of origin, transit and destination to prevent, suppress and punish trafficking in persons, especially women and children;

131 b. Support the ongoing negotiations on the draft protocol to prevent, suppress and punish trafficking in persons, especially women and children which supplements the UN Convention against Transnational Organized Crime;

131 c. As appropriate, pursue and support national, regional and international strategies to reduce the risk to women and girls, including those who are refugees and displaced, as well as women migrant workers, of becoming victims of trafficking; strengthen national legislation by further defining the crime of trafficking in all its elements and by reinforcing the punishment accordingly; enact social and economic policies and programmes, as well as information and awareness raising initiatives, to prevent and combat trafficking in persons, especially women and children; prosecute perpetrators of trafficking; provide measures to support, assist and protect trafficked persons in countries of origin and destination; and facilitate their return to and support their reintegration in countries of origin;

132 a. Improve knowledge and awareness of the remedies available for violations of women's human rights;

132 b. Promote and protect the human rights of all migrant women and implement policies to address the specific needs of documented migrant women and, where necessary, tackle the existing inequalities between men and women migrants to ensure gender equality;

132 c. Promote respect for the right of women and men to the freedom

of thought, conscience and religion. Recognize the central role that religion, spirituality and belief play in the lives of millions of women and men;

132 d. Encourage co-operation between governmental authorities, parliamentarians and other relevant authorities and women's organizations including NGOs, as appropriate, in ensuring that legislation is non-discriminatory;

Note: To be Moved to National Level

132 e. Encourage, through the media and other means, a high awareness of harmful effects of certain traditional or customary practices affecting the health of women, some of which increase their vulnerability to HIV/AIDS and other sexually transmitted infections and intensify efforts to eliminate such practices;

132 f. Take necessary measures to protect individuals, groups and organs of society engaged in promoting and protecting women's human rights;

132 g. Encourage States parties to continue to include a gender perspective in their reports to the treaty bodies; also encourage these bodies to continue to take into account a gender perspective in the implementation of their mandates, taking into account the need to avoid unnecessary duplication and overlapping of their work; further encourage human rights mechanisms to continue to take into account a gender perspective in their work;

132 i. Take measures to enable all older women to be actively engaged in all aspects of life, as well as assume a variety of roles in communities, public life and decision-making, and develop and implement policies and programmes to ensure their full enjoyment of human rights and quality of life, as well as to address their needs, with a view to contribute to the realisation of a society for all ages;

Note: To be Moved to National Level

132 i. bis. Support innovative programmes to empower older women to increase their contribution to and benefit from development and efforts to combat poverty;

133a. Promote comprehensive human rights education programmes, *inter alia* in cooperation, where appropriate, with education and human rights institutions, the relevant factors of civil society, in particular NGOs and the media networks, to ensure widespread dissemination of information on human rights instruments, in particular those on human rights of women and girls;

133 b. Take measures, through *inter alia*, supporting and strengthening existing mechanisms entrusted with prosecuting perpetrators of violations of human rights of women, to eliminate impunity;

133 b. bis. Take measures to eliminate violations of international law and the United Nations Charter. Many of these violations have a negative impact on the promotion and protection of human rights of women;

133 d. Address the root causes of armed conflict in a comprehensive and durable manner as well as the differences in the impact of armed conflict on women and men and take them into account in relevant policies and programmes, in order to, *inter alia*, enhance the protection of civilians, particularly women and children;

133 f. Consider signing and ratifying the Rome Statute of the International Criminal Court;

Note: To be Moved to National Level

133 g. Ensure release of hostages, particularly women and children, including those subsequently imprisoned, in armed conflict;

133 h. Develop and support policies and programmes for the protection of children, especially girls, in hostilities, in order to prohibit their forced recruitment and use by all factors, and to promote and/or strengthen mechanisms for their rehabilitation and reintegration, taking into account the specific experiences and needs of girls;

Note: To be Moved to National and International Level

133 i. Improve and strengthen the capacity of women affected by situations of armed conflict including women refugees and displaced women by *inter alia*, involving them in the design and management of humanitarian activities so that they benefit from these activities on an equal basis with men;

133 j. Seek to ensure the full and equal participation of women in the promotion of peace, in particular, through the full implementation of the Declaration and Programme of Action on a culture of peace;

133 k. bis. Provide support to and empower women who play an important role within their families as stabilizing factors in conflict and post-conflict situations;

133 m. bis. Strengthen efforts towards general and complete disarmament under strict and effective international control, based on the priorities established by the United Nations in the field of

disarmament, so that released resources could be used for, inter alia, social and economic programmes which benefit women and girls;

133 m. ter. Explore new ways of generating new public and private financial resources, *inter alia*, through the appropriate reduction of excessive military expenditures and the arms trade and investment for arms production and acquisition, including global military expenditures, taking into consideration national security requirements, so as to permit the possible allocation of additional funds for social and economic development, inter alia for the advancement of women;

133 n. Take measures to ensure the protection of refugees, especially women and girls, and their access to and the provision of gender sensitive appropriate basic social services, including education and health;

134 a. Cooperate and work with private sector partners and media networks at national and international levels to promote equal access for women and men as producers and consumers, particularly in the area of information and communications technologies, including through encouraging the media and the information industry consistent with freedom of expression to adopt, or develop further codes of conduct, professional guidelines and other self-regulatory guidelines to remove gender stereotypes and promote balanced portrayals of women and men;

134 b. Develop programmes that support women's ability to create, access and promote networking, in particular through the use of new information and communications technology, including through the establishment and support of programmes to build the capacity of women's NGOs in this regard;

134 h. Capitalise on the new information technologies, including the Internet, to improve the global sharing of information, research, strengths, lessons learned from women's experiences, including "Herstories" related to achieving gender equality, development and peace, and study other roles that these technologies can play towards that goal;

Note: Footnote to be Included to Explain "Her Stories"

135 (a) former 125 G. Take effective measures to address the challenges of globalisation, including through the enhanced and effective participation of developing countries in the international economic policy decision-making process, in order to *inter alia*, guarantee the equal participation of women, in particular those

from developing countries, in the process of macro-economic decision-making;

135 (b) former 125 D. Take measures with the full and effective participation of women to ensure new approaches to international development cooperation, based on stability, growth and equity with the enhanced and effective participation and the integration of developing countries in the globalizing world economy, geared towards poverty eradication and the reduction of gender-based inequality within the overall framework of achieving people centered sustainable development;

135 (c) former 125. A. Design and strengthen poverty eradication strategies with the full and effective participation of women that reduce the feminization of poverty and enhance the capacity of women and empower them to meet the negative social and economic impacts of globalisation;

135 d. Intensify efforts to implement poverty eradication programmes and evaluate, with the participation of women, the extent to which these programmes have an impact on the empowerment of women living in poverty, in terms of access to quality training and education as well as health care, employment, basic social services, inheritance, and access to and control over land, housing, income, micro-credit and other financial instruments and services, and introduce improvements to such programmes in the light of the above assessment;

135 (e) former 135 e. bis. Recognising the mutually reinforcing links between gender equality and poverty eradication, elaborate and implement, where appropriate, in consultation with civil society, comprehensive gender sensitive poverty eradication strategies addressing social, structural and macro-economic issues;

135 (f) former 135 g. Encourage the establishment, in partnership with private financial institutions where appropriate of "lending windows" and other accessible financial services with simplified procedures that are specifically designed to meet the savings, credit and insurance needs of all women;

135 (g) former 125 J. Undertake comprehensive actions to provide and support quality skills training for women and girls at all levels, on the basis of strategies developed with their full and effective participation, to achieve agreed targets to eradicate poverty, in particular the feminisation of poverty, through national, regional and international efforts. National efforts need to be complemented by intensified regional and international

cooperation in order to tackle the risks, overcome the challenges and ensure that opportunities created by globalization benefit women, particularly in developing countries;

135 (h) former 135 e. Establish, with the full and effective participation of women and in consultation with civil society, particularly NGOs, in a timely manner, social development funds, where appropriate, to alleviate the negative effects on women associated with structural adjustment programmes and trade liberalization and the disproportionate burden borne by women living in poverty;

135 (i) former 125 C. Identify and implement development-oriented and durable solutions which integrate a gender perspective to external debt and debt-servicing problems of developing countries, including least-developed countries, *inter alia*, through debt relief, including the option of ODA debt cancellation, in order to help them to finance programmes and projects targeted at development, including the advancement of women;

135 (j) former 135 f. Support the Cologne initiative for the reduction of debt, particularly the speedy implementation of the enhanced Heavily Indebted Poor Countries Debt Initiative, ensure the provision of adequate funds for its implementation, and the provision that funds saved should be used to support anti-poverty programmes that address gender dimensions;

135 (k) former 135 a. Promote and accelerate the implementation of the 20/20 initiative that integrates a gender perspective to fully benefit all, particularly women and girls;

135 (l) former 135 b. Call for continued international cooperation including the reaffirmation to strive to fulfill the yet to be attained internationally agreed target of 0.7 per cent of the gross national product of developed countries for overall official development assistance as soon as possible, thereby increasing the flow of resources for gender equality, development and peace;

135 (m) former 135 b. bis. Facilitate the transfer to developing countries and countries with economies in transition of appropriate technology, particularly new and modern technology and encourage efforts by the international community to eliminate restrictions to such transfers, as an effective means of complementing national efforts for further acceleration in achieving the goals of gender equality, development and peace;

135 (n) former 135 c. Recommend to the Preparatory Committee for the Millennium Assembly to make an effort within the context of gender mainstreaming in the UN system, to integrate a gender

perspective in all activities and documents related to the Millennium Assembly and Summit, including in the consideration of poverty eradication;

136 a. Create and strengthen an enabling environment, in accordance with national laws, to support the capacity of women's NGOs to mobilize resources to ensure sustainability of their development activities;

136 c. Encourage the establishment and strengthening of multi-stakeholder partnerships/cooperation at all levels among international and inter-governmental organisations, with relevant factors of civil society including NGOs, private sector and trade unions, and women's organizations and other NGOs, communications and media systems in support of the goals of the Fourth World Conference on Women;

136 d. Encourage partnerships and cooperation among governments, international organizations, in particular international financial institutions, and multilateral organisations, the private sector institutions and civil society including NGOs, especially women's and community-based organisations to support poverty eradication initiatives focused on women and girls;

136 e. Support the work of NGOs and community based organizations in helping disadvantaged women, in particular rural women, in having access to financial institutions in establishing businesses and other sustainable means of livelihood;

Note: To be Moved to National Level

136 f. Recognise the crucial role of and support women and women's NGOs and CBOs in the implementation of Agenda 21, by integrating a gender perspective in the formulation, design and implementation of sustainable environmental and resource management mechanisms, programmes and infrastructure;

136 g. Promote gender-sensitivity and social responsibility of the private sector, inter alia through management of work time, and dissemination of gender-sensitive information and advocacy campaigns;

Note: To be Moved to National Level

138 a. Promote programmes for healthy active ageing that stress the independence, equality, participation, and security of older women and undertake gender-specific research and programmes to address their needs;

138 c. As a matter of priority, especially in those countries most affected, and in partnership with NGOs, wherever possible, intensify

education, services and community based mobilization strategies to protect women of all ages from HIV and other sexually transmitted infections, including through the development of safe, affordable, effective and easily accessible female-controlled methods, including methods such as microbicides and female condoms that protect against sexually transmitted infections and HIV/AIDS; voluntary and confidential HIV testing and counseling, and the promotion of responsible sexual behaviour, including abstinence and condom use; development of vaccines, simple low-cost diagnosis and single dose treatments for sexually transmitted infections;

138 d. Provide access to adequate and affordable treatment, monitoring and care for all people, especially women and girls, infected with sexually transmitted diseases or living with life threatening diseases, including HIV/AIDS and associated opportunistic infections, such as tuberculosis. Provide other services, including adequate housing and social protection, including during pregnancy and breastfeeding; assist boys and girls orphaned as a result of the HIV/AIDS pandemic; and provide gender sensitive support systems for women and other family members who are involved in caring for persons affected by serious health conditions, including HIV/AIDS;

138 e. bis. Take effective and expeditious measures to mobilize international and national public opinion concerning the effects of different dimensions of the world drug problems on women and girls and ensure that appropriate resources are provided to this end;

139. Encourage partnerships between Governments and NGOs in the implementation of commitments made at the Fourth World Conference on Women and at other United Nations World Conferences and Summits in order to promote gender equality, development and peace in the twenty-first century.

Source: Twenty-third Special Session of the General Assembly of UNO entitled 'Women 2000: Gender Equality, Development and Peace for the Twenty-first Century' – Further Actions and Initiatives to Implement the Beijing Declaration and the Platform for Action.

Bibliography

Celine Rani, Emerging Pattern of Rural Women Leadership in India, New Delhi, Kalpaz Publications, 2002.

Kumar, Encyclopaedia of Women in Twenty-First Century, New Delhi, Anmol Publications, 2005.

A.K. Pandey, Emerging Issues in Empowerment of Women, New Delhi, Anmol Publications, 2002.

A.K. Pandey, Gender Equality, Development and Women Empowerment/edited, New Delhi, Anmol Publications, 2003.

A.K. Shukla, Political Status of Women, New Delhi, A.P.H. Publications, 2007.

Abha Avasthi and A.K. Srivastava (Eds.), Modernity, Feminism and Women Empowerment, New Delhi, Rawat Publications, 2001.

Abha Jain and Shalini Shekhawat (Eds.), Administration for Empowerment and Welfare of Women, Jaipur, Aalekh Publishers, 2007.

Abhilasha Kumari and Sabina Kidwai, Crossing the Sacred Line: Women's Search for Political Power, 1998.

Afsar Bano, Women and Social Change, New Delhi, Reference Press, 2003.

Ajit Kumar Sinha (Ed.) New Dimensions of Women Empowerment, New Delhi, Deep and Deep Publications, 2008.

Amal Mandal, Women in Panchayati Raj Institutions, New Delhi, Kanishka Publishers, Distributors, 2003.

Andal N., Women and Indian Society: Options and Constraints, New Delhi, Rawat Publications, 2002.

Anees Jung, Beyond the Courtyard: A Sequel to Unveiling India, New Delhi, Viking, 2003.

Angela R. Miles and Geraldine Finn (Eds.), Feminism: From Pressure to Politics, New Delhi, Rawat Publications, 2002.

Anil Bhuimali and Sampa Poddar, Development of Rural Women through Education and Empowerment, New Delhi, Abhijeet Publications, 2005.

Anil Bhuimali, Education, Employment and Empowering Women, New Delhi, Serials Publications, 2004.

Anil Dutta Mishra (Ed.), Gender Perspective: Participation, Empowerment and Development, New Delhi, Radha Publications, 1999.

Anil Kumar Thakur and Dalip Kumar, Gender Empowerment and Development/edited, New Delhi, Deep and Deep Publications, 2008.

Anita Banerji and Raj Kumar Sen (Eds.), Women and Economic Development, New Delhi, 2000.

Anita Srivastav, Women in India: Problems and Prospects, New Delhi, Indian Publications, 2004.

Anita Stephen, Communication Technologies and Women Empowerment, New Delhi, Rajat, 2006.

Anjana Maitra-Sinha, Women in a Changing Society,1993.

Anju Bhatia, Women's Development and NGOs, New Delhi, Rawat Publications, 2000.

Anju Bindra, Women and Human Rights, New Delhi, Manglam Publications, 2007.

Anupama Singh, Women Empowerment and Sustainable Development, New Delhi, Kanishka Publishers, Distributors, 2008.

Anuradha Mathu and Rameshwari Pandya (Eds.), Facets of Women's Development, New Delhi, Kalpaz Publications, 2006.

Aparna Basu and Anup Taneja, Breaking Out of Invisibility: Women in Indian History, New Delhi, Northern Book Centre, 2002.

Arati Mehta, Progressive Women and Political Identity, Reprint. New Delhi, Kanishka Publishers, Distributors, 2004.

Archana Ghosh and Stephanie Tawa Lama-Rewal, Democratisation in Progress: Women and Local Politics in Urban India, New Delhi, Tulika, 2005.

Arun Kumar, Empowering Women, New Delhi, Sarup, 2002.

Aruna Goel, Education and Socio-Economic Perspectives of Women Development and Empowerment, New Delhi, Deep and Deep Publications, 2004.

Aruna Goel, Violence and Protective Measures for Women Development and Empowerment, New Delhi, Deep and Deep Publications, 2004.

Aruna Sharma, J.C. Sharma, Rita Bakshi and Poonam Sharma (Eds.), Women, Education and Empowerment, New Delhi, Om Publications, 2006.

Asha Mukherjee and Kumkum Bhattacharya (Eds.), Conditioning and Empowerment of Women: A Multidimensional Approach, New Delhi, Gyan Publishing House, 2003.

Ashine Roy, Development of Women: An Assessment, New Delhi, Rajat Publications, 2003.

Ashine Roy, Women Empowerment and Gender Planning, New Delhi, Rajat Publications, 2003.

Ashine Roy, Women in Power and Decision Making, New Delhi, Rajat Publications, 2003.

Ashok Kumar (Ed.), Women in Contemporary Indian Society, 1993.

Ashok Kumar Jha (Ed.), Women in Panchayati Raj Institutions, New Delhi, Anmol Publications, 2004.

Ashok Kumar, Women and Development, New Delhi, Anmol Publications, 2005.

Asok Kumar Ray and Basudeb Dutta Ray (Eds.), Women Emancipation: Focus North East India, New Delhi, Om Publications, 2008.

B. Narayanaswamy, R.K. Samanta and K. Narayana Gowda, Self-Help Groups: Key to Empowerment of Rural Women, New Delhi, The Women Press, 2007.

B. Sambasiva Rao and Y. Indira Kumari, Empowerment of Women and Rural Development, New Delhi, Serials Publications, 2005.

B. Suguna, Empowerment of Rural Women through Self-Help Groups, New Delhi, Discovery Publishhing House, 2006.

B.D. Usmani, Women Education in Twenty First Century, New Delhi, Anmol Publications, 2004.

B.K. Singh, Women Empowerment through Self-Help Groups (SHGS), New Delhi, Adhyayan, 2006.

B.N. Singh, Rural Development and Women, New Delhi, Vista International Publications, 2006.

Balbir Soni, Empowerment of Women Workers: The Unorganised Sector, New Delhi, Dominant Publications, 2007.

Bedabati Mohanty, Violence Against Women: An Analysis of Contemporary Realities, New Delhi, Kanishka Publishers, Distributors, 2005.

Bharat Jhunjhunwala and Madhu Jhunjhunwala, Indian Approach to Women's Empowerment, Jaipur, Rawat Publications, 2004.

Bharat Singh, Working Women in India, New Delhi, Anmol Publications, 2004.

Bharati Ray (Ed.), Women and Politics: France, India and Russia, Calcutta, K.P. Bagchi & Company, 2000.

Bhawana Jharta, Women and Politics in India: Impact of Family and Education on Women Political Activists, 1996.

Bhola Nath Ghosh, Rural Women Leadership, New Delhi, Mohit Publications, 2002.

Bina Agarwal, Jane Humphries and Ingrid Robeyns (Eds.), Capabilities, Freedom, and Equality: Amartya Sen's Work from a Gender Perspective, New Delhi, Oxford University Press, 2006.

Bina Kumari Sarma, Role and Status of Indian Women through the Ages, Kolkata, R.N. Bhattacharya, 2006.

Binoy N. Verma and Madhuri Nath, Women and Rural Development Programmes, New Delhi, B.R. Publishing Company, 2004.

C. Hemalatha Prasad, A. Rizwana, A.V. Yadappanavar and R.P. Achari, Development of Women and Children in Rural Areas (DWCRA), Hyderabad, NIRD, 1996.

C.P. Yadav (Ed.), Encyclopaedia of Women Problems and their Remedies, New Delhi, Anmol Publications, 2007.

D.P. Singh and Manjit Singh (Eds.), Women and Empowerment: Experiences from Some Asian Countries, Chandigarh, Unistar Books, 2005.

Daniel W. Crowell, The SEWA Movement and Rural Development: The Banaskantha and Kutch Experience, New Delhi, Sage Publications India Pvt. Ltd., 2003.

Debal K. Singha Roy, Women, New Technology and Development: Changing Nature of Gender Relations in Rural India, 1995.

Deepak Bishoyi, Dimensions of Gender Problems: Policies and Prospects, New Delhi, Discovery Publishing House, 2007.

Devaki Jain, Women, Development, and the UN: A Sixty-Year Quest for Equality and Justice, New Delhi, Orient Longman, 2006.

Dharam Vir and Kamlesh Mahajan (Eds.), Changing Status and Emerging Problems of Indian Women, New Delhi, New Academic Publications, 2006.

Dharam Vir and Kamlesh Mahajan (Eds.), Women's Movements, Politics and Awareness, New Delhi, New Academic Publications, 2006.

Dharam Vir, Violence Against Women and Their Exploitation in India, New Delhi, New Academic Publications, 2006.

Dipangshu Chakroborty, Atrocities on Indian Women, 1999.

E.D. Setty and P. Krishna Moorthy, Women Empowerment through Entrepreneurship Development, New Delhi, Anmol Publications, 2007.

Ela R. Bhatt, We Are Poor But So Many: The Story of Self-Employed Women in India, New Delhi, Oxford University Press, 2006.

Evelin Hust, Women's Political Representation and Empowerment in India: A Million Indiras Now?, New Delhi, Manohar Publications, 2004.

Femida Handy, Meenaz Kassam, Suzanne Feeney and Bhagyashree Ranade, Grassroots NGOs by Women for Women: The Driving Force of Development in India, New Delhi, Sage Publications India Pvt. Ltd., 2006.

G. Narayana Reddy and D.V.V. Ramana Rao, Women Organisation and Power Struggle, 1995.

G. Palanithurai, T. Parthiban and J. Vanishree, Empowering Women: Grassroots Experience from Tamil Nadu, New Delhi, Concept Publishing Company, 2007.

G. Sreeramulu, Empowerment of Women through Self-Help Groups, New Delhi, Kalpaz, 2006.

G.S. Mehta, Participation of Women in the Panchayati Raj System, New Delhi, Kanishka Publishers, Distributors, 2002.

G.S. Pande, Political Participation of Women in India: Implementation of 73 and 74 Amendments, Lucknow, New Royal Book Company, 2001.

Geetanjali Mukherjee, Dowry Death in India, New Delhi, Indian Publications, 1999.

Gokulesh Sharma (Ed.), Feminine Jurisprudence in India: Women's Right, New Delhi, Deep and Deep Publications, 2008.

Gouri Srivastava, Women Role Models: Some Eminent Women of Contemporary India, New Delhi, Concept Publishing Company, 2006.

H.S. Krupalini and Vighnesh N. Bhat, Women in a Developing Country: Aspirations and Perceptions, New Delhi, APH Publications, 2003.

Hajira Kumar (Ed.), Status of Muslim Women in India, New Delhi, Aakar Books, 2002.

Hajira Kumar and Jaimon Varghese, Women's Empowerment: Issues, Challenges and Strategies—A Source Book, New Delhi, Regency Publications, 2005.

Indra Gupta, India's 50 Most Illustrious Women, New Delhi, Icon Publications, 2003.

Indu Grover and Deepak Grover (Eds.), Empowerment of Women/ edited, Udaipur, Agrotech, 2002.

J. Meenakshi (Ed.), Women and Panchayati Raj, New Delhi, Omega Publications, 2007.

J. Nirmala and V. Dhulasi Birundha, Empowerment of Women, New Delhi, Serials Publications, 2005.

J.L. Singh, Women and Panchayati Raj, New Delhi, Sunrise Publications, 2005.

J.N. Choudhary and Sangeeta Choudhary, Empowerment of Peasant Women, Jaipur, Ritu Publications, 2008.

Janardan Prasad, Women Education and Gender Justice: A Multi-Dimensional Approach, New Delhi, Kanishka Publishers, Distributors, 2006.

Jasodhara Bagchi (Ed.), The Changing Status of Women in West Bengal, 1970-2000: The Challenge Ahead, New Delhi, Sage Publications India Pvt. Ltd., 2005.

Jasprit Kaur Soni, Women Empowerment: Exploring the Facts, New Delhi, Authors Press, 2006.

Jaya Arunachalam, Women's Equality: A Struggle for Survival, New Delhi, Gyan Publishing House, 2005.

Jill M. Bystydzienski and Joti Sekhon (Eds.), Democratisation and Women's Grassroots Movements, New Delhi, Kali for Women, 2002.

Johanna Brenner, Women and the Politics of Class, New Delhi, Aakar Books, 2006.

Jyoti Mitra (Ed.), Women and Society: Equality and Empowerment, 1997.

K. Baby Sarojani, Women Empowerment Self-Help Group, Ambala Cantt., The Associated Publications, 2006.

K. Elango, A. Ayyan Perumal and J. Mohan Raj, Emerging Issues on Gender and Women Development, New Delhi, Abhijeet Publications, 2008.

K. Shanthi, Women in India: Retrospect and Prospect, New Delhi, Anmol Publications, 2005.

K. Uma Devi, Women's Equality in India: A Myth or Reality, New Delhi, Discovery Publishing House, 2000.

K.C. Vidya, Political Empowerment of Women at the Grassroots, Reprint. New Delhi, Kanishka Publishers, Distributors, 2007.

K.L. Chanchreek and M.K. Jain (Eds.), Eminent Women Politicians, New Delhi, Shree Publications, 2007.

K.L. Chanchreek and M.K. Jain, Eminent Women Administrators, New Delhi, Shree Publications, 2007.

K.S. Saxena, Women's Political Participation in India, 1999.

K.V. Singh, Women Issues: Empowerment and Gender Discrimination, New Delhi, Vista International, 2007.

Kalpana Kannabiran (Ed.), The Violence of Normal Times: Essays on Women's Lived Realities, New Delhi, Women Unlimited, 2005.

Kamal K. Misra and Janet Huber Lowry (Eds.), Recent Studies on Indian Women: Empirical Work of Social Scientists, New Delhi, Rawat Publications, 2007.

Kamlesh Mann, Tribal Women : On the Threshold of Twenty-first Century, 1996.

Kanchan Mathur, Countering Gender Violence: Initiatives Towards Collective Action in Rajasthan, New Delhi, Sage Publications India Pvt. Ltd., 2004.

Kanta Sharma, Women Power in Twenty-first Century, New Delhi, Anmol Publications, 2004.

Kavita Mishra, Women's Role in Politics in Modern World, New Delhi, Omega Publications, 2006.

Kiran Prasad (Ed.), Women in Rural Development: Contemporary Social Policy and Practice, New Delhi, The Women Press, 2006.

Kiran Prasad, Communication and Empowerment of Women: Strategies and Policy Insights from India, New Delhi, Women Press, 2004.

Kiran Saksena (Ed.), Women and Politics, New Delhi, Gyan Publishing House, 2000.

Kiran Sankar Chakraborty (Ed.), Empowerment and Status of Women in Tripura, New Delhi, Akansha Publications, 2008.

Kirit K. Shah and Radhika Seshan, Visibilising Women: Facets of History through a Gender Lens, New Delhi, Kalpaz Publications, 2005.

Kumkum Sangari and Uma Chakravarti (Eds.), From Myths to Markets: Essays on Gender, New Delhi, Manohar Publishers, 1999.

Kumkum Sangari, Politics of the Possible: Essays on Gender, History, Narrative, Colonial English, New Delhi, 1999.

Kusum Datta, Women's Studies and Women's Movement in India Since the 1970s: An Overview, Kolkata, The Asiatic Society, 2007.

Lakkineni Ratna Kumari, Economic Discrimination against Women, New Delhi, Abhijeet Publications, 2007.

Lalit Latta, Women Development in India: A Statistical Profile, New Delhi, Manak Publications, 2005.

Latika Menon, Female Exploitation and Women's Emancipation, Reprint. New Delhi, Kanishka Publications, Distributors, 2004.

Latika Menon, Women Empowerment and Challenge of Change, Reprint. New Delhi, Kanishka Publishers, Distributors, 2008.

Lena Dominelli, Women and Community Action, Reprint. New Delhi, Rawat Publications, 2007.

Linda Mayoux (Ed.), Sustainable Learning for Women's Empowerment: Ways Forward in Micro-Finance, New Delhi, Samskriti, 2003.

Lipi Ghosh, Ishita Mukhopadhyay and Suchandra Chakraborty (Eds.), Women Across Asia: Issues of Identities, New Delhi, Gyan Publishing House, 2006.

Lisa D. Brush, Gender and Governance, Reprint, New Delhi, Rawat Publications, 2007.

Lotika Sarkar, Kumud Sharma and Leela Kasturi (Editors), Between Tradition, Counter Tradition and Heresy: Contributions in Honour of Vina Mazumdar, Noida, Rainbow Publications, 2002.

M. Chatterjee, Violence against Women, Jaipur, Aavishkar, 2006.

M. Koteswara Rao, Empowerment of Women in India, New Delhi, Discovery Publishing House, 2005.

M. Lakshmi Narasaiah and S.A. Haseena Sulthana, Women Development Programmes, New Delhi, Discovery Publishing House, 2007.

M. Lakshmi Narasaiah, Empowerment for Women, New Delhi, Discovery Publishing House, 2004.

M. Lakshmi Narasaiah, Women and Development, New Delhi, Discovery Publishing House, 2006.

M. Lakshmi Narasaiah, Women and Microcredit, New Delhi, Sonali Publications, 2004.

M. Lakshmipathi Raju (Ed.), Women Empowerment: Challenges and Strategies, New Delhi, Regal Publications, 2007.

M. Meera Bai (Ed.), Women and Economic Reforms: Kerala Experience, New Delhi, Serials Publications, 2006.

M. Ramanjaneyulu, Economic Empowerment of Women in India, New Delhi, Anmol, 2006.

M. Razia Parvin, Empowerment of Women: Strategies and Systems for Gender Justice, New Delhi, Dominant, 2005.

M.G. Chitkara, Women & Social Transformation, New Delhi, A.P.H. Publications, 2001.

M.P. Boraian, Empowerment of Rural Women: The Deterrents and Determinants, New Delhi, Concept Publishing Company, 2008.

M.R. Biju, Women's Empowerment: Politics and Policies, New Delhi, Mittal Publications, 2006.

Madhu Jha, Women in Decision-Making Positions: Where Numbers Matter, New Delhi, Kanishka Publishers, Distributors, 2005.

Maitreya Dixit, Women and Achievement: Dynamics of Participation and Partnership, 1998.

Malavika Karlekar (Ed.), Visualising Indian Women 1875–1947, New Delhi, Oxford University Press, 2006.

Malavika M. Deshpande, Political Culture of Indian Urban Women: A Case Study of Hubli-Dharwad City, New Delhi, Mohit Publications, 2006.

Mamta Rajawat, Women Education and Social Empowerment, New Delhi, Reference Press, 2005.

Manas Chakrabarty and Vidyawati Agarwala, Women and Politics in India, Ambala Cantt., The Associated Publications, 2006.

Manisha Pathak Shelat, Communication for Gender Sensitisation: The Value Discussion Approach, New Delhi, Concept Publishing Company, 2004.

Marilyn Carr, Martha Chen and Renana Jhabvala (Eds.), Speaking Out: Women's Economic Empowerment in South Asia, Dhaka, University Press Limited, 1997.

Marjorie Agosin (Ed.), Women, Gender, and Human Rights: A Global Perspective, Reprint. New Delhi, Rawat Publications, 2003.

Martha C. Nussbaum, Women and Human Development: The Capabilities Approach, New Delhi, Kali for Women, 2000.

Meena Anand, Dalit Women: Fear and Discrimination, New Delhi, Isha Books, 2005.

Meena Bhargava and Kalyani Dutta, Women, Education, and Politics: The Women's Movement and Delhi's Indraprastha College, New Delhi, Oxford University Press, 2005.

Meenakshi Malhotra (Ed.), Dimensions of Women Exploitation, New Delhi, Isha Books, 2004.

Meenakshi Malhotra (Ed.), Empowerment of Women, 3 Vols., New Delhi, Isha, 2004.

Meenu Agrawal (Ed.), Women Empowerment: Today's Vision for Tomorrow's Mission, New Delhi, Mahamaya Publications, 2007.

Meera Kosambi, Crossing Thresholds: Feminist Essays in Social History, New Delhi, Permanent Black, 2007.

Minakshi and Sudarshan Mehta, Empowering Rural Women, New Delhi, Anmol Publications, 2006.

Mira Seth, Women and Development: The Indian Experience, New Delhi, Sage Publications, 2001.

Molly Joseph, Women Participation and Development Strategies, Reprint. New Delhi, Kanishka Publishers, Distributors, 2007.

N. Kulkarni, Women and Leadership, Jaipur, Pointer Publications, 2006.

Nalini Keller, Women under the Cross: Changing Gender Roles in Christian Families, 1997.

Navaneeta Rath, Women in Rural Society: A Quest for Development, 1996.

Neela Gokhale and Vaishali Prasad, Women in Twenty-First Century, New Delhi, Shree Publications, 2007.

Neelam Satiya, Encyclopaedia of Women Rulers and Political Authorities, New Delhi, Omega Publications, 2008.

Neelam Satiya, Encyclopaedia of World Great Women Leaders, 2 Vols., New Delhi, Omega Publications, 2008.

Neeta Lodha, Status of Tribal Women: Work Participation and Decision-making Role in Tribal Society, Jaipur, Mangal Deep, 2003.

Neeta Tapan, Need for Women Empowerment, New Delhi, Rawat Publications, 2000.

Nilima Srivastava, Women's March on the Path of Progress: A Study of Decadal Change in Role Conflict, New Delhi, Serials Publications, 2005.

Nirmala Sharma (Ed.) Dynamics of Women Development, New Delhi, Alfa, 2006.

Niroj Sinha (Ed.), Women in Indian Politics: Empowerment of Women through Political Participation, New Delhi, 2000.

Niroj Sinha, Empowerment of Women through Political Participation, New Delhi, Kalpaz Publications, 2007.

Nita Kumar, The Politics of Gender, Community and Modernity: Essays on Education in India, New Delhi, Oxford University Press, 2007.

Nivedita Menon (Ed.), Gender and Politics in India, Reprint. New Delhi, Oxford University Press, 2001.

Noorjehan N. Ganihar and Shahataj Begum, Gender Issues and Women Empowerment, New Delhi, Discovery Publishing House, 2007.

Om Raj Singh Vishnoi, Women Police in India, 1999.

P.K. Kar and P.P. Panda, Awareness of Women's Rights: Projection in Mass Media, New Delhi, Dominant Publishers, 2005.

Padma Iyer, Women and Social Revolution, Jaipur, Pointer Publications, 2007.

Palanithurai, G., Process and Performance of Gram Panchayat Women and Dalit Presidents (With 38 Case Studies of Tamil Nadu Panchayats), New Delhi, Concept Publishing Company, 2005.

Pamela Singla, Women's Participation in Panchayati Raj: Nature and Effectiveness: A Northern India Perspective, New Delhi, Rawat Publications, 2007.

Partha Chatterjee and Pradeep Jeganathan (Eds.), Community, Gender and Violence, Reprint. New Delhi, Permanent Black, 2007.

Parvathi Menon, Breaking Barriers: Stories of Twelve Women, New Delhi, Left Word Books, 2005.

Pauline Kolenda, Caste, Marriage and Inequality: Essays on North and South India, New Delhi, Rawat Publications, 2003.

Pitam Singh, Women Legislators in Indian Politics, New Delhi, Concept Publishing Company, 2003.

Poonam Pant, Role of Women in Medieval Indian Politics: 1236-1627, Lucknow, Tarun Prakashan, 2001.

Poonam Vats, Political Participation and Attitudinal Transformation of Rural Women, New Delhi, Abhijeet Publications, 2004.

Pradeep Kumar Swain and Surjya Narayan Tripathy (Eds.), Urban Women in Contemporary India: A Reader, New Delhi, Sage Publications India Pvt. Ltd., 2007.

Pradip K. Bhowmick and R.N. Bhattacharya, Empowerment of Rural Women: A Study Across the Three States Jharkhand, Orissa and West Bengal, Kolkata, 2005.

Pran Nevile, Beyond the Veil: Indian Women in the Raj, New Delhi, Nevile Books, 2000.

Preeti Misra, Domestic Violence against Women: Legal Control and Judicial Response, New Delhi, Deep and Deep Publications, 2006.

Prem Chand Patanjali, Development of Women Education in India, New Delhi, Shree Publications, 2005.

Premlata Pujari and Vijay Kumari Kaushik, Women Power in India, 1994.

Promilla Kapur (Ed.), Empowering the Indian Woman, New Delhi, Publications Division, Government of India, 2001.

Puran Chandra (Ed.), Political Dynamics of Women, New Delhi, Akansha Publications, 2005.

R. Letha Kumari, Women in Politics: Participation and Governance, New Delhi, Authors Press, 2006.

R.B.S. Verma, H.S. Verma and Nadeem Hasnain (Eds.), Towards Empowering Indian Women: Mapping Specifics of Tasks in Crucial Sectors, New Delhi, Serials Publications, 2007.

R.C. Hiremath, Women and Gender Issues, Jaipur, Pointer Publications, 2005.

R.C. Hiremath, Women in a Changing World, Jaipur, Pointer Publications, 2002.

R.C. Mishra, Women in India: Towards Gender Equality, New Delhi, Authors Press, 2006.

R.K. Dutta, Crime against Women, New Delhi, Reference Press, 2003.

R.K. Dutta, Women Empowerment, New Delhi, Reference Press, 2003.

R.K. Sahoo and S.N. Tripathy (Eds.), Self-Help Groups and Women Empowerment, New Delhi, Anmol Publications, 2006.

R.K. Samanta, Empowering Rural Women: Issues, Opportunities and Approaches, New Delhi, The Women Press, 2005.

R.K. Upadhyay (Ed.), Women in 21st Century: Problems and Challenges, 1996.

R.S. Narayan, Advancing Women and Human Rights, New Delhi, Indian Publishing House, 2007.

Raj Kumar Manisana Singh, Discrimination Against Women In India: A Gender Study, New Delhi, Akansha Publishing House, 2008.

Raj Kumar Pruthi, Rameshwari Devi and Romila Pruthi (Eds.), Education, Employment and Empowerment of Women, Jaipur, Mangal Deep Publications, 2001.

Raj Kumar Pruthi, Rameshwari Devi and Romila Pruthi (Eds.), Women in Law & Politics, Jaipur, Mangal Deep Publications, 2001.

Rajani Sinha, Status of Women and Economic Development: Some Econometric Evidence, Jaipur, RBSA Publications, 2004.

Rajib Lochan Panigrahy and Dasarathi Bhuyan (Eds.), Women Empowerment, New Delhi, Discovery Publishing House, 2006.

Rameshwari Pandya (Ed.), Women in India: Issues, Perspectives and Solutions, New Delhi, New Century Publications, 2007.

Rameshwari Pandya (Ed.), Women Welfare and Empowerment in India: Vision for 21 Century, New Delhi, New Century Publications, 2008.

Rameshwari Pandya, Women in Changing India, New Delhi, Serials Publications, 2008.

Ranabir Samaddar (Ed.), The Politics of Autonomy: Indian Experiences, New Delhi, Sage Publications India Pvt. Ltd., 2005.

Ranjana Harish and V. Bharathi Harishankar (Eds.), Shakti: Multidisciplinary Perspectives on Women's Empowerment in India, New Delhi, Rawat Publications, 2003.

Ranjani K. Murthy (Ed.), Building Women's Capacities: Interventions in Gender Transformation, New Delhi, Sage Publications India Pvt. Ltd., 2001.

Rathindra Nath Pramanik and Ashim Kumar Adhikary (Eds.), Gender Inequality and Women's Empowerment, Delhi, Abhijeet Publications, 2006.

Rinki Bhattacharya (Ed.), Behind Closed Doors: Domestic Violence in India, New Delhi, Sage Publications, 2004.

Rita Bakshi, M.S. Rathore, Meenu Agarwal and Manjula Tyagi (Eds.), Economic Empowerment of Rural Women in India, Jaipur, RBSA, 2003.

S. Ganesan, Status of Women Entrepreneurs in India, New Delhi, Kanishka Publishers, Distributors, 2003.

S. Murty and K.D. Gaur, Women Work Participation and Empowerment: Problems and Prospects, Jaipur, RBSA Publications, 2002.

S. Nagendra Ambedkar and Shilaja Nagendra, Role of Women in Panchayati Raj, Jaipur, ABD Publications, 2006.

S. Nagendra Ambedkar and Shilaja Nagendra, Women and Panchayati Raj, Jaipur, ABD Publications, 2008.

S. Nagendra Ambedkar and Shilaja Nagendra, Women, Empowerment and Panchayati Raj, Jaipur, ABD Publications, 2005.

S. Ram (Ed.), Women and Social Change, New Delhi, Commonwealth Publications, 2004.

S. Vats and Shakuntala Mudgal (Eds.), Women and Social Development in India, 1999.

S. Wal and Shruti Banerji (Eds.), Encyclopaedia of Women as Human Resource in 21 Century and Beyond, 4 Vols., New Delhi, Sarup, 2001.

S.B. Verma (Ed.), Status of Women in Modern India, New Delhi, Deep and Deep Publications, 2005.

S.B. Verma, Shiv Kumar Jiloka and Kumari Jyoti Kushwah (Eds.), Rural Women Empowerment, New Delhi, Deep & Deep Publications, 2006.

S.C. Joshi (Ed.), Women Empowerment: Myth and Reality, New Delhi, Akansha, 2004.

S.D. Mudgal, Feminism and Status of Women, Jaipur, Book Enclave, 2007.

S.K. Ravikumar, Indian Women: Status, Role and Empowerment, Jaipur, Mangal Deep Publications, 2006.

S.N. Rao, Women in Decentralised Governance: Status and Empowerment, Jaipur, Mangal Deep Publications, 2007.

S.N. Tripathy (Ed.), Women and Rural Development, New Delhi, Sonali Publications, 2006.

S.R. Bakshi, Empowerment of Women and Politics of Reservation, Jaipur, Book Enclave, 2002.

Sakuntala Narasimhan, Empowering Women: An Alternative Strategy from Rural India, 1999.

Samirendra Nath Dhar, Micro-Finance for Women: Necessities, Systems and Perceptions, New Delhi, Northern Book Centre, 2005.

Sandhya Narang, Coping With Role Conflicts: Employed Married Women,1996.

Sangeeta Nagaich, Changing Status of Women in India, 1997.

Sangeetha Purushothaman, The Empowerment of Women in India: Grassroots Women's Networks and the State, 1998.

Sarala Ranganathan, Women and Social Order: A Profile of Major Indicators and Determinants, 1998.

Sarita Sahay, Tribal Women in the New Profile: *Vis-à-Vis* their Non-Tribal Twins, New Delhi, Anmol Publications, 2002.

Sarojini Nayak and Jeevan Nair, Women's Empowerment in India, Jaipur, Pointer Publications, 2005.

Sarojini Vats, Women's Participation in Rural Development, New Delhi, Abhijeet Publications, 2004.

Saryu Ruhela (Ed.), Understanding the Indian Women Today: Problems and Challenges, New Delhi, Indian Publications, 1999.

Savitri Goonesekere (Ed.), Violence, Law and Women's Rights in South Asia, New Delhi, Sage Publications India Pvt. Ltd., 2004.

Sawalia Bihari Verma and Shiv Kumar Singh (Eds.), Rural Development Through Women's Participation and Electronic Media, Jaipur, Pointer Publications, 2004.

Sawalia Bihari Verma, Poverty Alleviation Approaches and Women's Participation, Jaipur, Aavishkar Publications, 2003.

Seema P. Salgaonkar, Women Political Power and the State, New Delhi, Abhijeet Publications, 2006.

Shakuntla Gupta, Women Development in India: A Comparative Study, New Delhi, Anmol Publications, 2005.

Shanta B. Astige, Role and Status of Working Women, New Delhi, Anmol Publications, 2006.

Sharada Rath and Navaneeta Rath (Eds.), Women in India: A Search for Identity, New Delhi, 1999.

Sheela Gulati, Women Education in 21 Century, Jaipur, ABD Publications, 2006.

Siddhartha Sarkar and Anil Bhuimali, Disadvantaged Women in Informal Sector: A Study of Domestic Help and Bidi Workers, New Delhi, Abhijeet Publications, 2005.

Singh and S. Narayan, Empowerment of Women Through Panchayati Raj Institutions: A Study, Kolkata, Towards Freedom, 2008.

Smita Mishra Panda (Ed.), Engendering Governance Institutions: State, Market and Civil Society, New Delhi, Sage Publications India Pvt. Ltd., 2008.

Smita Tewari Jassal, Daughters of the Earth: Women and Land in Uttar Pradesh, New Delhi, Manohar Publishers, 2001.

Snehalata Panda, Political Empowerment of Women, New Delhi, Raj Publications, 2002.

Sonia Bathla, Women, Democracy and the Media: Cultural and Political Representations in the Indian Press, 1998.

Subhadra Channa (Ed.), Women's Role and Status: Gender Politics, Rites of Passage, Reproduction, Prostitution, Women Careers, Conflict, New Delhi, Cosmo Publications, 2006.

Subhasini Mahapatra, Status of Women: Towards Empowerment, New Delhi, Rajat Publications, 2006.

Subhasini Mahapatra, Women and Politics, New Delhi, Rajat Publications, 2001.

Subhasini Mahapatra, Women Participation in Labour Force, New Delhi, Rajat Publications, 2002.

Sucheta Sen Chaudhuri, The Bodo Movement and Women Participation, New Delhi, Mittal Publications, 2004.

Sudhir Varma, Women's Struggle for Political Space: From Enfranchisement to Participation, 1997.

Sujit Kumar Dutta and Dilip Kumar Ghosh, Empowering Rural Women, New Delhi, Akansha Publications, 2002.

Sukanya Nihal Singh, Prospectus for Women's Empowerment: Dynamics of Enablement. New Delhi, Commonwealth, 2001.

Sumati Karmakar, The Better Half: Mothers, Sisters, Wives and Homemakers, New Delhi, Dominant Publications, 2001.

Sumi Krishna (Ed.), Women's Livelihood Rights: Recasting Citizenship for Development, New Delhi, Sage Publications India Pvt. Ltd., 2007.

Sumit Sarkar and Tanika Sarkar (Eds.), Women and Social Reform in Modern India: A Reader, Ranikhet Cantt., Permanent Black Publications, 2007.

Sumitra Kumari (Ed.), Dynamics of Women Empowerment, New Delhi, Alfa, 2006.

Sunanda S. Shirur, Emergence of Elite Women in Politics, New Delhi, Mohit Publications, 2005.

Sunita Dhaka and Rajvir S. Dhaka, Behind the Veil the Veil: Dalit Women in Panchayati Raj, Delhi, Abhijeet Publications, 2005.

Sunita Singh-Sengupta, Women Leadership in Organisations: Socio-Cultural Determinants, New Delhi, Gyan Publishing House, 2003.

Surendra Singh and S.P. Srivastava, Gender Equality through Women's Empowerment: Strategies and Approaches, Lucknow, Bharat Book Centre, 2001.

Sushila Vaidya, Role of Women in Maratha Politics, New Delhi, Sharada Publications, 2001.

Sushma Yadav and Anil Dutta Mishra, Gender Issues in India: Some Reflections, New Delhi, Radha Publications, 2003.

U. Jerinabi, Micro Credit Management by Women's Self-Help Groups, New Delhi, Discovery Publishing House, 2006.

Udai Prakash Sinha and Rekha Sinha, Women Empowerment and Family Management in Tribal Region, New Delhi, Concept Publishing Company, 2007.

Udai Veer, Crime Against Women, New Delhi, Anmol Publications, 2004.

Usha Sharma, Women Empowerment through Information Technology, New Delhi, Authors Press, 2003.

Usha Sharma, Women in South Asia: Employment, Empowerment and Human Development, New Delhi, Authors Press, 2003.

Utpal Kumar De and Bhola Nath Ghosh, Issues on Empowerment of Women, New Delhi, Mohit Publications, 2004.

Utpala Nayak, Women's Development and Social Conflicts: Historical Perspectives on Indian Women: Study in Orissa, 1999.

V. Mohini Giri, Deprived Devis: Women's Unequal Status in Society, New Delhi, Gyan Publishing House, 2006.

V. Mohini Giri, Emancipation and Empowerment of Women, 1998.

V.M. Rao, Tribal Women in India, Jaipur, ABD Publications, 2006.

V.S. Ganesamurthy (Ed.), Empowerment of Women in India: Social, Economic and Political, New Delhi, New Century Publications, 2008.

V.S. Ganesamurthy (Ed.), India: Economic Empowerment of Women, New Delhi, New Century Publications, 2007.

Vaikunth Mehta, Women and Political Issues: An International Perspective, Jaipur, ABD Publications, 2006.

Vani Prabhakar, Women in Rural India, New Delhi, Dominant Publications, 2004.

Varalakshmi Janapathy, Indira Gandhi: Woman of India's Destiny, New Delhi, Kalpaz Publications, 2005.

Veena Gandotra, Krishna Oberai and Promila Sharma, Appropriate Technology for Rural Women, New Delhi, Dominant Publishers, 2008.

Veena Jain, Educating Scheduled Caste Women, New Delhi, Indian Publications, 2005.

Vibhuti Patel, Women's Challenges of the New Millennium, New Delhi, Gyan Publishing House, 2002.

Vijaya Khader, Empowerment of Fisher Women: In Coastal Ecosystem of Andhra Pradesh, Karnataka, Kerala and Tamil Nadu, Udaipur, Agrotech Publishing Academy, 2008.

Zainab Rahman, Empowerment of Rural Indian Women: Study of Uttarakhand, New Delhi, Kalpaz Publications, 2007.

Zenab Banu, Disempowerment of Tribal Women: Perspectives on Seventy-Third Constitutional Amendment, New Delhi, Kanishka Publishers, Distributors, 2004.

Zenab Banu, Tribal Women Empowerment and Gender Issues, New Delhi, Kanishka Publishers, Distributors, 2001.

Zubair Meenai, Empowering Rural Women: An Approach to Empowering Women Through Credit-Based Self-Help Groups, New Delhi, Aakar Books, 2003.

Index